VOYEUR VOYANT
A Portrait of Louis-Ferdinand Céline

VOYEUR VOYANT

A Portrait of Louis-Ferdinand CELINE

by Erika Ostrovsky

 RANDOM HOUSE · NEW YORK

ISBN: 0–394–46524–5
Library of Congress Catalog Card Number: 76–159362

Translations not otherwise acknowledged are by Erika Ostrovsky.

Acknowledgment is gratefully extended to the following for permission
to reprint short excerpts from their works:
Delacorte Press: From *Castle to Castle* by Louis-Ferdinand Céline,
translated by Ralph Manheim. Copyright © 1957 by Editions Gallimard.
Copyright © 1968 by Dell Publishing Co. Inc. A Seymour Lawrence Book/
Delacorte Press.
Librairie Plon: From *Entretiens familiers avec L.-F. Céline,* by Robert
Poulet.
Librairie Arthème Fayard: From *Histoire de Vichy,* by Robert Aron.
Permission to translate excerpts from Céline's *Nord* and *Rigodon* has
been granted by Seymour Lawrence, Inc./Delacorte Press. Editions Gal-
limard has granted permission to translate from *Féerie pour une autre fois,*
I (© 1952 by Editions Gallimard) and from *Le Pont de Londres* (© 1964
by Editions Gallimard).
Short excerpts, totaling approximately 2,000 words from the following
Céline works, in translation by Erika Ostrovsky and Ralph Manheim, are
reprinted by permission of New Directions Publishing Corporation: *Journey to the End of Night.* Copyright 1934, © 1961 by Louis-Ferdinand
Céline. *Guignol's Band.* Copyright 1954 by New Directions Publishing Cor-
poration. *Death on the Installment Plan,* translated by Ralph Manheim.
Copyright © 1966 by Ralph Manheim.

Manufactured in the United States of America
by H. Wolff Book Manufacturing Co., Inc., New York

2   4   6   8   9   7   5   3
FIRST EDITION

TO

N.L.

AND

L.N.

A biography . . . is something one invents.

Life, also, is fiction. . . .

CÉLINE

CONTENTS

Prologue

Prologue

1

Here we are, alone again.
It's all so slow, so heavy,
so sad. . . . So many people
have come into my room. They've
talked. They haven't said much.
They've gone away.

(DJP, 15)

AUGUST 1961

Summer heat. Paris in stagnation: a near necropolis where only strangers come. Closed bakery shops from which the odor of bread has faded, and sewers ripped up for repair. All the inhabitants have gone—to celebrate the yearly exodus to familial pastures, the revels of harvest and pig-slaughter.

A time of stillness, dust, and rasping cricket sounds. Days waning past the summer solstice. When the newly dead have all been wept for and there is surfeit of weeping. A dry month. The sun below its zenith. When apathy blots out the word's clamor and even the shrillest cry is stifled. A time for silence to descend on those also whose entire life has been a refusal to be silent.

Even Louis-Ferdinand Céline, at last, was buried.

The voice that used to chide, guffaw, threaten, prophesy,

mesmerize, no longer rang out. (Even the newsboys had stopped chanting his name.) The earth had settled around his grave; the cemetery gates were rusty and the keeper begrudged their opening. It seemed that everything was done with. And he could now sink into the long oblivion.

Nothing remained to mark his passing but a few monuments (rigid, stark, shrouded in fixity): a gravestone; books with stiff covers; a gray house on a hill. Sparse fossils preserved from time's torrential flow. Vestigial remains of all the yearnings, pride, passion, screams, battles, betrayals, and laughter of more than sixty years.

How could the live voice be wrenched from such silence; the mind, the eyes—especially the eyes—of such piercing clarity, be reclaimed from the fast-falling dust?

> Our journey is entirely imaginary. Therein lies its strength.
>
> It leads from life to death. Men, beasts, cities and things, all is imagined. It's a novel, nothing but a fiction.
>
> (*VOY,* Epigraph)

The place where his journey had ended, offered the sole point of departure for recovery of the man. The path led to the house where his fictions still clung to the walls, where everything echoed the edifice of his imagination.

BELLEVUE

The small suburban railway station seems asleep. A faded placard ironically marks the place. Steel shutters conceal the ticket booth. Flies climb over the hands of a huge clock. 2 P.M. Digestive torpor. The village square is deserted. No guide appears to point the way.

Past the crossroads, the Route des Gardes stretches ahead in the sun; descends into a haze; winds from Versailles to the far Louvre Palace. The ancient route of the kings of France. Now flanked by modest pavilions and the Renault factories below. Only the cobblestones of former days remain, as does the continuing splendor of the Seine's valley.

The road drags on, past stone fences and cottages in bad repair. Then rises to a narrow side-path, almost hidden from view. Detour or hidden passageway?

A steep walk leads to three identical houses—genre Louis-Philippe—separated by gardens and old trees. They dominate the landscape below, reminders of nobility in another age. The last ("Villa Maitou") is shut off by high yellow gates. Rosebushes and geraniums spot the lawns, less brilliant than the blood-red plaque that hangs on one side of the entranceway:

LUCETTE ALMANZOR
DE L'OPÉRA COMIQUE
DANSES CLASSIQUES ET DE CARACTÈRE

While on the other side, a sign gray with age announces a quite different calling:

DR. L.-F. DESTOUCHES
DE LA FACULTÉ DE MÉDECINE DE PARIS
DE 14H À 16H SAUF VENDREDI

The uninitiated would never suspect this to be the house of Louis-Ferdinand Céline.

A bell rings shrilly, but far away. It sets off barking inside the house, coupled with odd rushing sounds. Large dogs come panting down the hill, hurl themselves against the gate. (The horde of hellhounds people often spoke about? Which, it was rumored, he sicked joyously at intruders.) They now seem old, worn as the peasant woman who follows.

The face of an adolescent dancer appears for an instant at a door. Sulkily withdraws.

* * *

The heavy gates swing open, grate on the gravel. Dogs leap, surround, calm down as the old woman's voice chides them softly, calling them by name: "Delphine . . . Totom . . . Cri-Cri . . ."

A path leads up flagstones, past the side entrance of the house which leads toward a dim kitchen, into the back garden. There, in profusion, ship's lanterns and bells, watering cans and flower jars, wicker chairs and low reclining beds —not unlike Roman couches—covered with furs and terry cloth; washlines full of colored leotards, a primitive outdoor shower; cages filled with sound and decked with the bright artifacts of weaver-birds. A clothes rack on which a gray parrot is perched, eyeing the trespasser with veiled gaze. His rose-colored tail feathers move, as if prepared for a leap; his beak menaces with clicking sounds. —Toto, last companion of Céline. Confidant and defender. Trained to attack, with word or claw. Pinch unwelcome legs or hurl anathema at uninvited guests. Tutored to put intruders to the test; preside sternly over trials by fear. His impassive eyes pierce all appearances; the ugly voice cuts polite formulas in two.

A light step approaches. The parrot relents; holds excommunication in abeyance. The dogs go ambling more gaily down the hill. The woman steps out into the garden: Lucette Almanzor-Destouches-Céline.

A slender high-domed head; the reddish hair constrained by a turban. Face of imp or Flemish saint. Smiling, uncertain, ready to flee.

Her body has remained young. Barely clothed, it reclines in leisurely graces, merges its shape with the Roman couch.

Bidding all visitors to do the same (feet up for freer circulation, not crossed and cramped in mundane ways). Her trained eyes appraise the other's body. Weigh, assess, approve or turn away; judge shape of knee, tightness of waist, skin tone, the bearing of the head.

While noting the reactions of the animals that hover about —the parrot, dogs, and numberless small birds. Testing. Probing. As he would have done. Diagnosing with furtive glance, on the threshold of welcome or retreat.

The parrot does not attack.

The dogs place heads on paws with low sighs. The gaze softens. The trial of entry is over.

The doors of the house can now open; the first barrier be crossed; the wandering through labyrinth of rooms begin.

Into a kitchen, incomprehensibly transformed into a bath (its original contents probably relegated to the dank cellar room one passed on entering). The bedroom, strewn with animal skins, perfume flasks, boxes of talc, gilt brushes, and teapots wrapped in fur. Music drifts out of a corner—its mechanical source hidden by screens—envelops the room; but seems arrested at the door.

Across the hallway, his study waits. Stands very still. All connotes recent death. The objects, more inanimate than elsewhere in the house, appear frozen into fixity. The table stares, covered with sheets of paper (some of which are fastened together with clothespins), surrounded by baskets full of words. The chair—half drawn—conjures up the bent shoulders and massive head, a clawlike hand that moves with effort across a final page.

("Today, the paper will remain white," he had muttered; and died the very same night.)

Bookshelves with sparse contents stand undisturbed.
Coal dust lies immobile in the fireplace, its screen an elaborate lacework of brass. The sofa against the wall shows no
indentation. Only a slight depression remains where his cadaver had lain, the hemorrhaged head turned to the wall.
There, maps of seafarers still hang, their love of ships no
greater than his.

The eye moves. Swings back to the table—dissecting,
delivery, work table—assuming his eye's position. Follows
the landscape outside, the darkening trees, the Seine valley
below. Inevitably ends at the river.

(River to cross his life innumerable times and become
the source of many a fabled journey.)

Across the river to the other side.

Time is distended. Last gaze and first now meet. Bellevue obliquely faces Courbevoie-sur-Seine; the Route des
Gardes rejoins the Rampe du Pont where he was born; the
garden path winds toward the Sentier des Bergères where
he had once lain at his wet-nurse's lush breast.[1]

Bridge of mind and time.

> I was born over there, so near here . . . in Courbevoie,
> on that other bend of the river. . . . And all around
> the bridge, the seagulls, graceful in their winter sojourn,
> palpitating flakes of the infinite, embraces from space to
> calm our misfortunes, crumbs in the wind that sweeps
> everything away! . . .[2]

Circle of water now closed. Which once had flowed into
oceans and far-off streams; borne the ships of his imagination. Three-masted schooners of delight and transatlantic
giants; barges and galleys; freighters, tugboats and destroy-
ers; even dread Charon's bark upon the river Styx.

Ring of water, now locked over the journey's end.

*   *   *

Above the silent room, the dancer's studios rise. Stairways lined with Degas; reclining couches on each landing; mirrors reflecting everywhere.

Music of India suddenly streams through the house. An evening raga with yearning drone, and drumbeats so intricate that the human pulsebeat becomes confused. In the first room, circled by mundane ladies attempting to achieve ritual poise, Lucette sways with elaborate grace.

Metamorphosis of her face: a Hindu now, as long ago when—wrapped in saris, a royal dot of red painted between her eyes—she had toured Europe with Ravi Shankar, Standra Kali and his troupe, disguised.[3] (A glorious Mardi gras. Despite her family's fears that such *mascarade* might put her Catholic soul in peril.)

Only remnants of that glory remained. No longer young, relegated from center to backstage, from floodlight to semidarkness, she clung to her exacting craft. Patiently corrected her pupils' stance, perfected gestures, assessed posture—her fleeting art in need of being constantly renewed. For each movement, sketched in air, lingered the space of an instant, no more. Beauty stated and wiped out; no trace of its perfection preserved.

> With beauty at least, one knows that it must die. And that way, one knows that it lives. . . .
>
>   (*EG,* 253)

> But old age is coming . . . ! The stage is out of the question now—Lessons, that's all that's left—. . . . She who had won first prize at the Paris Conservatory. . . .[4]

The second room resounded with castanets. Transformed into a Spanish dancer now, her body moves with contained violence. A sharp pulsing rhythm grows from her hand; ex-

tends to the floor, making the boards vibrate in the house.
As when, vying with doomed gypsies, she had made the
woods of Germany resound:

> [She] puts the strings around her fingers and trrr! . . .
> they know instantly she's an artist! . . . those flights
> of trills! . . . gusts! . . . pizzicati! light! light! . . .
> lighter! . . . still lighter! . . . and then stronger! . . .
> stronger! . . . *furioso!* . . . the whole forest is vi-
> brating . . . trrr! a truly magnificent echo for such
> small castanets . . . trrr! ter! tac! . . .[5]

> Few women in the world play the castanets as she
> does. . . .[6]

The students follow: lesser shapes. Move with clumsy effort
to mimic her uncanny skill. Point out, by contrast, the hard-
won mastery of her art.

The whirring passion stops.

She glides swiftly from the room.

> She emanated grace, every movement was lovely. . . .
> She was a mirage of charm. . . . When she left the
> room, you felt a void in your soul, your heart slipped
> down to the basement in sadness. . . .
>
> (*DIP*, 241)

Into another room. Foam mats and bars. Wooden lad-
ders line the walls. The low sounds of a minuet establish
calm. Bodies sway in supple rhythm, expand, breathe, and
contract. A flow of muscles; air inhaled and forced out. Reptilian motion, fluid and slow. In others, faltering and out of
joint. Limbs strained or flopping uncontrolled. Ill-shaped
bellies and thighs that will not respond to the call. To the
soft voice's urgings:

> Let yourself fall . . . far . . . far . . . glide forward
> . . . slowly . . . sink into the ground . . . breathe in
> . . . deep . . . deeper . . . reach upward . . . with

your throat . . . up . . . up . . . feel the pull . . .
fall back . . . breathe out . . . and rest.

Among the dancers, the sulking girl's face which had
appeared at the door, then vanished. In full view, she seems
a young double of Lucette. Their flowing bodies form a
single motion, one continuous line of grace made flesh. Her
breathing, her gestures patterned upon the others', she has
become a mirror image of the older woman's art. In perfection of limbs also (limbs wrought from raw materials found
in an impaired body—one deformed leg preventing dance
or walk; cold hands that were too weak to trace the simplest
gesture). Long years of stringent exacting toil had brought
forth these pure forms; produced an instrument capable of
complex and demanding harmony.[7] Marie-Claude. Servant or
priestess. Reclaimed anomaly, now pledged in the cult of
forms. Golem or Galatea.

She also would vanish one stormy night. Fly off into
the wind on newly fleet legs. Leaving the house to its silence.

Below, the sound of a hundred birds. The bath swarms with
their wings. The sink, the tub, are covered by sheets; the
mirrors, spotted over with white droppings, seem blind. Their
cries, their variegated colors everywhere. Screens at the windows check their outward flight. Inside the room, however,
they whir about, shift in continual motion. A kaleidoscope
of feathers, dizzying in its endless round.

Even with the door shut, their voices penetrate the
house. Mingle with those in the garden, where the weaver-
birds live who wind bright-colored strands into strange artifacts. Bird tapestries of hidden meaning, responding to age-
old inner calls. Artisans in this building of artifice.

Vying with the gray parrot's powers.

He roams free. Thrones on his perch, clicking ugly beak

with menacing air. Grave now, calling the dogs to heel; then laughingly aping a teakettle's sound.

A long silence while he hangs upside down, eyeing the world with veiled, inverted gaze. Voyeur or seer.

Suddenly, a curse cuts through the air. Upright, with red eyes blazing, he echoes his master's harsh words. —Last judgment pronounced upon our cockeyed universe.— The long hours of companionship are etched in his small bird's brain. He holds a live fund of unwritten words in that fragile skull. Survivor for many years to come, more faithful than all mechanical devices that might capture and preserve the dead man's voice, he will go on screaming the last thoughts shared; sing raucous songs; reflect the dread loneliness, now silenced.

From beyond the grave, a parrot's voice.

The sound cracks the shell of fixity. Cuts through the house; sweeps off dust covers; unshrouds the mirrors. Prompts the turning of pages; the search of a life gone by.

Doors open that seem to have been stuck in sand. The parrot's master suddenly looms large in this overgrown garden. His voice rings out, as though it had never faltered. Or died.

The books seem no longer contained in stiff, monumental covers. A vast, lava-like flow issues forth. It kindles everything it touches; illuminates the house, the trees, the valley below; causes the Seine to boil and rise from its banks. Glows with harsh radiance. Breaks the barriers of extinction.

The story of their creator can now begin to unfold:

ONE

Treat this bunch of anecdotes . . . like
fragments of a tapestry . . . you go ahead
and patch them, fit them together as
well as you can. . . .

CÉLINE

My vice . . . that need to flee from
every place, in search of I don't
know what. . . . as if life
would rob me, hide what I most
wanted to know, existence at the
core of darkness . . . so that, at
the end, I would lose everything
for lack of strength, and I'd be
deceived just like all the others,
by Life, the true mistress of
real men.

CÉLINE

2

RITES DE PASSAGE

---

*The sky . . . the gray waters . . . the
mauve banks . . . all caresses . . . one
within the other, neither commanding
. . . you drift, softly drawn into their
circle, further and further into other
dreams . . . ready to perish in beautiful
secrets, you move into other worlds
formed of veils and mists. . . . Do you
follow me?*

(GB, 47)

LONDON, 1915

Undoubtedly, it was the watery nature of the city that
drew him: the fog or swift promise of fog in the air; the frail
masts that showed suddenly above a roof, some tavern sign,
beside church steeples; the siren calls that trailed now and
then through the labyrinth of streets.

He tended constantly toward the docks. No matter
where he walked in this unknown city, where street names
were just so many signs that led one astray, he found himself
turned in the direction of the sea.

> Hollyborn Street . . . Falmouth Cottage . . . Hol-
> lander Place . . . Bread Avenue! . . . suddenly a si-
> ren rang from far, from over there! . . . from the end
> of the roofs . . . the cry of a ship! . . . all the way
> from the other end of things! . . .
>
> (*GB,* 41)

His feet led him always to the docks where commerce with
far shores and a profusion of wares and language centered.
The eye suddenly came up against mountains of wool, burlap
and silk. Mysterious bales rose and descended in puppetlike
rhythm dictated by cranes. Locomotives and birdcages were
lifted and deposed with equal ease. The rise and fall of waves
was no more puzzling than this mechanical feat which mimed
their motion.

He never tired of their uncanny maneuvers, or the variety of objects that described an airy arc before his eyes.

The other senses were subject to bombardment also.
Whole oceans of odors assailed one, in the vicinity of the
docks: coffee, turmeric, and brine; oil bubbling amid heavy
perfumes; tar, onions, and urine, seaweed, damp stone, and
the acrid smell of rope under friction. The voices were as
varied as the rest: curses of sailors and cabin boys in numberless tongues and dialects; the calls of chip-sellers and tarts
(hawking quite different wares to keep the chill of the London air away).

Raucous, sweat-drenched life bordering the vast cool,
and silence of the sea.

He strolled gaily down the slippery lanes, arms linked with
boisterous companions. Painters and pimps, inventors and
whores, trespassers and stowaways cast up by war—a crew
as motley as any that a storm might strand on an island of
concrete such as this.

Among the followers, there was a group of soldiers in uniforms faded beyond recognition, but bright with medals (hung about the neck or pinned—at heart level—on the thin coats). Whether deserters or heroes, no one knew; if decorated for shell shock, mutilation, or the successful escape from trench warfare, they did not say. All of them, however, sported their "hardware" with disdainful nobility, to elicit free rounds of stout in chilly British pubs.

"Give them an eyeful of yours, Ferdine," they shouted, having calculated the weight of his impressive "war cross" in terms of brimming glasses raised in the bar before them. He jingled the other decorations in his trouser pockets—the medal of honor and various citations (that nearly cost him his head, and sounded no heavier than a load of copper pennies now). Then answered, bantering: "But I'm a voyeur, no exhibitionist,[1] my lads!" And smiled his sly smile.

Immense in the doorway of the pub, he appraised the audience within. Blue eyes narrowed, he paused, as if weighing advance in battle. Flung words over his shoulder at the rest of his crew: "But then, I'm an actor too, not a spectator, my hardies!"

With comedian's indifference, he strode forward to the center of the floor and put his bandaged right hand on the counter top.

"Drinks, all around!" he ordered in staccato tones, his English accent impeccable. (A vestige of harsh apprenticeship in adolescent years:

In 1908 he had been sent to Diepholz to master German.
In 1909, he spent a year in England.[2]

Both trips were meant to prepare young Ferdinand Destouches for a successful commercial career. Unfortunately, he was sent back to his dismayed parents in both instances, due to "youthful indiscretions." [3]

Short stay and huge disgrace. Seduced boarding-house ladies and schoolmistresses had complained of his excessive ardor —in its first flowering of post-pubescent years. In a manner so unlike that of their transposed selves that would adorn his novels, many years from now, when their screeching complaints had been stilled, filtered and refined and they would yield a creature such as the silent, graceful Nora of Meanwell College who, having sapped his semen, could float —as gently as Ophelia—to her watery British grave. . . .)

His boon companions drank deeply. He would not touch a drop, but feigned to drain his tankard dry. Hatred of alcohol already formed in his mind. A confirmed "water drinker" from youth to old age, he was not yet ready to thunder his disdain as in later years when he would chide his countrymen for their sodden, benumbed ways (which, for a Frenchman, amounts to treason and may be judged as severely as the betrayal of the Maginot line).

Now, he still dissembled. Only the slight curl of his lip revealed his contempt for their drunken sprawl. An unlit cigarette—another prop for dissembling, since clouds of to-bacco were as revolting to him as alcohol fumes—hung from one side of his mouth. That side of his face seemed amused; the other, in shadow, harbored opposite thoughts. Two vis-ages in one, almost never revealed at the same time. A Janus-face which would grow more complex during long years of trial. Already sketched in the youth's barely formed traits.

Sitting masked among them—sharp gaze veiled with reptilian cunning—he noted, observed.

The hours dragged on. His glance did not soften. But recorded the orgiastic night in his mind, in all its grotesque, intricate detail.

They're rolling on the benches for fun. . . . They un-derstand nothing. The night watchmen laugh like crazy too. . . . They no longer have jackets, nor shoes,

they're almost naked with drunkenness, wearing only
their gunbelts, they walk on all fours on the women.
They bark from joy. Great messing around! Great filthy
heap! . . . That's what I was thinking! . . .

                                                        (*PL,* 371)

Near closing time, the ribald crew stretched and began to
rise. Put hands in pockets, miming gestures of willingness
to pay.

They were waiting for Ferdinand to do his act. He
caught the cue. The mask shifted, revealing the clown. At
the propitious moment he rose; threw all his hero's medals
on the zinc bar. They asked in shrill, mocking tones:

"In England, is this currency still good?" [4] Instant silence.
Attentive stupor of the audience about. The bartender
stopped, twirled around, bent over the counter, peered at
the metal shapes. Finally, with sweeping grandiose gesture
of his hand, conceded the rounds of stout.

The rowdy occupants of the bar concurred. Among
shouts of approval, Ferdinand and his companions lurched,
laughing, into the night.

The room at 71 Gower Street was small. The two men, once
out of their cots, could hardly move about. With its clutter
of books, torn trench coats hung from nails driven into the
door, the remnants of the night's scanty dinner turned cold,
it seemed more like a refuge of transients than a resting place.
A den to wander out from, without inviting return.

The second cot had been added in haste.

The day Louis-Ferdinand had suddenly appeared, flung
his canvas bag down, offered no explanation for his presence.
Seeing the ravaged face, Georges had asked no questions.
His friend's armored eyes discouraged all probes, even the
most discreet. All that was evident—even to the most cur-

sory examiner or the blindest in officialdom—was that for
Ferdinand the war had ended. Whether in desertion or hero's
dismissal, he dared not ask.

His wounds seemed to suggest the latter. The right arm
was almost paralyzed. A hole as large as a pigeon's egg deformed one shoulder. Several incisions showed, barely scarred
over, before he swiftly covered them with his shirt. "Oh, I've
been a boarder at all the best places," Ferdinand said. "From
the emergency ward at Hazebrouck to the Val-de-Grâce in
Paris, and the Paul-Brousse in Villejuif to the Michelet hospital in Vanves[5] . . . the whole world of stretchers, cranked-
up beds, and slanted tables is no mystery to me . . . and all
those gentlemen doctors who had such a ball noting, observing, operating, noting again, treating me with alternating
currents and galvanic shocks! . . . and putting sutures in
my radical nerve and pulling out bullets like magicians pull
rabbits out of a hat . . . ah! what mastery! They tried to
straighten out my hand so that it wouldn't look so much like
a monkey's paw. Then they pinned me with medals to cover
up the holes. And sent me here to rot!"

Their lives were a form of entrenchment. The days spent in
secret tasks—which some report as no more hazardous than
the construction of airplane wings,[6] the nights devoted to the
exploration of bordellos and music halls.

In fact, the daylight hours were shadier than those of
the night. Attached to the Passport Bureau (which, in turn,
had its connection with British Intelligence and the Espionage Services), Ferdinand had his fill of odd encounters:
minor criminals and expatriate pimps, deserters in search of
asylum, turncoats and double agents. All eclipsed by Mata
Hari, queen of spies. A labyrinth of offices where the omnipotent sound of a rubber stamp could decide a closed trap

or exit, the flourish of his pen determine liberation or seal an uncertain fate. World of double lives, masks, disguises and hidden trails—parallel to his own penchants, the underground workings of his mind.

The crowning event was an invitation to dine with Mata Hari at the Savoy.[7] The orders were to accord her a visa after making her dangle for a while. —The game which held the greatest enchantment, was to outwit her undisputed mastery in deceit, coupled with the enjoyment of her beauty and seductive skill. A chess match in which the queen would soon disappear from the board.

His elation over the encounter lasted well into the night.

Then, he plunged into the half-lit world of dancers and whores. The marginal zone on the edge of this great city, where one could roam unhampered by stale bonds or clay idols that rose, threatening, from the past. A place out of time and battlefield. Where the self could slowly emerge. Where, despite the still aching flesh, he could erect a storehouse of artifice. Gather impressions, amass sounds, record scents in his mind, imagine words that could exorcise the stifling visions pent up inside.

Besides, there was the secret life of books which could be drained in lamplight. Nietzsche, Hegel, Fichte, and old Schopenhauer[8] were pressed beneath the springs of his cot. Mocked in bright day among thieves and spies, cast swiftly aside to make room for an erotic night, they nevertheless sated the more contemplative appetites he sometimes discovered in himself.

As did the dancers his thirst for perfection of form.

Their uncanny limbs—sculptured and luminous— haunted him for days on end. To encompass this grace . . .

to penetrate the inner core of this flesh . . . innundate it with hot bursts of desire! He spent hours among them, gathering as many of the muscular beauties as he could hold. Devoted whole nights to the study of each perfect skin fold, in order to explore, probe, discover every hidden orifice. Then leaped and enjoyed, in orgies of light unending until dawn.

He preferred them by twos. Engulfed in liquid pairs of thighs, their nymphs' feigned evasion—countered by ruse or brute strength—brought him utmost delight. He mounted each in turn while the other, languorously draped across the sheets, observed. Mingling joys of the eye with those of the flesh. Actor and voyeur; satyr and reed flute fused into one.

The trained limbs of dancers, however, were not enough. He considered them best complemented by those of whores. Whose mastery—he often felt—was equal in scope. Skilled hand, mouth, genitals: all perfectly controlled. Bodies trained to excite to frenzy, manipulated with consummate craft, they performed acts that rivaled works of art. And, like true artists, vied with each other. Compared timing, boasted of magnitude and speed records in getting the sperm to gush forth: Mireille, while leaning against a tree (a lamppost sometimes had to do, in urban scenes); Annette, best when bent low over a chair; Rita, wielding her belt with relentless hand.

Sorceresses of sex, initiated into manifold secret desires.

Who transformed bidet and rubber syringe into the sacred tools of their craft; twitched their asses, or rubbed their silky thighs together with ritual skill. Cunts that could transform dingy hotel rooms into phallic altars of delight. Half artisan, half priestess—the least of them could turn a few seconds' delirium to gold; perform the alchemy of sex, which puts all other occult operations to shame.

The act accomplished, they moved on, free of constraints, toward the next night's journey.

Outside the tyranny of space and time, the whores and dancers sailed: three-masted schooners of delight, marginal, magical.

Had one of them joined him; made him an adept of her craft; become the first to be called his wife? Rumors and silence. Some furtive reference to such a bond. Most often dismissed as young man's folly, arranged to the satisfaction of everyone by the traditional intercession of paternal wisdom.[9]

Apsaras of London docks! Whore or dancer; early companion of artifice. Who blew the breath of hot life into his war-torn body and opened his flesh to feelings much keener than shrapnel could produce.

> One is as virgin to Horror as to sensual joy.
> *(VOY, 17)*

Now his encounter with death was balanced by a living presence. Even though the woman herself might be forgotten, she would not fail to reappear—in various guises—in his books: Lola, Molly, Nora, Sophie.

Prophecy of women to come. First, fiery touchstone of delight.

Gone now. Vanished into the London night. As other women would be lost in the mists of far cities: Los Angeles, Antwerp, Rome, Madrid, Moscow, Vienna. . . . Preserved only within the pages of his books. Enlarged, illumined by absence. Word statues. Lifted out of their metamorphosed mold. Rescued—timeless—from the awful flow of time.

POELKAPELLE, FALL 1914

> I wonder if the most real sacrifices don't consist of shoveling manure in the wan light of grimy lanterns. . . .[10]

Time passed most heavily before dawn. The cavalry barracks lay silent in the rain. Here and there the horses stirred, shook invisible manes or whinnied harshly in their stalls.

Probably because of their sores that festered, unattended, giving off a sweet cabbage-like smell.

Destouches walked toward them. Carefully, remembering his dread when he first had to mount the treacherous beasts.[11] When he examined their sides, the raw flesh showed in blotches that looked like bloodstains in the night. Sometimes, his companions' open mouths, while sleeping, had the same look. The young men who snored at his side, volunteers as full of blind rage and revulsion for their past life as he, caught in the same nightmare. Slaves of war, livestock for the slaughter, they were chained to their barracks as surely as the horses fastened to their stalls. Confined to dens which

> stank enough to make the guards faint, odors that went to the bottom of your nostrils and made your head spin . . . that made you sniff all cockeyed, it was so pungent and acid. . . . Meat, piss, chewing tobacco, turds, that's what that violent stench was, plus bad coffee gone cold and horse shit, plus something else like dead rat in all the corners. . . .
>
> *(CP,* 8–9)

Like rats caught in the huge madness, without the dignity of rodents who claw at the trap for escape or bare their teeth in desperate terror.

Instead, they lined up each morning with brass buttons shined, hiding their nausea beneath bravado and harsh smiles. Knights of falsehood, who gaily mounted their steeds and rode off into the dawn. Heads high, spurs digging into the horses' already lacerated sides.　　—

Many did not return or were brought back diminished: parts of their bodies lopped off; limbs hanging formless at

their sides. In a democracy of death, officers and lowly enlisted men sometimes embraced—their flesh mingled.

> . . . the colonel . . . had been thrown on the grass by
> the explosion and into the arms of the cavalryman, the
> messenger, who was finished also. They both kissed, for
> this moment and forever, but the rider no longer had a
> head, nothing but an opening above the neck, with
> blood bubbling in it like jam in a pot. The colonel's
> belly was ripped open, he made a nasty face. . . .

> All these meats bled enormously together.
>
> (*VOY*, 15)

In the whole countryside, there was a stench of gangrene
mixed with that of blood. Thick clouds of smoke filled the
air.

When their morale ran low, rumors of deserters' executions were circulated. Also, a "beautiful" telegram recently
sent by General Foch was cited as often as seemed appro-
priate:

> My left flank is demolished, my right one is weakening;
> situation excellent: I shall attack.[12]

The cannons continued their intermittent sound; punctuated by mines and loud dying. The wounded screamed
like horses in a slaughterhouse.

When night fell, all sounds diminished. Most of the
victims had already died; the others moaned softly under
morphine or heavy sleep. Then the huge bonfires of villages
appeared. They lit the clouds—in patterns almost as lovely
as those of northern lights.

> It was gay. A little nothing of a hamlet which you'd
> never even notice in the daytime, stuck way out in the
> sticks, well you can't imagine at night, when it's burning,
> what an effect it can have! You'd swear it was Notre-
> Dame! And the fire lasts all night, even from a tiny vil-

lage, at the end you'd think it was an enormous flower,
then only a bud, then nothing.

It smokes and then it's morning.

(VOY, 23)

A smell of burning flesh and timber floated toward the camp.
The mares reared in their stalls, maddened eyes turned up-
ward, straining to break through their chains.

The futile pawing of their hoofs accompanied the thunder of cannons. And lulled the exhausted warriors to sleep.

YPRES, OCTOBER 25, 1914

Dawn. And the sickening awareness of another day. A
glare of light hits the bloodshot eye. Eye still filled with the
last days' carnage. Gorge ready to rise. The innards aching
to vomit, spew forth their contents of disgust and fear. Latrines and feed buckets could not hold it; the whole battlefield did not have trenches deep enough to contain this flow.
Only the turned back, the flight to the hinterland planned
with animal cunning, offered a way out, escape. . . .

A sentry called.

The echo rose to the trees . . . above the buildings
. . . all the way to the shadows, to the enormous stage-
sets erected above everything . . . in front of the sky
. . . all black there, noisy, swollen, full of whispering
dreadful monsters . . . it's fear which comes from the
leaves . . . from the night which moves. . . .

(CP, 37)

Desertion! Solace of cowardice.[13] To abandon oneself
to the soft urgings of the flesh—still intact, screaming to remain thus. Skin vulnerable to the slightest cut; eyes, balls,
belly, throat—all unprotected, already aching in anticipated
pain. The nape of the neck had gooseflesh on it. In dread

projection, lead penetrated to the bone, shattering the wind-pipe. The brain envisaged its own liquid putrefaction.

The legs turn watery, bend, flail about as in some strange element. Move crablike with amazing speed. Carry the will-less body toward the trees.

Refuge there . . . hide until darkness falls.

Then move stealthily onward. From tree to blacker tree. Into the sheltering woods. Where the sound of battle slowly retreats. And dies. Away.

Dawn. And the sickening awareness of another day. Light pries open the bloodshot eye. Eye filled with the past day's carnage. The gorge works to hold down nausea. Sphincters tighten against the irresistible urge to let go, dissolve, in ex-cremental abandon. Although,

> To soil one's pants . . . is the beginning of genius!
> (*EG*, 85)

The back stiffens. Legs move mechanically, as in a con-trolled dream. Forward to headquarters. The hand is raised in rigid salute. Timor mortis petrified.

With hard metal helmet drawn over the face, but other-wise unarmored, he rides forth. Urging his horse on. Scream-ing a battle cry. The sound of hoofs like machine-gun fire. Onward, from tree to tree. Aware of danger from every side. Forward, to reconnoiter. Each move calculated to bring news of the day's fight.

Terror contained. Body walled in to stave off the soft entrails' plea. Eyes flashing with pride at having subdued the instincts, stifled the awful and most human cry.

The scream rose, despite him. Spears of shrapnel tore into his side. Pierced arm and shoulder. Threw him from his high horse to the ground.

The mud was spattered with blood. Earth and slime filled his eyes. His mouth seemed glued against a red slippery rock. A slow trickle of excrement soiled his thighs. He felt numb yet watched himself writhing with pain. Cut off from his own body, yet acutely aware of its grotesque plight. He was lying in a circle of blood and filth, his weak head ready to sink into the ground. A web formed before his eyes.

Was he dying?

An angry howl, unlike any he had ever heard, rose from somewhere. He heard it again. It was coming from his mouth. Then consciousness faded. He lay motionless in a pool of his body's outflow.

When evening fell, they came to gather him up in canvas sheets. When the mutilated body had been brought back to camp, it was shipped on to Hazebrouck. He had not regained consciousness. In his morphine dreams he saw—once more —his rearing horse's mane, flying pale against a white sky, each hair as fierce as a lead shaft. The wind was lacerating as shrapnel. A red sunburst of pain followed. As did the knowledge of a world about to end.

But he recovered. And found himself suddenly a hero. (Depicted with flashing eyes and plumes flying, undaunted, unafraid—on the front page of the *Illustré National*.) A taste of glory. Awed companions surrounded him; he was no longer the clumsy recruit of yesterday, fearful of horses in an outfit of cavalry. He had been decorated and cited for bravery by the great Joffre himself:

The Military Medal has been awarded to: Destouches, Louis, sergeant in the 12th Armored Division.

He volunteered to carry, under heavy fire, an order which the liaison officers of the infantry division hesitated to transmit, for the purpose of effecting communication between his brigade and an infantry division.

In the process of this mission, he was gravely wounded.[14]

He began telling the story of his exploit to eager listeners—enlarged, embellished, almost attaining the level of a legend. His verbal spell held them for hours.

And thus discovered a weird new talent in himself: he was a natural at creating oral epic (as some bards he had heard about), at releasing a great free flow of words that came as easily as any bodily function. He would say later:

> I can fabricate legends with as much facility as other men take a leak. . . .[15]

Now he was full of amazement at his own powers—this new alchemy which could transform shame, fear, or pain, into a network of artifice. A simple rite of metamorphosis, which he would never again allow to fall into disuse. But perfect into its written shape, into the craft based on trial by fire. Whose roots lay deep in his body, embedded in layers of fierce pride and despair.

FROM DESTOUCHES' "BLACK NOTEBOOK," 1914[16]

The first written attempts were testy, secretive, awkward. Jotted down in a black moleskin notebook which could easily be slipped into a pocket of his uniform at the sound of footsteps approaching. Pages scrawled in infantry barracks, amidst manure smells, in grimy lantern light. Full of forebodings for future years. Pages of passage. Painful first initiation into the world of words.

> I couldn't say what makes me want to put my thoughts into writing.

I am filled with a melancholy in which I move about like
a bird in the air or a fish in water. . . .

I have suffered, and for real, both from the present ills
and from my inferiority as a male . . . I felt that with
my back to the wall I was nothing more than a poor
transplanted guy who had lost half his faculties and was
using the remaining ones just to note his total absence
of strength. It was then, at the bottom of my abyss, that
I could devote myself to studies of my self and my soul
which can only be scrutinized profoundly I think when
it is battling with itself.

I'm a being with complex and sensitive feelings the least
lack of tact or delicacy shocks me and makes me suffer
for way inside I hide a fundamental pride which frightens
me. I want to dominate not by imaginary power like military fame but I do want, one day or as soon as possible,
to be a complete man. . . .

(Alas) will I be forever free and alone, having too complicated a heart to find a woman whom I could love for
long? I don't know. But what I want above all is a life
filled with adventure . . . which I hope providence will
put in my path and not to end up like those who've established one *single* pole of amorphous continuity on
earth and live a life in which they never take detours. . . .

. . . if I should undergo those great crises which life is
already preparing I'll perhaps be less unhappy than the
next man for I want to know and understand. . . .

. . . in a word I am proud is that a fault I don't believe
so I know that this pride will bring me serious troubles
or perhaps great *Fame*.

Naïve phrases, but keys to much that will follow; fears
and hopes of a young man which would determine many of
his acts. Questions of strength and absence of strength, pride,
multiplicity, detours and adventures, great crises, Fame.

A skilled fortuneteller could not have laid out his future more clearly before him.

Doctor, writer, adventurer, hero.
Luftmensch, madman, traitor, exile.
Soldier, cripple, prophet, prisoner.
Alchemist, miser, regicide, clown.
High man, low man, everyman, man.

Everything he was, would be, or was claimed to be.
His complex fate was beginning to unfold:

Doctors had always fascinated him. From earliest childhood he observed them, studied their moves, drawn as if by enchantment.

> A man . . . came to the Passage Choiseuil to see my sick mother or father. . . . To me, he was a miracle man who cured people, who did amazing things with a body that was out of order, I thought it was marvelous. He seemed so wise . . . that's what I thought, absolutely, a magician.[17]

He began to dream of their exploits. To desire such powers also. An absurd hope took hold of him as he carried wares from store to store, in his apprentice's smock, that he might one day join their ranks. Make magic equal to theirs. —Besides, did they not hourly watch lovely women undress, examine their most intimate parts? —A dream which would have been considered preposterous, even subversive, by his parents and their kind. Which therefore had to be nurtured in silence and cunning.

While apprenticed (to Lacloche, rue de la Paix, and Robert, rue Royale, then Wagner, rue Vieille-du-Temple), he secretly worked on his studies. If he could prepare the

baccalaureate, the first step would have been made. The witchcraft which they practiced might one day be within his reach.

In the meantime, though, he settled for some minor magic:
toward 1911 he probably landed in the establishment of
Henri de Graffigny—the wonderfully eccentric inventor Courtial des Pereires of *Mort à crédit*—whose literary double
would emerge some twenty-five years later. The scientific and
pseudo-scientific experiments delighted him endlessly. All the
varied means for defying gravity, sea pressure, sterility of
crops, seemed just so many ways of magically changing life.
(The sordid, narrow, pained confines of existence which
medicine also appeared to overcome.)

In 1912, the first part of his baccalaureate was finished.
The road now appeared smooth and open.

A violent fight with his parents overturned all this. He
enlisted. The second apprenticeship was that of war.

By 1915, the dream of medicine had been inverted. Severely
wounded, he now became the patient rather than the practi-
tioner. As such, he had to undergo their magical and not-so-
magical interventions: observations, probes, examinations
and re-examinations, surgery, transfers from hospital to hospital, stays in convalescent homes, galvanic shocks, post-
surgical care, sutures, drains. All this, only to leave his right
arm deformed, invalid. And its owner 70 percent mutilated.

(One day, his wounds would become—as in a legend—
magnified. To the right arm's injured nerves that made pain
radiate to the ear and head, a skull wound would be added.
Resulting in the supposed trepanation so much talked about.
The myth of silver disc and head injury would arise from the
fusion of a literary double with the living man. Or the confu-

sion of a character's ruse with his author's manifold masks and disguises.[18]

Ladies would someday swear that they had touched the metal plaque as they held his head in their soft arms.

A mask of pain or covering shield, maintained by Céline in years of fame and infamy to come. Worn with an actor's skill and the fierce, protective instinct of the porcupine. So well portrayed that most were mystified—or perhaps preferred explaining his acts by means of a silver plate within his skull. Where far more dangerous secrets lurked, that would make creation break forth.)

1917, THE CAMEROONS

He continued to receive rather than give medical care. His wounded right arm needed further treatment; as did the chronic enteritis which he had contracted while in the service of the Sangha-Oubangui Company at Dipinkar. The resident physician recommended evacuation to France.

1917–1920, FRANCE

So far, he had only succeeded in acquiring the sick man's view (his illnesses were all chronic). He decided it was time to see medicine from both sides now. Even if it meant beginning his career as something of a charlatan, showman, or local witch doctor.

He joined a traveling troupe of health officers—a cross between physicians and performers—who went from town to little town in Britanny, to lecture on tuberculosis to local potato growers and fishermen. Their circus-like shows were run under an imposing banner (the Rockefeller Foundation's). Destouches, to his delight, was allowed to disguise himself in an American army officer's uniform:

. . . with decorations by Pershing, if you please! The whole farce! I was the leader of this group of propaganda-agent-lecturers à la Charlie Chaplin! [19]

With their rickety equipment packed in trunks, they moved like itinerant gypsies from place to place; set up their primitive film shows in village schoolhouses, and invited the natives to attend. Who, for lack of other entertainment, gladly came—especially on market days.

> . . . most of them spoke only the local dialect and didn't understand our explanations . . . but they listened obediently, without saying a word. . . . Most of all, they came to the films! . . . Very educational, films! . . . One could see flies wandering over the surface of milk. . . . The filmstrip broke every five minutes, or jumped the track. It didn't matter . . . we repaired it. . . .[20]

His real studies of medicine, however, began in 1919. He was as naïve and untutored as his classmates, but had more bravado than the rest: only a few months later, he invited professors and resident physicians to a lecture on tuberculosis—given by him! [21] (In innocence or through fool's pride. Or perhaps only because this adventure seemed no more serious than the rest. For why should the hazards of an amphitheater outstrip those of war, espionage circles, or jungle trails? He was still young enough to view them all as simple avatars.)

The medical student's life—then, as always—mingled gravity with laughter, death with light banter. It went from fishing parties in the formaldehyde pool where cadavers were speared with hooks and pulled to shore, to winding roads on which he drove his huge motorcycle wearing goggles beneath a cowboy hat, or the Army Polygon at Rennes where he could ride the fieriest horses.[22] Laughing, as the corpses slipped across the tiled floor, his sidecar swerved and tore at hawthorn bushes, or his swift mount cleared an impossible hurdle with ease. —Frenetic outings into life, paralleled by cohabitation with death.

The result was explosive: wild pity alternated with ironic disdain; black humor gave way to tricks of incubi as, in the night, he revisited the morgue and death-wards he had seen.

One incident (seen or imagined) haunted him for years: a young girl lay dying of meningitis; her mother occupied the next cot. The child's screams were almost continuous for weeks. The mother, broken with grief, lay masturbating for hours to shut out the sounds. Even when it was finished, she could not stop.[23]

The only truly miraculous medical maneuver he retained for life was the injection of morphine:[24] As soon as the regulation "2 ccs" reached the bloodstream, twisted limbs relaxed, the mask of pain was lifted, a gentle ease closed the eyes. Thus to still pain—what greater magic could one acquire? He was determined to own the means of such power.

No matter what the price. Compromise, hypocrisy, calculated smiles—any path would be worth taking.

Even courting the daughter of the director of the medical school.

What matter, if it would bring him the great gift of stilling pain. His own body did not seem too great a price—why another's then?

RENNES, 1918

A circle of ladies drank tea in the salon. Carefully placed china cups among petits fours, served by young women trained to domestic tasks who gingerly inquired after distant relatives' health and temperatures in various provincial towns. And hid impatience beneath attentive smiles, while yearning to run under trees in summer heat, gather outlandish quantities of flowers, roll in the grass with local blades.

The slow afternoon stretched on.

Platitudes thickened the air. In the room, now like a stagnant aquarium, gossip floated lazily about, circled mildly scandalous themes. Was turned over with delectation, lapped, nibbled by the flabby lips of old women. Once exhausted, the topic floated to the surface, white belly upturned. To be replaced by matter equally slimy and appealing. The open sewers of the provincial scene all seemed to empty into this room, and were picked over with rapacious care.

Boredom and summer heat fermented the brew.

The polite circle of ladies turned into a lethargic witches' round. They nodded with torpor. Dropped wrinkled, bejeweled hands into fat laps. From time to time, one dull eye opened, to survey the young women lest they slip. Into the vice-filled streets. Where life lurked. Ready to pounce.

The door was violently thrust open. A young man almost filled its frame. With battle jacket unbuttoned, motorcyclist's gloves hung from his neck on a string, large feet stuck into heavy boots, he strode without greeting into the dim room. The door stood ajar behind him.

A stream of cool air lifted the tablecloth, swept up lace napkins, rattled the china, touched the young woman's face. Intrusion like a sudden gust at sea. Which brought fresh motion into the ordered house and words that cut like razors into stale thoughts.

"Where's Dr. Follet?" he rasped. The syllables hit the air like missiles. "I must speak to him about a pulmonary case, and quickly."

Her father's new assistant, whom he often spoke about: Louis-Ferdinand Destouches, self-taught, outrageous, with an innate talent for medicine, nurtured by struggle, and not the usual bourgeois dream.[25]

"A natural, this boy. Not like the dolts I usually teach," her father had thundered. "A born physician—except for his girl's squeamishness in the dissecting room, which I'll soon knock out of him."

Edith looked up at the arrogant, unsqueamish face above her. The blue eyes hardened in disdain, as he surveyed the polite ladies—clothed cadavers in an upright pose, who hid their imminent decay under silk corsets and flowered robes. He glanced at her briefly, but his probing gaze lingered enough to cause her unease. And flush of blood from breasts to face.

His face had changed when she next saw him. It was weary now, as if touched by the pallor of death or by contact contaminated. The blotches beneath his eyes recalled contusions of corpses; shadows, resembling bruises, outlined his chin. The hands were clenched, as in rigor mortis communicated.

He was walking slowly from the autopsy room.

He stumbled with somnambulist's gait into the street. Blinked, mole-like in the brightness. Shook his head as though to clear unseen webs out of his hair. Lurched to a tree; bent down; vomited long into the grass. Until he had emptied his innards, expelled the taste of formaldehyde and the sight of pale, rotting flesh. He leaned against the tree trunk, waiting for the nausea to pass.

When suddenly he saw her there. His expression changed. A mask of disdain instantly covered the face. An invisible visor dropped. He advanced, smiling. With an airy wave in lieu of greeting, he let his mocking eyes linger unabashed on her thin dress. Without a word he took possession of her arm and propelled her toward the river. For a long

time they watched the waters flow. The powerful barges
strain toward the sea.

"Men piss into the water," he muttered, "like sailors,
with a feeling of eternity." [26]

He stared into the distance, his face averted. Seemingly
unaware of her warmth at his side. Then pulled himself up
suddenly and turned to her with a demonic smile.

"But Mademoiselle Edith, the great Dr. Follet's daughter, will surely be compromised, wandering through the
streets with a rake like me."

Unheeding her gentle objections, he piloted her home.
Before she could speak again or question, he was gone. Moving away stealthily in the evening light. As if swallowed up
by jungle growth. —A jungle such as he had recently explored. According to the complex rumors, either as trader,
tracker of spies, adventurer or double agent; in a German
colony of the Cameroons. What the true story was, no one
seemed to know. The only trace, etched in his body and
which none could dispute, was the tropical disease from
which he was said to suffer. The rest was wrapped in silence.

1916, DIPINKAR IN THE CAMEROONS

The silence was never complete. Animal sounds—even
in the dead of night—continually filled the air. Often un-
identifiable, they swelled in complex unison, subsided, then
rose again to affirm the omnipresence of the jungle around.
He was alone in the forest hut where merchants' wares lay
piled up to the straw roof. The natives had long left the site.

> It was in the tropical forest. . . . Now you can't im-
> agine it anymore. . . . Africa is so near now that peo-
> ple go there for the weekend, so the tourists can see the
> jungle. . . . At that time, there were no tourists. . . .
> Nothing but straw huts and misery for the natives, for

us. . . . Nothing to eat except a bit of manioc. In the
part where I was, the ground can't be cultivated. . . .

So I lived in a straw hut, I learned how to make houses
out of palm leaves, I went down streams in the canoes
of the blacks. . . .

I took care of the cocoa harvest. . . .[27]

The harvest had also been one of disease.

He turned on his narrow cot which rattled as the fever
mounted, then fell. Almost in harmony with the forest sounds
or the chanting of the rivermen who paddled hollowed-out
tree trunks in waters filled with hippos and crocodiles. His
breath, as shrill as the parrot voices in the night, formed part
of the vast unity of the jungle. The individual fever dream
joined with the damp nightmare of the region about. Where
prey was stealthily tracked down and the hunter's prize was
always bloody.

What paths had he followed in the jungle night? Silence
would soon cover all the tracks left in the hot mud. Fire or
torrential rains wipe out the memory of his acts. Only dim
echoes would remain of his first, enigmatic contact with the
African soil. Never to be elucidated fully. Mute denial or
skillful disguise would screen out this time and place.

Sixteen years later, it would reappear—in literary guise
—and Dipinkar become fused with other sites to form Bam-
bola-Bragamance, in those hallucinatory pages of the dark
continent which Bardamu explored in his voyage.[28]

The only live evidence of his stay was in the intermittent
bouts of malaria which remained. Illness as fluctuating as his
face. Quiescent for long periods of time, only to break out—
in full flower of violence—when the microbe seemed conquered. Disease crowned by grandiose fever dreams, that
would become the springboard of his art.

A doctor . . . knows what malaria is . . . you've got
it all your life and that's that. . . . You get the "solemn
shivers" . . . and you shake your bed till it creaks
and cracks! . . . one fit after another . . . as regu-
lar as clockwork . . . first the shivers . . . and then
right away . . . you start raving . . . you rave and
rave. . . .

Over 102° you see everything . . . fever must be good
for something! . . . I never forgot a thing! . . . never!

(*CAS*, 108, 121)

Delirium at once dreadful and precious, sprung from
deep within the body. Hallucinogen more powerful than
opium, truer than any artificial paradise. —So much more
primitive than Proust's elegant *madeleine*. —Dark fruit of
the interior Africa he had come to know, while walking on
its outer soil. Its rituals shaped into an enduring private rite.

QUINTIN, AUGUST 11, 1919

The marriage rites were simple; stripped to essentials
at his imperious demand.

A garden reflected the radiance of Edith's face. He,
debonair in a dark suit, smiled mockingly at photographers
and sparse wedding guests. Trying to mimic Robinson Cru-
soe astride a provincial island.

He took his bride swiftly away. The car turned at the
crossroads; by-passed her home where they had laughed at
her old nursemaid's fright over his "satyr's" ways.[29] And
steered toward Paris.

His city. Where he could submerge her in unchartered
domains.

Dizzy with new sights, excited by his presence, she
moved across wide boulevards, a dim passageway that had
once been his home, up winding stairways that trailed off into
the clouds. Toward the summit of Montmartre. There, she

discovered street corners like stage sets, lit by a single gas lamp; secret squares; a hotel named Paradise; bars full of odd habitués—a whole underworld of sight, odor, and sound. Painters and pimps; sleight-of-hand artists from music halls, musicians and taciturn mimes; cutthroats and mythographers; tricksters and giants. The city's treasures in microcosm—and all the varied facets of its face.

He seemed to revel in this diversity.

Most of all, though, he was drawn to the dancers. In each new setting, they insinuated their body's grace. Until it appeared to her as if they were spinning out some invisible thread which led him, from street to street, enticed. While she was will-lessly drawn along, into a labyrinth of unknown sensations.

Did one of these join them during their first night, imposing complex sensuality upon her simple girlish dreams? Thus establishing his stake in more worlds than one; preclude adherence to a single being or state. —A fearful, yet tantalizing initiation. Which could only deepen the paradox, the magnetism of his nature. But also forebode loss and early failure of marriage, escape from the circular trap of provincial fame.

She asked herself desperately if there were no bonds that would hold, or snares strong enough to lure him into quietude.

He was restless during the long nights. The fluidity of his body—like that of his face—was both desirable and terrifying. A rush of hot flesh rocked her, then swiftly ebbed away. Each thrust combined with the threat of sudden escape. Present and absent at the same time, he gave and took away in one swift motion. She felt him slip through her locked arms. And wildly searched for something that could still this awful flow.

A child.

(Had he not moaned, as he possessed her, "I will get you with child. . . . Oh, I shall make you a child!")

She was soon pregnant.

During the months that followed, life was simplified; turned inward toward her growing womb. As if the arc of her belly described every horizon and united all opposite poles.

He often appeared suddenly at her side. Sometimes, to question her in physician's tones; sometimes, to feel the quickening life within her. Joy and perturbation were mingled in his eyes. Often, he foresaw grave dangers in her coming labor.[30] Plagued her with midwives' tales; conjured up anomaly, stillbirth, or childbed fever. Death or death-in-life seemed imminent when he spoke.

Perhaps the words he was soon to write—uttered by Semmelweiss, that initial projection of himself—were thoughts he harbored in those long months:

> I must admit that my life was hell, that the thought of death was unbearable to me, especially when it interfered with the two greatest joys of existence, being young and bringing forth life.[31]

She calmed him, moved by his solicitude. Confident in her youthful powers. Untutored still in failure or in loss.

When her time came, he could not be present. He sat without moving in their room; stared at the water below. In his mind, many horrendous fantasies were formed. (Some never to be forgotten, but appearing in his books only many decades later.) He remembered once hearing of a maternity hospital located on a street named Schlachtgasse[32] (Slaughter-Street); thought of the long lines of women he had seen in wards who "spawn, bleed, confess, scream. . . .";[33] constructed scenes from a play in his mind, such as this:

Bardamu

This daughter of the policeman . . . (he picks up the forceps), I got a grip which I thought was pretty good. . . . I squeeze (he squeezes the forceps), I pull, I thought I had it, I slipped, and caught it there . . . (he points to the eye) above the eye. I pulled it out; it was a girl, but she was dead . . . and the eye was hanging out. . . .

(EG, 246)

Edith was, however, easily delivered. When the gigantic wave of strength and pain had passed over, she found a child breathing warmly in her arms. She searched its body swiftly with her hands: fingers and toes intact; the head unmarred by its passage; eyes—his uncanny eyes—staring up into her face.

A girl: his counter-image. The living refutation of his fears.

Jubilant, they sent announcements of her birth, the formal verbiage lightened by his humor.[34]

June 16, 1920

Mr. and Mrs. Louis Destouches are happy to announce the birth of their daughter Colette.

6, Quai Richemont
Rennes

With red ink, he had drawn a child's nipple beneath the starkly engraved words. Balancing the dread mystery of birth with laughter. As later (in his works), death scenes would be attended by antics of clowns, and satyr plays mitigate the tragedies. Creation—or extinction—thus heightened by the power of farce.

In secret, though, he sat watching his child with terrified
eyes. (For there had been little reassurance in the fact of her
being baptized in a lace gown which the *Roi de Rome* had
once worn.)[35] Divining all her coming pain: the long years
of separation, a life which—as every creature's—stretched
forward into putrefaction. Under his gaze, the mild unformed
traits began to twist, dissolve, as if about to disintegrate.

She began to cry; then scream, with inconceivable fury.

What cries, God! What cries! I couldn't stand it. . . .

Eh! I said to the little howler, don't be in such a hurry,
you idiot, there'll always be time later for screeching!
. . . Don't worry, you little ass! Hold it! There'll always be enough misery to make your eyes, your head,
and the rest of you dissolve. . . .

(*VOY,* 271)

He did not say it. But the feeling of impotent rage at life's
suffering would not leave his mind.

AT THE INSTITUT PASTEUR, 1920–1924

Research began to preoccupy him now. Perhaps because
its calm and removed realm provided some relief from bedside and amphitheater.

His stay at the Institut was long enough for him to scru-
tinize the premises with his sharp gaze (as the fine satirical
description of the Institut Bioduret Joseph in *Voyage* would
one day show), and learn disdain for the omniscient pose of
scientists. —Another lesson in demystification. —Nevertheless, he also decided to play the game: he produced what he
referred to as some "little written bits"—*Physiological Observations on Convoluta Roscoffensis* (1920); *The Prolonga-
tion of Life in Silk Worms* (1921). Written in apparent
haste, full of scientific naïveté, without concern for past re-

search or bibliographical sources.[36] But reflecting more than mere medical curiosity: a need to explore what was paramount in his own life then (though in oblique, devious ways). For the first "paper" dealt with a symbiotic relationship between sea worms and algae, in which the former took on the latter's coloring (thus sacrificing its own identity); the second dwelt on hibernation and its effects on longevity. —Problems not unrelated to the form of his existence at that time, the fears, questions and dangers with which he wrestled.

But he continued to pursue his medical studies relentlessly. By June of 1923, he had passed his final examinations and chosen to undertake his internship at the Tarnier Maternity Hospital under Professor Brindeau.

1923–1924

> Through medicine . . . I grew much closer to men, to animals, to everything.
>
> (*VOY*, 240)

He now turned away from the woman and his child. Colette was growing. On summer days, in the hills surrounding Rennes, he listened and marveled at her childish talk, its charming deformations of common words. In him, however, something was also growing—a metamorphosis of words on quite a different plane.

In his study, creation (as unrelenting as a cancer) began to transform the ordinary cells of life into a monstrous growth.

Perhaps he had already diagnosed its presence as his black notebook grew; or suspected spreading contagion when it uncovered itself in an early tale—"The Waves," 1917.[37] What other works, now lost or jettisoned, had warned him of the progressive danger of creation? All the symptoms were there for him to read.

Now it broke forth. Enveloped every thought, staked out its claim during the dead of night.

The story of a life (distant from his, yet so strangely similar) was taking life within him. Feeding upon his body. Flesh of his flesh. It clamored for birth. With threat of anomaly or destruction; promise of delivery and joy. Child of his pain. Slowly forming within male entrails. Fruit of parthenogenesis which swelled a womb made fecund by its own powers —mingling male and female in creation. Hidden hermaphroditic joining in the night. The ancient story of the making of a world.

Although he would one day say:

> I always had the medical calling, but literary vocation meant nothing to me. I considered it something totally grotesque, pretentious, idiotic, not made for me. It meant nothing. . . . So, when I had to write a thesis, and write it fast, I came upon a memory and I said to myself, I'll jot down a thesis about medical history and Semmelweiss. . . .[38]

He could not deny his double calling. He knew that he must speak, that terror could, for him, be exorcised only by words:

> It's been said that dreadful things happen in our cellars.
> There are other things there also which only a doctor
> can see and understand. . . .[39]

If he would keep the black notebook's promise of ten years ago, to "know and understand," he must now speak of what he had since known. Express a vision which held grave dangers and would be the beginning of his fame. For he knew that:

> The saddest hour always comes when Happiness, that
> absurd and glorious confidence in life, gives way to truth

in the human heart. . . . is it not our lot to look this terrible truth in the face. . . . Perhaps it's this calm intimacy with their greatest secret that men's pride will least pardon us for.[40]

The long labor ended. Paralleled and exceeded the woman's toil. The final, pulsating thrust took place unaided by strange surgeon's hands. *Accoucheur's* self-delivery of an *accoucheur's* tale. Rent from his innards with the harsh forceps of his craft. Difficult first birth. Out of a wound that would continue gaping.

Birth into death.

Bystanders came to examine and marvel. Comment on likeness and heritage; predict several future fates; conjecture about further births; appraise the creature.

They awarded him a medal (yet another; for very different sacrifice from the first) made of bronze.

1924

The work lay in his hands, complete. Each word intact; the pages perfectly spaced; the title staring fixed and finalized into his eyes: *The Life and Work of Philippe-Ignace Semmelweiss (1818–1865)*. His Doppelgänger. Within this thin book lay the germ of the entire, vast body of his work.

Strange tale of sorrow. Which, despite removal in space and time, was to be echoed by his own: re-lived and deepened, grimly enlarged into the image of his life.

Here is the terrible story of Philippe-Ignace Semmelweiss.

Nothing is free in this world. Everything must be expiated, good as well as evil has to be paid for sooner or later. Naturally, the good costs a great deal more.

(SEM, 9–10)

Semmelweiss, first double of Louis-Ferdinand Céline, moving one step ahead, into the shadows, to point the way (as Robinson would lead Bardamu on the next literary journey). Semmelweiss—discoverer and *accoucheur;* rebel on incendiary paths ("Semmelweiss is fire," his author says); angry healer; impatient, venomous martyr; voyeur and seer; driven to explore each circle in the hell of life. Fated to end his long night vigil in exile and ignominy. Dead by his own folly, in the too thorough exercise of his craft.

1925

Success came easily in Rennes. The apprentice years were over now; his gilt-framed diploma hung on the wall. (Although the battle to win it had been almost as arduous as the first, its effect upon the audience of patients seemed far greater than any citations of war.)

The office on the Place des Lices was nicely appointed.

He also. So that he was much solicited by patients—especially the ladies of this provincial town. More than the precision of his diagnoses, they appreciated his rugged good looks which always cheered them in their difficult days. He, in turn, assisted them gladly in their struggle against ugliness and old age. None empathized as well as he with menses, miscarriage, birth-pangs and menopause—the sad plight of the female flesh fighting against sterility and rapid deterioration: skin subject to passage of time; ovaries swollen or drying; smooth hair and shining eyes, shapely ankles and thighs, all subjugated to the ephemeral. All that passed, never to return, excited his pity. (His other passions were faster aroused by perfect musculature and forms unblemished by time, found in non-patients of the town—to whom he also, on occasion, ministered.)

Children elicited his warmth. Was it because for a short

and wondrous span of years they seemed so exempt from sordidness and vice? Though their beauty and spontaneous joy were intact for a moment only ("until the age of eight," he said, "then they become as vicious as we, as twisted and full of rot . . ." [41]), they drew him by their spell. And were equally spellbound by him.

His voice, his gentle hands, soothed, drove away fear. He could inoculate against disease, open infected sores, calm fever dream and nightmare by his presence. When nothing else availed, he could always play the clown.

> The kid wore glasses. I sat down beside her bed. She's sick all right, but even so she was playing with her doll, kind of. I thought I'd cheer her up. I'm always good for a laugh when I put my mind to it. . . . I take a piece of string and make a kind of swing for the miserable doll. Up and down she goes, from the bed to the door-knob and back. It was very funny . . . that was better than talking.
>
> (*DIP*, 17–18)

Rennes was pointed out to him as the closest thing to Eden on French soil: his flourishing medical practice, under the protectorate of Dr. Follet; a family circle, full of free-flowing adulation and warm conjugal fare; his child's eyes— so like his own—adoringly upon him.

Warmth and quiescence could now spread their nets over him, slowly, insidiously. The curtains of his office were carefully selected and hemmed.

"Outside, there's freedom . . . ," he murmured to a visiting friend.[42] And looked past them, into the night.

He contented himself with writing another little scientific "paper"—this one called *Quinine in Therapeutic Use*. Did it reflect the struggle going on in his mind? The drug, which conscientious practitioners must laud for the prevention and cure of the exotic disease he himself had known, was also the killer of those hallucinatory flights which he must indulge in for his work, and thus as remedial, soothing and contraceptive to the dream as the lace curtains on the windowpanes.

Their glass now seemed to shut him in. As under a bell. The space that contained his life became used, stale, stagnant. The protective shield turned into a cage, solicitude into a stifling mold.

Although he would mockingly chide himself for his impatience in later years and say:

> . . . my father-in-law, old man Follet . . . was pretty rich, the bugger, five hundred thousand gold francs' income a year and the same again out of patients! My craze for independence made me split from that haven where I only had to sit tight . . . and me, who was born into such poverty! It's unpardonable . . . morons never learn! . . .[43]

Then, all he could sense was a closed passageway from which he must flee. Insulation that had to be broken through, in order to breathe, to gulp in the cold cutting air outside. To wander once again in the real night.

PARIS, 1912

Another place had once also confined him: no. 64, Passage Choiseuil. In the middle of Paris, it formed a small, secluded tunnel (such as would delight the Surrealists, but did not cause rapture in the young Destouches). True, its glass roof, while patched and soiled by pigeon droppings, shut out the rain; and shops boasting of petit-bourgeois success, formed a snug bulwark against the misery outside. There, the shopkeepers vied with each other for coquettish presentation of their wares; the smug storefronts disguised sordid, hidden toil. His mother's lace, carefully collected and restored, exhibited skill of artisan and connoisseur's eye. Paternal prestige was visibly established by employment in the Phoenix Insurance firm.

Son of clerk and artisan, he could vegetate in relative ease. (They even bought him a small boat in which to row at Ablon on the Seine on Sundays,[44] for the hygienic value of the exercise.) The Passage covered his life with a protective lid. Limited the world to small glories and petty cares.

Glass tent of his adolescent years, from which he had only ventured out on two short journeys—England, Germany —that ended abruptly and left him once again wedged into his tight lodgings. Among streams of incessant talk and recriminations that always climaxed in the threat that he would never attain the glorious post of buyer in one of Paris' major department stores. The climb up the bourgeois ladder was depicted in all its arduous glory; the peaks of commerce mapped out in the distance, aglow. And life defined as the attainment of other, and far grander passageways.

> . . . the Passage was an unbelievable pesthole. It was made to kill you off, slowly but surely, what with the little mongrels' urine, the shit, the sputum, the leaky gas pipes. The stink was worse than the inside of a prison. Down under the glass roof the sun is so dim you can eclipse it with a candle. Everybody began to gasp for breath. . . .
>
> (*DIP,* 70–71)

Pictures of objects decaying, rotting under glass, started to fill his mind. A whole storehouse of asphyxiation. The stench around him began to grow stronger. Stagnation hovered in everything about: in the lace christening gowns, crowding his mother's showcase, to which the urine of long-dead infants clung; the yellowed Valenciennes that bordered antique handkerchiefs, containing the phlegm of ages accumulated; the toddlers' bibs, artfully embroidered, that had collected the spittle of generations; and initialed wedding sheets where vanished couples had embraced—all the ejaculations of time, preserved and regurgitated.

Even the dust reeked of decay.

Despite his mother's efforts to fight off olfactory menaces by the use of white, farinaceous foods:

> . . . all my life I've eaten noodles. Noodles because you see, my mother used to mend old lace. And one thing that everybody knows about old lace is that odors stick to it forever. And the customers, well, you can't bring your customers smelly lace. So what didn't make any odors? Noodles. I ate whole washtubs full of noodles, my mother made them by the washtubful. . . . I ate boiled noodles, oh yes, oh yes, my whole childhood, noodles and bread soup. Those things were odorless.[45]

Despite attempts to render life aseptic, the smell of death clung to the passage walls.

Outside . . . outside was freedom. And swift currents of air. To sweep dust and cobwebs away. To whirl one about —unhampered—infuse breath and motion into one's life.

He broke out of the Passage Choiseuil. As he would flee across continents, whenever a trap threatened to close. In this first, untutored rending of attachments and safety rails, panic made him enter new servitudes to shake the old: thus, he exchanged cavalry barracks for glass-covered cage, stables for storefronts, the forest of Rambouillet for the commercial Paris jungle. In hope of feeling easier among the mares and roughshod stallions than behind counters of lace.

The hardest was to ignore his mother's tears, sticky and sweet as bird-lime; build barriers that shut out the flood of her imploring voice; escape the snares of her caress.

Only by brutal means could one be certain of escape.

1925–1926

Edith neither cried nor implored.

For a long time she thought that she would die. His leave-taking was brutal—but no more so than the first eruption into her life. Without warning, he walked into the night, as easily as he had invaded the drawing room some years ago. She was once again stranded on a provincial island in a circle of lamplight and family councils, where now she and the child had become easy marks for pity and shame.

She only knew that he roamed across Europe, from Geneva to Liverpool. Someone informed her that, through the Rockefeller Foundation, he had found his way into the League of Nations and become a doctor for the World Hygiene service. Now as before, he crossed far seas in quest of exotic diseases: to track the course of sleeping sickness and malarial fever, hunt down bacteria with quinine and pursue the tsetse fly.

While her own body ached, unrelieved.

When her family's urgings grew unbearable, she had to submit to "reason" and relent. They obtained a judgment of divorce.[46]

He was informed of the decree, while on the high seas.

Was this what he had searched for, to be free and polymorphous, devoid of civil state and ties of flesh, adrift on forever unchartered waters?

He moved on, relentlessly. Stood astride numberless decks; boarded a variety of ships whose prows were pointed to ever further ports of call. As in a dream, where all that mattered was to remain fluid without end. Alien in each new setting; rootless, never touching ground; *Luftmensch* or

wandering Jew; itinerant bard. Perhaps simply a man in need
of shifting realities, prone to that free-floating panic for life
which does not permit standing still, for fear that the earth
under one's feet will decay.

> While one stays in one place, things and people fall
> apart, putrefy and begin to stink, expressly for you. . . .
>
> (*VOY*, 272)

At every new departure, a siren call rent the air, brought
forth his huge laughter. Each time it blew, he uttered the
raucous sound, as if delivered. The powerful blast of the
horn wiped out past and future, swelled to envelop all the
dimensions of time. Swept along all lesser noises in its deep
wail.

Mournful and majestic, it affirmed the rites of passage.
Signal for leave-taking, more moving than a thousand agitated handkerchiefs or floods of women's tears. The vibrations coursed through him. His body's rhythm responded to
the call, thrilled in unison with the shattering organ sound.

And yet, the vessel hesitated, landlocked, captive.

> . . . it would move off, if the men weren't straining to
> hold it back with a hundred thousand ropes, it would
> lift itself up, all naked, from the docks, it would wander
> in the clouds, fly to the top of the sky, a live harp in the
> oceans of blue, that's how it would take off, as the spirit
> of travel, all indecent, all you'd have to do is close your
> eyes, and you'd be carried away for a long time, gone
> into the spaces of magic, of no-more-worries, a passenger
> of all dreams in the world! . . . Miracles are nothing,
> else but this! Ah, I want no other miracles!
>
> (*PL*, 319)

Suddenly, the ropes dropped one by one into the shallow waters. Cut by an ax. Each stroke severed attachments
to land. Then the tugboats came—like servants ministering
—to push the transatlantic giant into the deep.

The shore receded.

The vessel, gathering its own power now, swung out of the harbor. Relentless and slow. Unheeding of shelter, wake, or seagulls' cries. Prow turned toward the sea. The open, forever new. The birthplace of eternal passage.

NEW YORK, 1926

It was some surprise.

> Just imagine, it was standing up, their city, absolutely straight. New York is an upright city. Naturally, we had all seen cities before and some mighty beautiful ones too, and ports, some famous ones at that. But at home, the cities lie down, on the edge of the sea or river banks, they stretch out on the landscape to await the traveler, while that American one wouldn't swoon one bit, oh no, it was real tight, standing there, not at all ready to lie down for you, so rigid that it gave you a fright.
>
> (*VOY,* 184)

It was this city which awaited the traveler at "the other end of the world." The spaces of magic foundered on these unwelcoming shores. The twenties did not roar here, they simply echoed in stone chasms and died away in the long hotel corridors where liveried boys—like messengers from Hades—led one to rooms resembling isolation cells. Once the door closed, the occupant found himself walled in, unable to move or imagine furnishings otherwise disposed. Knowing that beyond this cubicle endless rows of others stretched, identical, inhuman as a hecatomb.

In terror, one would try the door. Find that, despite one's conviction it opened. Only to have the endless corridor, symmetrically perforated by doors numbered in thousands, lead one to another cubicle which moved in perpendicular fashion to the street. There, more numerical signs assailed the traveler. The thoroughfares had no names! Neither did the side streets. The crossroads resembled the points on a graph. Signifying nothing.

Lights suddenly glared, in harsh profusion. Spelled out a series of messages, of cryptic signals which no one appeared to heed. "Times Square" a street sign read, inexplicably resorting to words now. Time seemed to have lost its meaning here. In the middle of night, the sidewalks were bathed in artificial day; the crowds were as thick as during the noon hours. Restaurants beckoned everywhere, though once inside it seemed that it was all a huge error: the young women there resembled nurses in surgical garb, the plates contained shimmering, garish objects that appeared to have no imaginable relation to food. Yet people dissected them with knives, stuck forks into the rigid shapes, ladled a shivering heap of brightly colored cubes into their mouths, expressionless. Others put coins into a machine, which unlocked doors; they lifted out cellophane-wrapped things which they devoured swiftly, before one could identify them. Coins inserted in other places, followed by the pulling down of a lever, produced streams of hot liquid which spurted into a cup that fell, inexplicably, into place.

The natural impulse was to run. Back. To the hotel. It had an odd name: the Laugh Calvin;[47] or was that simply a trick of the imagination? An attempt at weak laughter which this city would soon wipe out. He found his way back. Perhaps from some blind instinct, like that of a mole returning to its burrow.

The room was better left dark. Then, the window seemed to lead out, to provide some perspective of escape, an illusion of extended space. Opposite, there were other windows. Perhaps a bit of voyeurism would provide relief. Or the reassurance that he had not landed on a totally dead planet. —In the rooms facing his, the shades were sometimes half drawn, sometimes left completely rolled up.

The women had very full, very pale thighs, at least those that I could see. Most of the men were shaving, while smoking a cigar, before going to bed.

In bed they took off their glasses and then their false teeth which they put in a glass, in full view. The men and women didn't seem to talk to each other, no more than on the street. They could have been big, docile beasts, quite used to being bored. I saw only two couples doing things that I expected, with the light on, and not wildly at all. The other women ate chocolates in bed while their husbands washed up. And then they all turned out the light.

(VOY, 198–199)

Night took over. From below, there came only the mechanical sounds of garbage trucks, the passing El, sometimes the eery wail of police sirens. Then the city shut like an oyster which not even the most jagged knife could pry open to longings or cries. It was impossible to sleep, to fall into the vertigo of silence, not to think.

That's exile and estrangement, this inexorable observation of existence as it really is, during those long, lucid hours so exceptional in the web of human time, when the habits of your former country abandon you and the others, the new ones, haven't sufficiently stupefied you.

. . . you see things, people, and the future as they really are, that is as skeletons, nothing but nothings, which nevertheless one must love, cherish, defend, animate as if they really existed.

(VOY, 214)

He suddenly understood the lemmings, their mad urge to break out of the burrow, go swarming in thousands and millions across the countryside, scourging the crops in their path, devastating all vegetation, to throw themselves—at last —headlong into the sea. Their mysterious blind flight toward annihilation. The only quiescence when, finally, their brown bodies formed a blanket on the waves. A statement of nothingness thus mutely spelled out.

But what was a man to do? Who did not have the rodent's single-minded despair. And was saddled with the proud burden of language.

He waited for the vertigo to pass. For the void to cake over once more.

In the meanwhile, he began groping for antidotes. Simple means. Primitive, halting copes that would permit time and habit to take hold: sleep, movies full of warm foetal darkness; women.

> It's only the women that are worth looking at in this place. They should make public gardens out of them, since their cities are so ugly. . . .
>
> (*EG*, 89)

At first he could not believe that they were real; that all the promises held out in films that he had seen would here be realized. Who would have thought that the revelation of such beauty would now explode before him in all its plenitude? He followed them in the streets, dazed. No longer aware of the cement labyrinth in which he dwelt. Their flesh hid the skeletal structure that lay beneath each morsel of existence. The solid flow of muscles was pitted against the flabby, amorphous mass of time. On beaches, the insubstantial forms of jellyfish were obscured by the blinding flash of bathers' limbs. The salt's savor slowly returned.

> Ah! Ferdinand . . . as long as you live you'll go searching for the secret of life between the legs of women!
>
> (*EG*, 223)

It was the best place he had yet found. The secret he sought at this point was simple—how to go on, and how re-

turn. The search, he knew, would lead him to greater nothingness still. He must have sustenance for this journey. Their
flesh was the luminous feast from which he could rise, re-
freshed and fortified.

Yet a phrase hauntingly recurred in his mind, a mocking chant: "love is the fear of dying," nothing more.

He took this fear and, having voiced it, laid it aside
among a store of secrets he had gathered. Used it to urge
him on, propel him on the path he had to take. Women
known or invented—Elisabeth, Lola, Vera, Molly—accompanied him, offering both yearning and relief from yearning,
malice and candor, spice and repletion. Whetting his appetite for life once more. Until he felt almost whole.

Now he could move on to explore other cities. Among them,
Detroit, the capital of the machine. Where the assembly-line
culture flowered; where one could use an epidemiologist's
skill to study the exotic diseases it had indubitably produced.
Perhaps isolate the virus at the root of modern times. Which
had been infecting whole populaces with astonishing speed.

It seemed to him that he had always intended this pil-
grimage. The first revelation had come at an age when other
children expressed their mechanical devotion by dissecting
their fathers' watches with a skillfully bent fork:

PARIS 1900—THE WORLD'S FAIR

Although I was still quite young, I nevertheless remember quite clearly that it was an enormous brutality. Especially the feet, feet everywhere and clouds of dust so
thick that one could touch them. Interminable lines of
people passing, hammering, crushing the Fair, and then
that moving sidewalk that squeaked all the way to the

gallery of machines, filled, for the first time, with metal
under torture, with colossal menaces, with catastrophes
held in suspense. Modern life was beginning. . . .[48]

DETROIT, 1927

A desolate place, even more hostile than French provincial towns whose windows all seem to turn from the
passer-by. At night, the blast furnaces shot up into the sky
with fierce bursts of flame; during the day, a slow rain fell
on the parallel streets. Not a curve anywhere in the plan of
the city; all angles, designed to jar or chafe. Gray frame
houses with loose boards squeaking in the wind. Drugstores,
displaying patent remedies, false teeth, and rubber rings for
preventing bedsores. A chain of Woolworth's. Bars that invited nothing, tiredly repelled trade by a display of plaster
sandwiches beneath neon signs naming local brands of beer.

In one part of town, he saw long lines of people, shuf-
fling, waiting to be admitted into a wooden enclosure, much
like a stockyard. A shapeless crew—immigrants with sweaty
feet and mouths full of decay; veterans with prosthetic limbs
or limp sleeves stuffed into pockets; a few trailing mongoloids
—assembled before the door on which a slate announced the
date and hours of hiring.

The heavy gates swung open. The men swarmed forward and were engulfed: into the palace of machines.

> . . . solid, glassed-in buildings, something like an end-
> less series of fly-cages, in which one could discern men
> moving, but just barely, as though putting up a feeble
> fight against some impossible foe. So this was Ford? All
> around and up to the sky, a heavy and manifold noise, a
> low rumble of machinery, harsh, the stubborn persist-
> ence of machines that turn, roll on, moan, always ready
> to break down but never breaking down.
>
>   (*VOY,* 223)

The men seemed no less stubborn. They limped, hobbled, groped their way to the examining rooms. Lisped,
drooled, ranted in a babel of voices, trying to convince the
doctors of their viable state. The white-coated examiners did
not seem difficult to please. After a perfunctory check, they
nodded, approved. The rumors were justified: Ford hired
anyone, anything—providing it could take its place in the
complex rotations of the machine. Imbeciles, cripples, syph-
ilitics, the blind, the halt, the insane were all received with
equal, indifferent benevolence. What mattered the hernias,
weak hearts, petit and grand mal, tuberculosis, heart murmurs, nephritis, or catatonia[49]—when all would be reduced
to the level of mute things. So partial would be their function
that a single sound limb sufficed, a Cyclops' eye would have
been a plethora, two ears a needless redundancy, a whole
man an overstatement.

The only failing to merit immediate dismissal, was the
propensity to think. An outrage such as this was paramount
to betrayal. Promethean defiance was, by comparison, the
mere prank of a disobedient child playing with matches during his parents' absence from home.

> You're not here to think, but to make the motions which
> we order you to execute. We don't need imagination in
> our factories. What we need are chimpanzees. . . .
>
> (VOY, 224)

The men soon sank much lower than chimpanzees.
(These primates, when bored, will invent games with their
own spittle trickling down a wall.) When the enormous brutality of mass production had enveloped them, crushed them
into silence with its relentless noise, they became themselves
objects. Utilitarian shapes of steel, devoid of any former
meaning. Inanimate. Indefinable. Solid and mute as things.

This was perhaps one of the lower reaches of hell which
he had wished to visit. The frozen center where life stood

still, was so diminished that one could hardly perceive it move.

He had seen enough.

The years of exploration were over now; he swung full circle back to the starting place.

Not, however, without having recorded his journey. The logbook of his internal discoveries had taken the shape of a play. (A bad one, a "real flop," according to his own appraisal.)[50] It was a curious outcome of his circumnavigation of the globe: a work in which three continents were demolished through the twin explosives of anger and laughter. Where no caste, race, or nation was spared; and the prime truth of life was, once again, revealed as death.[51]

How changed its tone was—how far from the earlier melancholy. The written word seemed to have acquired a hardness, a brilliance unalloyed by sentimentality, a power which came from violence shot through with flashes of dark laughter. He had found his authentic voice.

With which he would from now on speak.

Now he could take the path back. The swiftest ship was to his liking. He booked his passage as others put on a traveling coat. Knowing that all outward journeys had, for the time being, been made. The inward voyage could now begin.

1928—ON THE OUTSKIRTS OF PARIS

On the surface, it looked simply like a return to the place of his birth. He knew that despite the comeback from "the Other World" like some fabled hero from his journey, he had to once more take up "the thread of the days left hanging here, slimy, precarious. Waiting. . . ."[52]

*   *   *

One of the threads was medicine.

Not the comfortable practice at Rennes, where patients seemed to be entering a plush salon rather than a consulting room, and illness was one among many fashionable indulgences to tide one over when other pleasures failed.

He opened a small practice at 36, rue d'Alsace in Clichy —a suburb every bit as sordid as its literary portrait which he would soon paint.[53] There to become a doctor of the local poor which inhabit those disinherited regions that border Paris (which he would one day depict, almost tenderly, in all their abject horror):

> Poor Parisian suburbs, doormat in front of the city where everyone wipes his feet, spits heartily, passes on, who thinks of them? Nobody. Worn out by factories, stuffed with manure, cut up into rags, just some land without a soul, a damned labor camp where smiles are futile, all effort is lost, and suffering becomes insipid. . . . Permanent calvary of hunger, work, bombardments, who cares? Nobody of course. . . . Bitter suburbs that always bubble with a sort of revolt which no one ever furthers or ends, sick to death always, and never dying.[54]

This long agony he chose to watch over and perhaps alleviate.

He fixed his plaque upon the stone wall of a house in suburbs such as these. It then read:

DOCTEUR LOUIS DESTOUCHES
MÉDECINE GÉNÉRALE
MALADIES DES ENFANTS
IER À GAUCHE

And at night, began to write.

*   *   *

The metamorphosis of Dr. Destouches into Louis-Ferdinand Céline was about to take place. With the help of a secret formula no more obscure than ink, his night double would now arise. *Rite de passage* as irreversible as that which marks entry into manhood. And equally full of risks and promise. He was now ready—armed with sounds more ominous than bull-roarers amidst laughter—to take full possession of his craft.

. . . even looking hard, you won't find one
first-rate female in a thousand! I mean
it! . . . vitality, muscles, lungs, nerves,
charm . . . knees, ankles, thighs, grace! . . .
I'm difficult, I admit it . . . the tastes
of a Grand Duke, an Emir, a breeder of
thoroughbreds! . . . okay! we all have our
little weaknesses. . . . But I can tell you
this . . . the anemic, rachitic, cellulitic . . .
ageless and soulless monsters men run
after! . . . heavenly day! . . . with cocks aflame,
ah yes, my dear! . . . are enough to make the
most priapic gibbons cut their balls off
with neurasthenic disgust!

CÉLINE

3

THE SHADOWS OF WOMEN
ON THE WALL

MONTMARTRE, CA. 1934

The two girls played in his room. High up on the rue
Lepic, overlooking Paris with its steep streets curving downward between the frayed wings of the Moulin de la Galette.
Old wood gleamed here and there among the graceful furnishings, a gilded 18th-century Cupid hung from the ceiling,
circling lazily about. Paintings by friends—Vlaminck, Gen
Paul—enlivened the walls. The windows were flooded with
red geraniums.[1]

Eliane watched the older Colette, his daughter, explore
the various recesses of the room: leaf through a manuscript,
pause to examine a rare stamp on an envelope. She admired
the brazen freedom of her friend. Colette treated all topics
—sex, books, travel—with equal candor. Her father's tute-
lage had become evident. The younger girl, timid when in
the midst of Céline's domain as pilgrims are upon holy
ground, sat in a corner and explored only with her eyes.

She was soon struck by some inscriptions above his bed.
Graffiti which, in the past, she had associated only with
lavatories or grim schoolyard walls. Here, one could decipher
series of women's names, dates, and messages (banal reminders of love or cryptic signs) scratched into the white

plaster. Colette, noticing her puzzlement, shrugged knowingly and said: "My father's ladies . . . they come and go. Those are their shadows on the wall."

Eliane marveled, with childish awe, at the great daring which had led them to write upon the wall—forbidden wish of her early years when she had yearned to cover such tempting expanses of whiteness with pictures growing in her mind.[2]

Names, dates, and shadows . . . more ephemeral than lines carved in the bark of trees or silhouettes of Balinese puppets (soon to be effaced, or painted over by future occupants of these walls). Long cortege of women, lost in the mists of time. Only a few among them would ever be more than nameless shades, those whose forms were retained in the printed memory of letters or books: Eveline . . . Erika . . . Lucienne . . . Elisabeth . . . Karen . . . Arlette . . . Natasha . . . Lucette . . . Lili. . . .

In banter and gravity joined; summed up in another inscription scrawled on the wall (facing the occupant of the bed squarely):

Come, let us be bored together!

which a king had spoken long ago, as he beckoned a plump maiden to his side.[3]

CLICHY: 36, RUE D'ALSACE
MONTMARTRE: 98, RUE LEPIC
1928–CA. 1933

He had named her "The Empress." A title which all who saw her, found apt. Tall, regal, obviously of foreign birth, she had that removed elegance which elicits conjectures of the most varied kind. Some thought her an exiled countess who dwelt incognito among them in this shabby

suburb of Paris; others held that she was a queen among call-
girls in some great American city (for Frenchmen believe
that the fleshpots of Egypt have moved to New York or Los
Angeles, as fervently as Americans locate them in the French
metropolis); the butcher's wife was certain that "the stranger"
had come to perform orgiastic dances in the doctor's flat, so
savage that they made the ceilings groan and bedbugs flee in
terror throughout the house. —When four years later he
moved because of an invasion of these insects, she nodded
wisely, her suspicions about the origins of their migration
finally confirmed.

By her aloofness, she made all their attempts at elucida-
tion grow and cloak her, like gauze veils, in silence.

Actually, Elisabeth Craig was a dancer. It was the
source of that subtle grace they had all tried to define and
ascribed to such a variety of roles. The anonymity pleased
her. She flitted swiftly through the halls, avoided the concierge's innuendos, paused hardly long enough on the stairs
for anyone to get a glimpse of her face.

Her portrait however, would remain etched in a painter's mind:

> Large cobalt eyes, small finely shaped nose, a sensual
> rectangular mouth, long reddish-gold hair that flowed
> down to the shoulders, firm arrogant little breasts, the
> legs of a dancer. . . .[4]

In other words, all the womanly traits which Destouches—
throughout his life—desired: the Nordic beauty he prized,
but most of all, those marks of nobility to which he ascribed
an uncommon importance:

> I remember as if it were yesterday . . . her long blond
> legs, magnificently slender and muscular, noble legs.
> True human aristocracy, I don't care what anyone says,
> is conferred by the legs. . . .

> (*VOY*, 227–228)

And if to him her limbs were regal in repose and matter for
impassioned scrutiny, in motion they provided utter delight.

> She had that winged, supple, precise walk which is so
> frequent, almost habitual in American women, the walk
> of the great beings of the future whom life carries
> ambitiously yet lightly toward ever new forms of ad-
> venture. . . . Three-master of tender joy, en route to
> the Infinite. . . .
>
> (*VOY*, 463)

(His love for women and ships made him, quite naturally,
link them in image. He and a painter-friend developed a
system of classification by which females were identified in
nautical terms: young girls were "skiffs"; next came "schooners"; finally, the great "three-masters" or "clippers." —Elisabeth Craig was definitely a "clipper," they concurred, and of
the finest design.)[5]

She had sailed into his life with dancer's lightness. Into
an adventure which did not lack in ambition nor variety of
form. With dancer's swiftness, she would one day leave him.
To vanish into the far continent from which she had come,
across the sea. Leaving no trail, nor wake. But only a voice
in his memory (with the slight accent that gave such charming estrangement to the French words she spoke) echoing in
his mind long after she had gone. And her perfumes embedded in the walls, where a line from Shakespeare had been
inscribed that spoke of men as moving shadows.

Now, however, she reigned with the power of a Tarot Empress over his secret domain, and the profound changes that
were taking place. Threshold demon or accomplice to the
metamorphosis which transformed Dr. Destouches into Louis-
Ferdinand Céline (or "Dr. Jekyll" into "Mr. Hyde," as he
would one day jokingly say).[6] A strange transfiguration—

although it produced no other hairy beast than the manuscript he referred to as his "bear." From simple male to complex androgyne.

For he now chose to join his masculine first names to a female pseudonym (drawn from his mother's middle names: Marie Marguerite Céline Destouches, nee Guillou).[7] If pressed, he offered a variety of explanations—that it was just a mask to prevent recognition by patients who might be wary of consulting a "cacographer and pornographer" about their ailments; a decoy that would lead intruders into his double life astray. In truth, though, it seemed an odd, transvestite refuge whose irony could not have escaped him. The deeper implications did not necessarily surface at once.

What could Elisabeth have thought of all this? Had she overheard one of his friends say: "He has the body of a dame. Not a muscle on him . . . "?[8] Or known him to insist that she, also, transcended the simple boundaries of sex (all neatly prescribed and classified, denying transgression and fusions, as if to effect these were the prerogative of perverts alone, and not the ancient privilege of those outside the common fold):

> I lived for . . . years with Elisabeth Craig. . . . She had the traits of a Molière turned woman, and all his wit! all his genius too. . . .[9]

Perhaps she sensed only that she was the complex companion he needed for the road which he was now about to take. For under her wide eyes, *Voyage au bout de la nuit* was taking form.

Heavy sheaves of paper soon cluttered the room. The wheel of his mind seemed to spin, unwind a thread of words in the dark Paris nights. With dizzying speed, it encircled whole

worlds, drove into the underground, dredged up emotions
—still dripping—from the unexplored treacherous deep.

She picked up the sheets of paper and hung them on
clotheslines around him (at his request), like laundry put
out to dry. With the docile air of a servant. Who could not
know that one day he would write of her:

> What genius in that woman! I would never have become
> anything without her—What wit! What finesse . . .
> what dolorous yet impish pantheism. What poetry—
> What mystery. . . . She understood everything before
> you'd said a word—Women who aren't basically rotten
> or servile, are rare—then, they're sorceresses or good
> fairies—.[10]

She felt herself receding into the background. Sorcery
and fairies' spells had no power over him now. Her embraces
remained unanswered, while he labored. Like limbs that are
lopped off in midair but continue the gesture intended. Or
severed heads that persist in speaking (as in the story he had
once told her, of a head that lay in the basket below the
guillotine and when asked, "Does it hurt . . . Where does
it hurt?" tried to mumble something, before dying in his
hands).[11]

His body's juices were all spent upon the paper; the
fountain of his sex turned inward; the exploration of her flesh
was as nothing, when compared to the penetration of the vast
labyrinth within.

The quest for monsters demanded monstrous denial.

Thus, she would become "Sabeth, the Forsaken," to
his friends.[12] Magnificent and futile, she roamed the streets
of Montmartre; drank nightly in the bars; let them caress her
in his stead. In his presence even.

To no avail. Unheeding, he continued his search. In the
morning, she wearily gathered the sheets of paper which were

the sole harvest of the night. Once, passing one of the large African statues near the door (the one that held out its hand), she remembered his bantering comment: "That's the gesture of the gods. They're begging for alms!" [13] The resemblance between them continued to chafe her. Each motion of her hands seemed suddenly like a mendicant's plea.

When the huge manuscript was finished, it bore her name in dedication. . . . Love's labors not lost but transformed into paper. Her limbs an offering upon the word altar; her quivering woman's flesh transfigured into verbal artifice.

She shook her blond *fauve's* mane and fled.

For the first time.

(When questioned, she would reply that she had been disinherited on the other side of the sea, as if that was where the true loss had been incurred, adding that her birthright and other inalienable rights were at stake. The legal proceedings were long, she wrote, and would undoubtedly detain her for quite a while. The threat of material deprivation—so quickly bought by those for whom Americans were money-lovers above all else—was so much easier to spell out than alms-taking.)

For months she wandered aimlessly: New York, Chicago, Los Angeles, and back. Knowing that despite everything she was still bound. Remembering also that she had once heard him say: "To feel pain . . . keeps one occupied." Oceans would not shut out his enigmatic face, the fierce spell of his hands and gaze. She knew that she must return if only to bring Colette a sky-blue robe,[14] which would —for an instant—still the pain in his child's eyes.

*   *   *

Back in Paris, much had changed. He had left Clichy for
Montmartre. The old house in the suburbs reeked of "Fly-
tox" and "Mortis," an even more potent insecticide. All the
occupants of 36, rue d'Alsace had joined in the epic sport of
bedbug hunting, armed with knitting needles, newspaper, and
kerosene. Springs crowded the halls, their four iron legs
sticking stiffly into the air, as those of shot animals. Bed-
spreads trailed like banners on the landings.

Their apartment stood empty, the door ajar. The furnishings had been hastily removed. The masks and statues
were gone, there were no longer any marigolds at the bay
window; the walls looked shadowy in the late afternoon light.
Already foreign, their familiar meaning blanked out.

When she found him, he seemed just as empty and
changed. Drained of his substance. The haggard face and
halting walk, the hands that seemed suddenly those of an
ascetic—all made him appear hollow. Now that the book
which he had carried to term was delivered, he had become
as slack as the abdomen of a post-parturate.

She heard from a friend that his father had died in the
interim.

And also, the story surrounding the discovery of his
work:

How the bundle of pages had been thrown upon the
table of the young proofreader who was their neighbor in
Clichy; her faithful preparation of his "bear" for its first
showing; the simultaneous submission of the manuscript to
Gallimard and a bright young team of publishers named
Denoël & Steele. How Denoël had devoured "Voyage au bout
de la nuit" in one long night and had exclaimed in the morning, "I must have that man!" [15] The rest of the tale began to
sound like the anecdotes people fondly relate about the dis-

covery of famous works of art: Denoël realized that he had
no notion of the author's identity. The brown paper parcel in
which the manuscript had arrived bore only an address
(98, rue Lepic) and a woman's first name (Céline). Further
confusion arose from the submission of another manuscript
(this one, by a lady author). Denoël was said to have raced
to the address in Montmartre and inquired at the concierge's
for a Madame Céline. The good woman claimed to know no
one by that name. A lot of explanations followed, coupled
with conjectures, eliminations, hints of possible identity. The
attempts at sleuthing seemed to no avail, when suddenly the
concierge exclaimed (so the story goes): "My God, it must
be that nut who lives on the fourth floor!" [16] And proceeded
to identify that bizarre personage who healed by day and
wrote at night. They raced to the dispensary in Clichy where
he worked as Dr. Destouches; unmasked him; and signed the
contract on the spot. It was that signature which would
launch him into world-wide fame.

The printing was now beginning. He seemed so tense that
Elisabeth scarcely dared to approach him. (Although he had
welcomed her as if she had returned from the underworld,
triumphant—a self-styled Eurydice without benefit of songs
or lyre.)

  He started out early in the mornings for the abandoned
chapel on the rue Amélie, which Denoël & Steele used for
their offices. It had been stripped of all its religious vestiges,
except for the wood altar which served as Denoël's desk and
a few pews on which visitors (such as Antonin Artaud) [17]
would lounge, deep in conversation.

  Céline prepared for these outings by a series of maneuvers which were as bizarre as the setting for which they were
destined. She saw him lower motorcyclist's goggles over his

eyes; put on a large sheepskin coat; chain the brief case containing his manuscript to his wrist, and fasten it with a large padlock (with such gravity that one of his friends remarked, "If anyone wants to steal his baby, they'll have to cut off his arm!")[18]

Yet, when it came to the printed version of his work, he vacillated between extreme concern and total indifference: he proudly read long passages—just off the press—to the assembled company, acting, laughing, gesticulating, giving the words their rightful accents and infusing them with life; but also threw down the proofs, exclaiming with disgust that a book was just a form of death; and considering it necessary to protest:

> I never reread Voyage and I never will. I find it all boring and flat enough to make one puke. . . .[19]

As the publication date approached, he became more and more anxious. Almost panic-stricken. He planned a trip out of Paris, made Denoël promise to keep the secret of his identity, predicted dire consequences from the appearance of his book: "I shall go to prison . . ." he muttered,[20] and would not accept reassurances. He seemed intent on prophesying his own future—with gaze as fixed as if he were staring into a private crystal ball—in which the manuscript chained to his wrist would accompany him like a convict's manacles (changing its shape but never its weight).

In the fall of 1932 *Voyage au bout de la nuit* finally appeared. He would not let his mother read it, despite her name. Instead, he took one of the first copies to Jeanne, the young proofreader; in it, he had placed a piece of fine old lace. "It comes from my mother's," he said, "hold on to it, little one,

one day it'll be worth a fortune." [21] (Not specifying whether he meant the book or the square of lace.) She was most struck by his weariness. He had the air of someone illuminated, an inward look; but also the heavy gait of a convict in irons. "It's been seven years," he grumbled, "and the next one is already under way." Apparently, he could no longer lay his pen down. One labor had ended, but the procreative process had already begun anew. A constant inner growth fed on his body and would not relent, until it had forced its way into the light.

The book caused an immediate sensation. As did the nature of the man. All the newspapers seemed filled with accounts about this startling new work and its strange author. Attacks and adulation alternated with unrelenting speed. Catchwords to characterize his novel appeared everywhere (garbage, mud, scatology, vulgarity, sadism, despair, public danger— but also, modern Rabelais, Montaigne, Voltaire, Villon, Zola, Jarry, Dostoyevsky . . .)[22] Valéry would sum it all up neatly: "A book of genius, but criminal." [23]

Photographers began to appear at his house and at the clinic in Clichy—to capture his face, as though he were some unknown beast fit for a side show. He felt stripped, almost deflowered.

Especially when the more brazen suggested that he should pose at his worktable. (The most shameful place.) In a position which he had, years ago, already considered revolting:

> One must never allow oneself to be photographed at
> one's writing desk—First of all, it's disgusting to write,
> it's a form of excretion. Does one allow oneself to be
> photographed in the middle of taking a crap?
>
> (*EG,* 112)

Now they invaded every corner of his life, even the most
intimate. He did not know where to hide. His face stared at
him from every newsstand. He felt trapped. And began
thrashing about wildly, looking for a way to escape: he
thought, alternately, of growing a beard, committing suicide,[24] or leaving the country. Anything to make them forget
him, to feel less bruited about, not so much like a "slut." [25]

(Not that he minded being feted in a manner befitting
some great woman of the world. It was a distinction which
remained vital to him until the end of his life. "I'm a *femme
du monde*, Sir," he would insist, "not a whore. I choose!")[26]

Now, however, the choice was not his.

The Goncourt Prize, a coveted award and worthy of the
most admired literary beauty, had almost seemed his. —He
had even allowed Denoël to print the brightly colored bands
that would adorn each book at his coronation. —But at the
last minute, it slipped through his fingers. A cautious jury
awarded the prize to a book now long lost in remainder sales:
Les Loups, of Guy Mazeline. Despite the fact that scandal
rocked the Academy as the celebrated patron of *Voyage*
(Lucien Descaves) walked out, slamming the door behind
him.

The Renaudot which Céline was awarded in the Goncourt's stead, seemed to him nothing but a consolation prize
such as is given in children's games, to keep the loser from
sulking.

He feigned indifference. And proceeded to lambaste
academies with even greater vigor than before, now that their
corrupt nature had been made totally manifest.

Beneath the mask, however, he was touched to the
quick. "Do not leave me alone," he said to Jeanne, the
evening the Goncourt was lost.[27] And shortly afterwards, fled
to Germany (in the company of his mother). He had con-
veniently obtained a mission from the League of Nations to

study the social problems of the workers there. But the timing of the trip seems to have been determined by one final, outrageous irony: the Galeries Lafayette (one of Paris' major department stores) had offered one thousand francs an hour if he would sign his book in public during its sale! [28]

Right after his return, he published an article to justify the book (the only one of its kind he ever deigned to write). It concluded with a quote from Thomas à Kempis—translated into the language of Céline:

> Do not try to imitate the lark or the nightingale, if you can't do it! If it's your destiny to croak like a toad, then go ahead! And with all your might! Make them hear you! [29]

But he also returned from Germany with a study that bore a Swiftian title: "To kill unemployment, will they kill off the unemployed?" (It was published at the same moment as his postscript to *Voyage* and came to similar conclusions as the novel: that peace and brotherhood were absurd illusions and that the fundamental question remained, "To be bored or not to be . . . .")[30]

The trip was followed by others. Elisabeth accompanied him most of the time. He moved from place to place as restlessly as Bardamu—his double. Antwerp . . . Geneva . . . Vienna . . . Breslau. . . . Sometimes, to see the Breughels that he loved for their black laughter, so well fitted to his mood:

> I only rejoice in the grotesque on the edge of death. All the rest seems futile to me.[31]

Sometimes, to stand staring at the sea-locks that led the ships, step by step, into the unformed deep. Releasing the hold of the land, as each progressive gate opened. (Did she, the "three-master" at his side, share this longing?)

Occasionally, his child was with them. She sensed the uneasiness within him with instinct as sure as that of the woman. And yet, Colette craved to be near and hear his voice take on those serious tones he knew how to take with children, that made them suddenly equals, accomplices, compatriots. It was only his silences that made her quake, the brooding mask of his face. Which suddenly descended on him, even at the edge of the sea.

Then she saw him scribble words such as these:

Dinard, August 1934

I am here with my daughter. Everything thrusts us forward and everything changes. The very dust ages. There are less and less sails on the sea. . . .[32]

Only when they were moving, did he seem more at rest. The rhythm of the wheels seemed to soothe him. He was suddenly in high spirits and agreed to play their secret game: invented especially for her, its principal actor was a monkey named Gologolo, full of horrid, uproarious tricks that defied decorum and genteel ways; a clandestine creature that they shared. (Little did she know that, in those lonely years far from her side, he had already created a Gologolo—an abandoned African child that Bardamu had adopted to accompany him in his journeys.)[33] She shrieked with delight in the long dim halls of museums as Gologolo spat at the paintings he did not like and outraged museum guards by his obscene mimes; and they pretended to flee in haste when footsteps warned them that the outraged curator was about to appear. —He was a fantasy all the more precious because it verged on danger. Without a doubt, her father's creature. Sprung from the fearful and wondrous recesses of his mind.[34]

But always, he would grow impatient with their stay.

Insist that they move on. As if at the end of each stop in their journey some other destination beckoned; or an invisible goal remained constantly in sight.

In the many trains back the child clung to Elisabeth's side. She studied the woman's face, gently outlined against the windowpane, the clouds of blond hair that conjured up echoes of forgotten fairy tales. Why did her father not seem to see her?

He sat staring, now into the moody Flemish landscape, now at the last bridges to span the Danube below. Lost to them. Always lost.

Geneva. And the lakefront in the dusk. They fed swans in the graying waters. On the edge of the city from which he had begun to venture forth into all the corners of the earth.

Evening fell. And swallowed up the distinctions between water and land. Creating a private limbo in which they moved.

A friend had joined them and while talking, enlaced Elisabeth's waist. The child, in surprise, noted her father's indifference. Then heard his harsh laugh ring out.

"She needs pleasure," he drawled. "Why not perform that little service for her?"

The woman raised her proud head, as if to snarl a response. Then, in weary resignation, leaned back upon the shoulders of the other man.

At night, from her hotel window, she watched him pace at the edge of the lake with his face turned to the cutting wind. (Had he purposely left her to the ministrations of the friend?) A series of previously unrelated facts began to arrange themselves in her mind, like the disparate pieces of a puzzle that suddenly combine into meaning:

Several years ago, she had seen him write to one of his

cronies: "Good health, man, good prick still? The 'dread'
age is upon us!" [35] (It had seemed odd to her that, at thirty-
six, he already spoke with dread of the waning of potency—
for surely that was what the letter implied.)[36] And at another
time, she had overheard a friend teasingly say, "Oh, Louis,
your eyes are bigger than your appetite!" as he devoured two
young girls with his eyes.[37] Was it then merely a question of
sparse appetite, of chosen morsels to be sparingly savored as
by a skilled gourmet? Or a need to pause, to remain apart for
long spells; preferring the role of "moderate stud" to that of
consistently priapic stallion? But there were also the fragments of a scenario he was writing which she had seen, telling
the story of love between women and that ended in a sadistic
orgy and death in the sea.[38]

Added to it all, was a rumor that malicious tongues had
spread—that the new literary technique he had lately developed (in which series of three dots created pauses, blanks
between phrases) was really nothing but a reflection of his
growing impotence; a trick which sprung from the dry sexual
heaves; the painful trickle of semen, wrung out drop by drop.

She was horror-struck. Fearing her body would be diminished until it shrank into oblivion.

She almost ran to the sea. Vanished without a clue;
somewhere across that vast ocean from which she had once
—Venus-like and full-blown—emerged. It seemed as if the
foam had now reversed its movement and swallowed her up.

When he came seeking, it was in vain. He pursued her
with grim determination, combing the cities where she had
gone in the past. To no avail. Her trail had become obscured.
Fragments of truth, half-truths, and blatant lies combined to
create a shadowy picture of un underworld existence into
which she had plunged. He soon felt that he was wandering
through a labyrinth, living "a hideous drama, so low, disgusting, and humiliating" [39] that he grew weary of his search.

It was obvious that she had been turned into a shade (not by a backward look, but through lack of any glance at all). Whether she dwelt in Elysian fields—to which a Jewish judge was rumored to have led her—or cavorted in Tartarus with gangsters, addicts and whores, he decided that she was irrevocably lost. And that, as Orpheus, he was decidedly a flop.

The grotesqueness of his quest was beginning to chafe:

> In the last month, such fantastic things have happened to me that I'm still sort of delirious. Fate has really fixed me. I even have a first-rate case of the boils! [40]

(Despite this, however, he tried to market one of his scenarios in Hollywood; visited a Danish ballerina performing in Chicago; and, on the return voyage, supposedly seduced a now-famous sculptress.)

By the end of summer, he was ready to take the path back from the "other world"—as he had called this portion of the globe in *Voyage*.

> I shall be in Le Havre around August 15. I have seen everything.[41]

> Now to return! One learns at any age! But we don't age . . . we don't know how! I would like to learn how to grow old.[42]

Did aging mean one accepted the passing of love? The graceful dismissal of women too long and not too well held? In that case, he had not learned the lesson. He continued to rage, to paint Elisabeth's descent into a limbo of liquor, drugs, and tobacco. And on his return, he announced (to a lady friend awaiting him in Antwerp, with tremulous arms outstretched):

> Here I am, back from the dead . . . I have gone through a dreadful adventure. . . .[43]

Yet, he had already lived through all this in his book; prophesied his leave-taking and his loss before they hap-

pened; embalmed the woman, while still alive, in her immobile literary pose. She had been turned into Molly long
before her actual demise; her presence stored up as some
buried gleam of light, to provide the gift of dreams and
render life in the future less abject and cold:

> I have kept so much of her beauty within me, so alive,
> so warm, that there's enough to keep me going for at
> least another twenty years, the time it takes to
> finish. . . .
>
> (VOY, 236)

(Although, twenty years later, the yearning had not been
stilled:

> If, by some chance (although the U.S. is an ocean), you
> meet someone who knows what has become of Elisabeth
> CRAIG—her last address—as far as I know was—2325
> Southhighland Avenue, Los Angeles—in 1935—She
> must be about 44 now, if she's still alive! She was living
> under a cloud of alcohol, tobacco and cops, in the lowest
> gangster circles, with a man named Ben Tenkle—cer-
> tainly well known by the special services bureau—Caro-
> lina Island, etc. . . . Well, all this just if by some
> chance—She's a phantom—but a phantom to whom I
> owe a great deal—[44])

But then, he had passed his last judgment upon her and
shut her within him. Into his private hell. A world had closed.
Another opened. A woman for a book. The dread bargain
was once and for all concluded. The contract with his demon
irrevocably signed.

CA. 1933–1937
Others came and went.
They moved in intricate patterns across his days—in

pairs, in stately minuet or wild saraband. Ballet of women, by chance encounters choreographed, which created shadow plays to fill the empty moments between creations.

(Some even found their way into actual "ballets" he wrote—Eveline in "La Naissance d'une fée," [45] needed only a minor change in her name to suit his fancy;[46] Erika in a little "legend" of love and death[47]—where they could prove their inability to survive in the real world and were swiftly destroyed.)

Women abandoned and taken up again. Distributed slyly in his various ports of call. He drew them for brief intervals to his side, only to release them brutally or push them —by more devious means—from his side. The shy young writer from Antwerp; a German student rescued in a Montmartre café; a Russian interpreter and guide; a famed Danish ballerina; the lovely pianist who attacked Mozart sonatas and glaciers with equal skill; a spinster whose long devotion was spent upon the paper of his books: Eveline, Erika, Natasha, Karen, Lucienne, Marie. . . .

Montage of faces, hands, thighs—composed and decomposed at will like the visions in a kaleidoscope, which by their variety might serve to fill his changeable needs. His thirst for twenty lives lived at once; the yearning to expand time sideways, until each instant became charged with the potency of years.

Yet, thanks to their dispersion in space, these women, or fragments of women, created pause and gaps of silence— the intermittent flux and reflux of encounter which had become the only form of closeness he could tolerate.

> He was going to leave again. These hours would pass,
> and there would again be months of waiting, and then a
> few hours of happiness, and so on, until there was no
> longer anything at all.[48]

And out of all these constraints, these flights, these brusque goodbyes, passion was reborn forever new, impetuous, spasmodic.[49]

He moved in and out of their lives; appeared to each in turn only to withdraw again; closed in and dodged aside; struck blows at the doors of their senses only to leave them standing ajar. Aching to be entered, to close and enfold. Engulf with warmth.

Arms and rooms of women. Full-fleshed and stifling. Shaded tents of desire, that left no air for nomadic drives.

> He would not let himself be stopped by anyone. To "lighten oneself," was one of his favorite expressions. He lightened himself little by little of human beings, he dropped them like pebbles along the edge of the road. One day he would divest himself of her also. It was futile to be patient, not to insist or demand: she weighed. She still weighed too heavily upon him.[50]

He pulled up stakes each time. Slipped away into the night, by stealth or brute force.

And yet, he kept a string of closeness always dangling —a thin thread of warmth within the vast solitude, for fear of "dying alone, like a dog." While panting with anguish at the feel of a sleeping woman at his side.

A cry of: "Leave me! . . . Oh, stay!" in circular motion. Paradox of opposites that constitute one human voice; and of the forces that draw and quarter a victim who has become his own executioner.

He used various forms of torment (or games men play) to parry the thrusts of indifference and passion, distance and presence, omnipotence and impotence: advising each of the women to take other lovers, seek varied adventures, marry or remain married, seek other women as sources of joy. Often, he preached the abjectness of jealousy, only to experience its pangs in his own flesh.[51] He also enjoyed giving "fatherly" counsel (almost as if he were issuing papal bulls):

Preserve your health—your thighs, your wit—

Be scrupulous, careful, and a bit more human if possible, at the same time nicer, gentler, more feminine. You're losing a great strength there. The strength of weakness, the strength of childhood.[52]

At other times, he played at combining their forms in his mind, superimposed one upon the other. Thus, he wrote to Erika, for example:

I am going to send you a little friend of mine to see you in Berlin . . . Elisabeth Craig, an American dancer, very subtle and very strange.[53]

Or introduced Lucette (who would one day become his wife) to Eveline:

. . . when he returned to Antwerp, he was accompanied by a dancer. He brought this dancer to her house.

. . . in the silence, she had time to look the young girl over. Dark and graceful, a sickly air, dressed in a vest and shorts of imitation suede, with bare thighs, and her hair drawn up into a striped turban.[54]

Often he contented himself with playing muse or patron saint: bought Eliane's first drawing; rigorously guided Eveline's pen; admired Lucienne's playing and her tenacity of craft; advised Erika how best to perfect her journalist's skill. Perhaps because these worlds of their own were both an attraction and distance assured: a domain which kept them apart from the mass of "heavy" inert beings, freeing and lightening them, thus making them easier to bear—and to leave. He set them, whenever possible, on their own course

with a swift wind to steer them, so that he would not have to
dread that, without sails, they would be marooned before him.
Dead vessels, fixed as a stare that does not falter or open eyes
of corpses that will not close.

Their shadows had to be kept in motion, glide forward
and away at a wave of his baton. Or else be swept, with
sudden violence, into a trap door on his stage.

The women come and go. (Talking of Breughel, Scarlatti,
or Diaghilev.)

Even Lucienne with the magic hands, as skilled at the keyboard as upon mountain peaks, who appeared and vanished
in as spasmodic fashion as he, combining presence and
absence, music and glacial silence, perfection of art with
grace of body. Whose portrait (though entitled *Nora*) would
illuminate the dark manuscript he now wrote.

> Her fingers were terrific . . . like beams of light. . . .
> <div align="right">(<i>DIP,</i> 248)</div>

Whom he observed, with voyeur's ecstasy, as she plied her
instrument.

> Nora always played the piano while she was waiting for
> us. . . . She left the window ajar. . . . You could
> hear her plainly from our hiding place. . . . She even
> sang a little . . . in an undertone. . . . She accom-
> panied herself. . . . Her singing wasn't loud at all.
> . . . Actually it was no more than a murmur . . . a
> little ballad. . . . I still remember the tune. . . . I
> never knew the words. . . . Her voice rose softly and
> floated down into the valley. . . . It came back to us.
> . . . The air over the river had a way of echoing and
> amplifying. . . . Her voice was like a bird, beating its
> wings, the whole night was full of little echoes. . . .

> We'd wait till she stopped, till she wasn't singing any-
> more, till she closed the piano. . . .
>
> (*DIP*, 256)

He did not wait. The real-life Nora became one day too
real and too alive. She would not, as did her paper counterpart, float away into non-being nor did the waters close over
her still face. Their parting had to be more painful, more
abrupt even than Nora's demise on paper. Only the woman's
shadow (he decided) was distant enough to be preserved, to
gleam like a reflection within the pages of his book.

The written word had once more triumphed over living
flesh—*Mort à crédit* commanded a price far higher than life
paid in full.

1936–1937

His second book (demolishing childhood as one smokes
out a wasp's nest) had now appeared. With it, his art had
come of age. And he himself, felt suddenly old.

He had divested himself of every shred of his past: his
former style; his youth; women's holds; professional ties (he
had recently even been fired from the clinic in Clichy); his
very home (having vacated the apartment in the rue Lepic,
he lived for a while at his mother's, then moved from place
to place as a substitute for various doctors).

The result was one of almost total isolation. At the mid-
point of his life (zenith or nadir?) he stood naked and ter-
ribly free. Looking about him with hideously unflinching
gaze.

> I'm lucid, that's my redemption. I see myself even more
> cruelly than others.[55]

There was no choice in what was left to him to do. The
hard downward path was now begun. The question was how
to descend the slope.

One doesn't change any more at my age.

To croak really free, at least that is work worthy of a
Man! having spit out all semblances. . . .[56]

Most others around him, however, had changed. Jeanne,
the faithful, left him to marry and go off to the same far
country where Elisabeth had already vanished. In his fury,
he had assailed her with one of his great withering maxims
(invented on the spot):

"An honest woman doesn't change her name!"

Which altered nothing. She was soon gone.

Erika too. She had moved to Cambridge and given up
her name (which was so colorful that he himself might have
coined it, and now had been supplanted by a tawdry commonplace one).[57] Almost gasping with astonishment, he
wrote to her there:

Married! A little child! a mother! So many things![58]

How far it all was from where they had begun: when
he had stood framed in Jeanne's doorway, owl-like and
nocturnal to bring her his huge bundle of words to deliver
(to be a midwife to his dream). How long ago also, the night
he had found Erika, wan and despairing on the Place du
Tertre; the months he spent in isolation with her (carefully
keeping his mother, his daughter, and Jeanne away) to cure
her *"mal de vivre."* How well she had seen through his disguises, his masks, his "fibs." How much they had laughed!
He remembered the long nights when they had crisscrossed
Paris in taxis or on foot, to end up at dawn in the Bois de
Boulogne where they had breakfast in a small café at the
edge of the lake. In the daytime hours he left her to work in
the dispensary in Clichy (not without placing money under
her pillow to spend on baubles or clothes, books or cinemas).
Once he had given her a green African dressing gown with

terrible and wonderful beasts contained in the fabric. Was it because she did not "weigh" upon him, to reward the desire to pursue her own paths?[59]

He followed her travels, full of advice, concern, affection—almost as if she were an adolescent daughter.

His own daughter was fast approaching adulthood. They would soon have to part.

All of them were gone or going. Some, because he had exiled them or cut the holds of entanglement. Others, because their lives diverged from his, took them to other lands and arms. Even Colette. Who had tried to live in the studio but, terrified by the way he stalked his workroom at night, talking and writing in frenzy, had fled back to her grandmother's tranquil fold.

Lucienne had gone to triumph over mountains and concert halls. The sound of her playing seemed to drift back to him, in waves of nostalgic exaltation. As when he had first seen her in the Salle Gaveau in 1934. How reticent she had been at first, when she thought him just another admirer. Only when she realized that he was "that man" (the author of *Voyage au bout de la nuit*) had she listened. Her face took on that thoughtful look which brought out all her beauty, as he said casually that her playing of the Chopin sonata ("La Révolutionnaire") that evening had set the right tone for a scene he was just writing, in which his hero tried to kill his father. It captivated her to hear his violence come through the words, as much as did his gentleness when he spoke to calm her sorrow about her dead daughter: "No phantoms, little one, no phantoms. . . ."

Many times, he sat on the sofa while she played, admiring her artisan's hands and the endurance which made her remain at the keyboard for hours without respite. Once, as she paused, he said in a hollow voice: "Do you hear the clock? Each tick brings us a second closer to our death." [60] Her anguished face instantly reflected his anguish.

Was this what he had meant when he had written, after one of her concerts:

> . . . it was totally admirable . . . a profound enchantment. . . . I can say no more except to beg you to begin again as soon as possible—it's all there, the mastery, the sureness, the fire. . . . Most of all, that magical recall, the secret I need so much. . . . I don't know what would happen to me if you no longer played . . . my dear little Double—[61]

Now she no longer played for him. Reality had been too much with them and he had fled. In an extension of the gesture of recoil he always made when anyone acted as though he were "the promised land." Fearing invasion, he would swiftly retort: "One mustn't become attached to me . . . I am nothing." If his iron rule of *chambre à part* was ever broken, and he found himself enclosed at night within the same walls as another human being, he twisted and panted in his sleep, battling as though assailed by succubi. —Almost as if he feared the violation of his person, a rape of body or mind. Which he depicted in all its horror in the book he was about to complete:

> She clutches me . . . I'm crushed, flattened under her caresses . . . I'm all ground up, there's nothing left of me. . . . The whole weight of her has come down on my head . . . it's sticky. . . . My face is wedged in, I'm suffocating. . . .
>
> (*DIP*, 265)

He fled, to wall himself up with his work. Hid from closeness behind that enormous heap of incidents and creatures that, he insisted, must be mended (like those piles of lace that lay on his mother's worktable, awaiting repair), arranged, pieced together, transposed into a network of words. Excused himself on paper and justified his withdrawal:

> What bothers me is having to devote myself to things that are not transposed, or shall only be transposable many years from now . . . many years. . . . I don't want to die without having transposed everything I've had to endure from people and from things . . . that's about all there is to my ambitions. . . . I still have . . . horribly much left to do.[62]

Thus, he set out to transpose living creatures: to move away, so that the wait of many years could instantly begin. In order for a woman to become an image (for Lucienne to be transposed into Nora) she had to be silenced and faded into absence—prepared for burial in a sarcophagus which would contain her, transfigured. (Nefertiti in her lifetime could not have hoped to produce the same magical spell as her statue.) With an almost necrophiliac passion, he bade her farewell. Projecting before her, the stillness reserved for his subjects:

> You'll see . . . everything passes . . . everything takes its proper place . . . nothing is essential, everything can be replaced, except that meager refuge where all is transposed and forgets its own existence.

And, at the same time, effacing himself also. Ready to vanish.

> I do not weigh heavily, despite my largeness . . . in reality, I weigh nothing. . . .[63]

The feeling of weightlessness and transparency must have increased after the publication of *Mort à crédit* which cut him loose from all his moorings.

He decided to go to England when the book appeared. And from there, to a country where he had never been before. Russia seemed enough of a far outpost to satisfy this need. Besides, the "bear" had won him much fame there (plus a good sum of royalties that must be spent on location). To think that it had all happened thanks to a surrealist and his wife! [64] Or the conviction (simplistic as all classifications) that he was a model leftist, and the hero of *Voyage* a kind of Job of the Communist bible! Why not then, spend a summer in the "Prolo-Paradise"?

It was an excellent way to still post-publication panic (for it would probably prove as salutary as his visit to Hitler's budding garden of Eden in 1932, when his first book had caused such outcries in the literary marketplace).

Actually, it was a hazardous move. One that would prepare his fall from leftist grace and leave him disenchanted; break down the illusions that had sustained him in the innocent past—when, to the amusement of his friends, he marched in May Day parades to the Bastille and seemed to have gone "red" in earnest.

What he found there, was a desert run by machines. Men that were as enslaved by promises of "progress" as some are by the clergy's illusory keys to heaven; an alter-image of the factories of Detroit, as faithful as if the two were reflected in a mirror and only distinguished by opposite labels.

All the Fords resemble each other, Soviet or not . . . ! [65]

Abjectness obviously took similar forms at all ends of the earth. There was no refuge from the harshness of life. (Unless it was in the domain of feminine beauty: Detroit had its brothels, and Russia flaunted an array of astounding cheekbones and athletic limbs—fortunately embodied in the person of Natasha, his translator, guide, and sometimes Beatrice.)

Upon returning, he had to conclude that asylums were absurdly hard to find.

They certainly did not reside in literary fame. All one

could hope to gain there, were the privileges accorded to any talented *enfant terrible:*

> I went to poor Denoël's office—and without even letting him read my manuscript—I said to him—1 million cash! and we'd make the exchange—[66]

But one also had to pay the price for one's diatribes, or for the "naughty" character of one's writing: submit to the deletion of passages judged too pornographic, too risky to be presented to a public with refined, delicate ears. The blank spaces in his new book—staring like blind eyes—were evidence of this figurative castration (so reminiscent of that famous German book for children where thumb-sucking results in having the guilty members cut off by a tailor with a pair of gigantic shears).

Then there were the critics! Some praised his second work—but not until they had intimated that it was surprising that Céline had anything else left in his guts after that first, horrendous outpouring—and one or two even proclaimed the undeniable genius of its author. Most, however, were too shocked, offended, or threatened by the totally blackened vision it contained, to be able to do anything but denigrate.[67]

Obviously, the book had been even less well understood than the first.

Perhaps a work such as *Semmelweiss* would mitigate the attacks by showing him in a less harsh light. —Denoël was willing. The early work of Dr. Destouches was certainly marketable, now that he had become Céline. —But oddly enough, the author wanted *Mea Culpa* to appear at the same time. His attack upon Communism—at the height of the power of the *Front Populaire*—was sure to throw the balance the other way and expose him to the violence which *Semmel-*

weiss, alone, might have calmed. It was as though he insisted upon maintaining the equilibrium between fame and infamy; upon keeping the double path of living constantly open (whether by means of bulldozer, machete, or persuasion).

It was at this time, also, that he began to search wildly for several forms of refuge: a woman; an island retreat; a safe cache for his gold.

The woman was the first to be found. He had noticed her several months ago, at Mme. Andreini's school where he sometimes went to watch the dancers train. (His penchant for dancers had in no way lessened.)

> I only want to write for dancers. . . . Everything for the dance! Only for the dance! Life seizes them, pure . . . carries them off . . . I want to lose myself with them . . . all of life . . . trembling . . . undulating. . . . They're calling me! . . . I'm no longer myself. . . . I give myself up. . . . I don't want to be shoved into the infinite! . . . to the source of all things . . . of all waves. . . . The reason for existence is there. . . . Nowhere else. . . . To perish in the arms of a dancer! . . . I'm old, I'm going to croak soon. . . . I want to collapse, to fall apart, to disperse myself, to become a mist, a tender cloud . . . in arabesques . . . within the void . . . in the fountains of the mirage. . . . I want to perish by the hand of the most beautiful one . . . !
>
> (*BAM,* 11–12)

Her youth and totally perfected grace made her stand out among all the others. As did her name—Almanzor—hinting at ancient Spanish or Arab lineage, while deeply rooted in the French soil that transpired in all its gracious gaiety in the syllables preceding it—Lucette.

Moreover, she had only recently returned from the far

continent into which Elisabeth had vanished. Her face was still bright with the neon lights of Broadway, the sparkle of uselessly illuminated skyscrapers at night. She spoke with the charming naïveté of a child of the Midtown Hotel where she had stayed (as of some sojourn in an oriental palace), and of the feverish throb of New York which kept her constantly awake. Her eyes shone as she spoke of her performances at the great Fisher Theater[68] (mocking yet timid eyes); instinctively, she thrust out her proud breasts and tightened her buttocks as does a race horse about to gallop.

They observed each other closely but did not speak. An awareness was forming between them. For him, by watching her move, enlaced with other ballerinas in poses recalling those of Naiads, as if she had been woven into garlands of women to create groupings of entwined delight. (While thus absorbed in each other, he could enjoy them with voyeur's pleasure.) For her, it was through the sense of his presence and the amazing, sea-colored eyes that fastened upon them all, yet singled her out. Sad eyes that suddenly blazed with life, as if the sun had touched the surface of waves. They drew her to him. As though she were choreographed to glide to his side.

Once he had claimed her, she did not leave him again.

In the spring, he took her to one of his favorite retreats: the Isle of Jersey. There, he assured her, ocean and sun combined to restore one, and one felt free from life's vicissitudes and petty machinations. —A refuge of calm.

Or so he thought.

But he had reckoned without his talent for complications; the fate that drew him forever into the arena.

In view of the coronation and the influx of visiting dignitaries to London, the British police had taken excep-

tional precautions. As a result, several incidents occurred. . . .

Louis-Ferdinand Céline, author of *Voyage au bout de
la nuit,* was suspected of wishing to assassinate George
VI and put under surveillance on the Isle of Jersey. His
passport was confiscated. Despite the protests of the
French Consul, the British police insisted on continuing
to search the island for Céline's "accomplices."

Everything was of course settled in the end, and the incident closed with an offer of apologies by the governor.

—"And to think," said Céline, "that I came to Jersey to
look for a possible refuge!" [69]

The next time he went to scout around another island,
he was more circumspect. (Attempted regicide was an amusing accusation only once.) He requested advice from the
French consul—with mock gravity—concerning the strictness
of customs officials in the matter of bicycles. And assured
him that his female "accomplice" was "very presentable,
very pleasant, and extremely discreet . . . not at all a personage who might alarm the British cops." [70]

Lucette laughed gaily. For her, it was the initial encounter with hostile authorities. She could not know that it
was only the first of a long series which would continue
during their years of wandering, the trials of exile and prison,
and pursue them even in the meager refuge of his declining
years.

Her light youth and buoyant ways brought out his
laughter; created the sensation that he had found an asylum
of grace.

"That's for my old age," he said musingly to a friend,[71]
eyeing her stretched out on the grass so lithe and unconscious
in her vigor. (An insurance policy against solitude, such as
his father had never underwritten in all the long years of

service to a company that bore the name of a bird forever born anew.)

Her strong legs shone in the sun. She stretched like a tawny cub, unaware of the men's presence. As she would dance, in clouds of talcum, across his various rooms; and create a mist of loveliness that effaced the majority of shadows on the walls.

He knew that she would follow him on all his convoluted paths, with an animal fidelity that had no roots in domesticated languor. Her silent presence—or birdlike, musical speech—suggested belonging without weight, union free of the taint of stagnation. For her gestures partook of another element than most: she flowed as swiftly as currents of air, unrestrained by laws of gravity, lighter than lace and liquid in repose.

Only later, much later, would he understand the variety of roles she played in his existence:

> She's Ophelia in daily life—and Jeanne d'Arc in moments of trial—all gentleness, generosity, concern, love —oh, I don't like saints—my saints have to dance and, by god, they'd better also have good thighs and good fun in them, and a strong dose of paganism. . . .[72]

Now, he delighted in her mute understanding, the sound of her swift footsteps within the house: a gliding reminder of her presence, ephemeral as the call of a ship; ebb and flow of her being, as restful as the companionship of the sea.

But he also took special pleasure in their outings. When they sat, like conspirators in Paris cafés (she, elegant and seemingly aloof to others; he, waiting for the opportune moment to scandalize the waiters—especially those stuffed shirts at the Café de la Paix) and watched the parade of passing women.

They'd comment on the shape of their ankles, knees, buttocks, as they filed by. She judged them with mockery and a professional eye, conferring grades of excellence upon them. And thus proved herself to be a true adept in the cult of form.

Yet, she seemed to remain unaware of her attraction to their bodies; while he encouraged her penchant with an observer's slyness.

Perhaps simply to keep a distance between them. True, her work was some insurance in this matter, though not necessarily conclusive (as experience with others had shown —the musicians, writers, and dancers, who had all seemed as dedicated as she). The sharing with other men had cost him Elisabeth. Perhaps, then, the greatest protection lay in a third realm—the desire of woman for woman (whether realized or sublimated). It seemed a natural, and had a variety of advantages and appeals—aesthetic, practical, uncommon.

Later that he would be able to formulate it all succinctly:

> I have always preferred women who were beautiful and lesbians. Very good to look at, without fatiguing me with their sexual demands! Let them have a ball, let them fuck each other, devour each other . . . for a voyeur like me . . . that's just right! perfectly fine! and always has been! [73]

And to spell out also the dangers for an aging man (as he had already designated himself at the age of thirty-six!) from randy women that clutched, clung, became almost carnivorous in their carnal desires, threatened fatigue or impotence with swift annihilation:

> The play is over, the curtain has fallen! . . . the most
> horrible blow to women is when men don't fuck any-
> more! . . . just like cats, I see how miserable the fe-
> males make life for altered toms! it's death, if they don't
> escape!
>
> (*NO*, 289–290)

Moreover, he was convinced that such behavior was exacerbated in times of crisis, when men such as he put sex aside
(as animals do when the forest around them is burning).
Women, however, found war and carnage a stimulus for
heightened erotic desire. It had been impressed upon him
during his earliest youth:

> The more cities burn, the more one massacres, hangs,
> draws and quarters, the crazier they are for sex. . . .
> I remember well that October 1914, when my regiment
> was camped on the right bank of the Lys waiting for
> dawn under continuous enemy fire, the numbers of
> misses and ladies, the bourgeoises and the working girls,
> who took advantage of the dark to come and feel us up,
> lifting their skirts, without a word being spoken, with-
> out a face being seen, going from one soldier to the
> other. . . .
>
> (*NO*, 205)

Now that his own period of greatest trials was approaching, and he would be exposed to carnage and war, he
knew that his companion must be free of such taint. That
she could offer warmth without cloying, a bond that did not
stifle, a presence without demands. That her youth and gaiety could endure hardship and horror, and thus sustain him.
She was exactly what he required—a carefree, lovely, and
courageous child-wife.

He married her when it seemed clear that their most
hazardous journey was imminent.

FEBRUARY 23, 1943

The threat of death dictated the ritual. Staccato menaces, flashed across the Channel, accompanied them as a wedding tune: a nuptial march that would continue its frenetic pounding rhythm throughout all the stages of their arduous journey (that led across Germany in flames to the steep rooftops of Copenhagen). An organ tone that prefigured the thunder of bombardments. Their names, signed in the mayor's registry of Montmartre, would soon acquire the character of solemn signatures affixed to a last testament.

Where was the superb, savage humor now with which he had smitten Jeanne's marriage rites; or disowned his own child when she entered the despised legal state ("There's no room in my house for two maidservants. Go!")[74]

One could no longer resort to sarcasm. The only refuge left resembled that of the porcupine: closed in upon itself, armed with barbs (in the form of contracts). The threat of extinction made him cling to a thin silver circle that gave Lucette his name, identified her as his companion of sorrow. It established, in the world's face, a bond that had long united them. And with it, willed her a widow's shield—that last dignity he could bestow, the only shelter he could still afford to provide.

The only other being the gold bars which he had cunningly stashed away in Denmark. (Guarded as jealously as Fafner's secret hoard, for this was not ordinary gold but earned by the alchemy of his books. A treasure to be protected from holocausts; buried, if need be, beneath the soil. —Foreseeing international strife and considering Swiss banks not safe enough, he had asked the Danish ballerina to hide "the child" in her garden. —Shielded, surrounded by superstition and ritual. Even in England, he had gone daily to see his gold weighed at his vault, watching the leaf of cigarette paper which had to be placed on the scale to equalize it with absolute precision.)[75] Now, all precautions seemed too slight. To reclaim his treasure, he did not shrink from a journey which led through the fiery heart of Europe. What matter, if the shelter where it lay, had to be reached by tortuous roads!

JULY 1944

It was a strange exodus.

They knew that the deluge was about to break loose; that their house would be put to the sack, his manuscripts pillaged, his blood-red motorcycle smashed to pieces (a modern killing in effigy).

There was no way back. No further throw of the dice to abolish the chance of their existence.

They hastily prepared for the journey: Bébert the cat was thrust into a gamebag; metal trunks were crammed full of documents proving identity and legal state—under a double bottom of a suitcase, such as conjurers use—cash, medical supplies, tools, negotiable minerals and ore. The baggage rattled suspiciously and weighed them down.

It was far from an elegant departure. Their actor friend Le Vigan objected slightly to this form of travel (being accustomed to the smooth roads of fame where such sordid details never obtruded). But he was sufficiently terrified to put up with such slights to his reputation. Besides, he saw the opportunity of playing a martyr's role—having once been a superb Christ, he could never forget the performance—in one of the most grandiose settings imaginable.

Lucette was delighted by the danger game. It might have been her youth which made her so sure of invulnerability; or simply her bird's curiosity combined with feline prowess. She kept their spirits high with her chirping banter. And explored ruins as others would go for a stroll in pleasure gardens. Bombed-out houses and castle halls held no terror for her but acted simply as a challenging backdrop for ever new adventures. She had a love of risk as exorbitant as that of a child:

> Heroism was natural to her! . . . I'd say she was drunk with courage. . . .
>
> If the house shakes . . . trembles . . . and grenades rock the walls . . . the ceiling cracks, the floor jumps, sways, explodes, she's in heaven, so to speak . . . it's all a ballet to her!
>
> *(NOR,* 64–65)

All that was forbidden charmed her: bomb craters, picnics during blackouts, underground passageways. She would brave danger with an impish smile. A dancing saint, full of pranks and tenderness. And that mute bravery that makes animals unflinchingly risk their lives in order to save their master.

As she would do when their only hope was to get aboard the last Red Cross train to Denmark:

> The Swedish train isn't stopping. . . . I'm all in a stupor. . . . Not Lili . . . the proof: before I have time to go ouf! . . . she's under the train . . . yes! she's thrown herself in front of it! . . . with one of those screams! . . . she who never screams, is she crushed? . . .
>
> *(RIG,* 274)

But her appetite for life left her entirely, when he seemed doomed. Thus, on that awful Christmas Day in 1945 when they were hunted across snow-covered rooftops, she was the first to think of dying. By the simplest of poisons—two tubes of aspirin, swallowed in rapid succession. As children do, in their wholeness of feeling.

*　　*　　*

Exile proceeded to age her, but for his sake, created a dogged wish of survival within her. Through days of prison, hospitals, and isolation, she kept up her rigorous training. To defend her body against slackness, and her spirit against apathy or despair. In order to give him the support of her form, when all was growing formless about them.

He wrote with pride:

> Lucette is holding up. She does her two hours of dancing a day.[76]

> Lucette . . . that unhappy, frozen dancer who nevertheless remains so lovely! [77]

> Out of corporeal beauty . . . dancers . . . I fashion myself a sort of artificial paradise . . . it's impossible for me to live far from the Dance. . . .[78]

She worked to maintain this force, this refuge of beauty for him. Only once, did her body fail. And cause him almost to despair:

> We have been through quite a storm again! . . . it lasted for 4 months! Lucette operated on in Copenhagen! for a fibroma! . . .[79]

As soon as her strength returned, she began to train once more; bathed each day in the Baltic, even though it often meant chopping the ice away to get into the water.

He watched her every movement. It was a joy merely to see her come and go; fetch the peat and light the fire. Each gesture confirmed the meaning of survival. And her simplest words kept the language of his country alive, amidst a babel of foreign voices. She kept up her patter, kept her body in shape, fanned and conserved the small spark of life remaining.

1951–1961

An old man's love bound him to her now.

It demanded constant closeness, her figure always at his side. He could be at peace only when the sound of music flowed through the house and she, among her dancers, moved across the floors. Or sat in silence by the fire at evening time.

When night fell, he shut her in his den. Often, he dozed off heavily on the sofa while she sat on a hassock at his feet. If they spoke, it was because he had asked her to tell him about the world outside (into which he almost never ventured now). Mostly, they were silent. Words were no longer needed between them.

He categorically refused to stir from the house. (In the beginning, he had sometimes gone to buy food for the dogs in town. But the ugly graffiti which had been painted on their garden walls, profoundly shocked him and made him hesitate to go beyond the gate.) So now they lived walled up, tormented by winter cold in the drafty old house. Retreating under the covers (layers of discarded overcoats which solicitous friends provided in a constant and unrelenting stream) to conserve the meager body heat which remained.

Sometimes she left or was lured away by friends—to buy supplies for her work, or see part of a new ballet (never daring to remain until the end, for fear of his loneliness). Always, when she returned, she found him waiting anxiously for her, below the garden wall.

> I was going to be alone again . . . Lili had to go to Paris . . . she never left me alone very long . . . of course she had to go now and then . . . errands . . . this and that for her pupils . . . especially her pupils . . . unbelievable the amount of slippers those pupils can wear out! . . . so Lili goes! . . . I stay home with

the dogs . . . I can't really claim to be alone . . . the
dogs keep me posted . . . they tell me . . . Lili's at
the station . . . they know when she gets off the train
. . . they never go wrong!

(CAS, 340)

He paced, wolflike in the dusk, until the dogs announced her
arrival. Came toward her with loping gait, grumbled about
the hour, led her swiftly back to the darkened house.

Yet he would not tolerate solicitude, shouted abuse if
she but spoke of his health, would not even let her help him
into his clothes. (The paralysis of his right arm had become
so pronounced that he could not pass it through a sleeve unaided; he insisted on wearing large capes and frequently slept
fully dressed for days.)[80] Even when he fell from weakness,
she did not dare to lift him up. She averted her face while
he dragged himself to a chair, tenacious and proud. His
mangy lion's head bent under the effort. Glaring at the least
sign of compassion; menacingly swinging his canes or lash-
ing out with tongue still full of the old venom.

The violence could only be stilled by her quietly moving shadow across a sunny wall; or the sound of evening
ragas streaming from under the roof. Then, his pen would
suddenly scratch across the yellow sheets, the words appear
—one by one—to make a book. The sheaves that piled up
laboriously would constitute the final offering he could make:
a threatening monument of paper that would one day serve
as her widow's shield. To guard her childlike, unworldly ways
when he was gone. And buy a string of many-colored dancing shoes for her sad feet (as gnarled and deformed by work
as the hands of old lacemakers).

1919–1961

Toward the end of life, a circle began to close. It was a furtive round, recomposed by him as though a bulwark of women could shield him from the cold of age.

He began to remember, to go backwards in time, to call up the phantoms of the past. Even those he had only glimpsed in passing, now took on an uncommon meaning, the importance of flowers pressed in a book that had but little value at the time of their picking:

In the 1930's, in one of the cafés he frequented in Montmartre (chez Manières), there was often a particular girl:

> . . . among the usual group of artists, at the tables along the wall, a very young woman (with painted eyebrows), a somewhat "Asiatic" face, a model I think . . . who really struck me. What a build! a goddess! . . . What could have become of her? It still haunts me. . . . She's surely a grandmother by now. I have my ghosts. . . .[81]

There were other "ghosts" he had attempted to conjure to his side: Eveline, whom he repeatedly called to him during the exile years[82] (while hiding this maneuver beneath furious protestations that denied the truth:

> She's been haunting me for 15 years, that bitch! . . . I haven't written her a word since 1940![83])

And Elisabeth, about whom he could inquire in less guarded fashion since she had almost certainly vanished, and her memory could safely be fed upon.

The terrible knowledge assailed him, however, that memories age, rot, perish as surely as the rest.

Only in his writings could he revive them; superimpose names of loved women until they formed a charmed circle that was perhaps safe against the ravages of time. Lucette merged with Lili (Elisabeth) and Arlette (Arletty); the last and the first were joined in an unending round.

But it was not enough. He must revive old kinships and attempt to resurrect those still undead. It occurred to him that he might write to Edith, whom he had forsaken long ago; recalling their early joys, the walks at the river, his child's first words, even the revolt and pain of their parting which seemed so futile, so dim now. With age, the fire and rage had softened. All that remained was the human need for closeness, for words that had been spoken long ago, now filtered through a veil of years.

What barriers could there be now between the bride of his youth and his youthful child-wife? In the stark hours of dying—or preparing to die—all that could matter was to harmonize the dark shadows that gathered each night on his walls.

The days must be crowded with youth. He waited to see Lucette's pupils ascend the stairs; smile, and pass. Just to observe them was enough. To know that "the rhythm of [their] life sprang from different sources than [his own]. . . ." [84]

Or have Eliane, now grown into a lovely woman, visit on a wintry afternoon. It was enough to make him suddenly come to life. Poke the stove, feed the fire, cook, and tell stories. For a moment, blood seemed to course in his veins.

Most of all, he would have wanted the beauty of children to surround him now. Their presence could inspire, and feed new visions into his tired brain.

I'm a pagan in my total adoration for physical beauty and well-being—I adulate healthy children—I swoon over them—I could easily fall madly *in love*—I said, *in*

love—with a little 4-year-old girl, full of grace, blond
beauty and health—[85]

But he would not avail himself of his own grandchildren—
a most natural source of joy. He had not softened in his harsh
attitude of long ago. Even in the lonely days of exile he clung
to the distance he had himself imposed:

> I haven't seen my daughter for 10 years [since her mar-
> riage in 1941]. I have five grandchildren who are un-
> known to me. I don't know whether I'll see them in
> Paris, because I have contracted such horror for argu-
> ments . . . which would be inevitable.[86]

His own daughter would also be kept at bay. He had only
followed her life from afar, known of her movements,
mourned her misfortunes, doomed by distance to impotent
dismay:

> I have remained dazed by some bad news. My daughter
> (5 children) operated on in Paris. I wanted to answer
> your letter, but the pen just stayed there, in the air. . . .
> I'm all in a stupor! . . . At such a distance [in Den-
> mark] . . . what can I do. Nothing. Always nothing.[87]

Nor would she be able to stand at his bedside, as he had done
in her faraway childhood days. Only when his closed coffin
was lowered into earth, was she there.

Neither his mother nor his child. (One dead, the other
exiled. They could not close his eyes and thus complete the
cycle of his life.)

1948 . . . 1961

First woman he had ever held. Woman whose name he
had taken like a shield, but also as a proud blazon engraved
on the cover of his every book. —Céline Destouches. Their
name. —Which he had feared for in exile, perhaps even more
acutely than for his life:

They have purged her tomb, they have effaced our name. . . .

(NO, 18)

Dead on a park bench in Paris, alone. While he was far from her side, in the frozen Danish countryside.

She died blind, moreover. . . . I will never console myself for it. I keep thinking of her terrible, solitary end. . . .[88]

Woman he had reviled and deformed in his books—who limped in hideous doglike submission through so many pages of *Mort à crédit*. Whose arms, outstretched to enfold, were thrust away in word or deed. And only sought for in moments of dread, confusion, or sorrow.

Kept in ignorance of her son's greatness; only vaguely aware of the role she had played: her workingwoman's hands, whose finesse and tenacity he had evoked (and perhaps wished to emulate); the torrent of her words, which may have unleashed his own (she, who seemed so silent in her husband's presence, was a notorious storyteller when he was gone).[89]

Only in death could he join her—echo her name on his tombstone, demonstrate the one truth which underlay all others: that only maggots unite us, and original nothingness is all we have to share.

Her lacemaker's art had vanished. His artisan's skill (derived from similar sources) would be preserved in paper. There, her portrait—grotesque and shadowy—would stand, etched in deep black letters of printer's ink. As harsh as any *faire-part*. While her secret, and more tender features lay buried within him.

*   *   *

Yet now, all tenderness and violence was stilled. Decomposed, the mother's teats; and breasts of other women (that had been so pointed in passion), nullified. Wombs fecunded —though the majority had remained unfructified; spasms of birth as well as of desire, all were superseded by the larger pulsations of dying.

First and last embrace merged. And were disengaged. Birth pangs and death throes had become equally nil.

All that remains is a procession of phantoms. Enlarged to dimensions so vast as to lose all meaning. The formless shadows of women pass over now inexistent walls.

The graffiti have become hieroglyphs, sunk into the sands. That soon efface all things. And deny us the right even to be bored together.

The work bursts into flame and its model dies.

GENET

4

DRAMATIS PERSONAE

*A photo isn't real. You create
reality by arranging, by cheating in the proper manner. . . .*[1]

"Did you know that I killed my father?" he said to
Marie, as they were crossing one of the last bridges on the
Seine. She looked up, perturbed. His face was serious, in-
tensely locked into a frown. She wondered if she was in
danger. At this hour, few strollers passed because of the harsh
winter winds. Then she saw the bundle of pages under his
arm—it must be a manuscript for her to type. She smiled with
relief. Realizing that what he had said (when translated into
pedestrian terms) was nothing more than: "Have you come
to the passage where my hero jumps at his father's throat and
runs off, thinking he's killed him?"[2]

It was often like this.

How startled she had been when, after copying long
pages that described his mother's deformed leg and the severe
limp with which she dragged herself up the spiral staircase
of her shop, she met Mme. Destouches one day. She was a
small, spare woman, dressed in black, who walked with perfect ease and showed not a trace of disability. Marie con-

tinued to stare at her legs with greater intensity than polite usage allowed. No matter how long she stared, she could discover no sign of the deformity she had come to believe to be so real.

He watched her slyly; with obvious relish. When they had left, he said in a drawling, offhand way:

> Reality revolts me . . . I find it unbearable . . . it drives me nuts, it's so hideous . . . so I transpose it, while dreaming, while walking. . . .[3]

"But why," she had wanted to ask but did not dare, "why always in the direction of darkness?" Why did transposing so often maim, or depict things as more hideous: deprive his mother of the use of her legs; transform his mild, eccentric father (whose wildest gesture consisted of wearing a captain's hat while he painted seascapes in the attic) into a raving demagogue; turn Rajchman of the League of Nations (who had been kindly disposed toward him and shared some of his most amusing capers) into an international intriguer of the lowest kind; cut off Gen Paul's other leg (when he had lost only one in the trenches) and confine him to the miserable platform of the double amputee? [4] But then, he also denigrated his own ancestry (the local gentry of Norman stock, once called the Destouches de Lenthillère)[5] and preferred a name common to workingwomen (Céline); assuring his friends that he was of "puny extraction" and had the lifelong "habits of a beggar," [6] denying the nobility which characterized both.

If he refused to spare himself, what would he do to others? She waited uneasily for her own portrait to appear. Certain that it would be horrendous, since even those closest to him had no claim to mercy.

None of it, however, had anything to do with mercy or the kind of fidelity photographers practice. The images he created (arranged, arrived at through "cheating," distorted by use of a poetic lens) had all the force of an El Greco portrait, the impact of a film in which trick cameras produce a heightened form of life. The characters born of this process had such vitality and color that one was seduced into regarding them as actualities. Even—as he did—to live in their midst, and act out a drama that had all the intensity of truth.

Naturally, he often came to resent the models from which his characters were drawn. He seemed to desire their annihilation, or at least their banishment. It was clear that, in order to come alive in his works, they must first be buried or submit to dismemberment. So that their separate parts— magnified or reassembled—might then be fused into a new whole.

Not all his friends appreciated this process.

(Although it seems that personal vanity makes being buried alive in an interesting pose, or a stage appearance in even the most mutilated role, preferable to burial in a mass grave, or the anonymous comfort of a spectator in the pit.)

Most of them were unaware of the death and trans- figuration they underwent in his mind, while they sat smoking and chatting in the long evenings of outdoor cafés. Their placid poses suggested none of the torments to which he secretly made them submit. —But then, hadn't his father died seeing only his son's grief-stricken face at his bedside; and his mother believed that she walked on two sound legs until the end of her days? And wasn't Gen Paul firmly convinced that he had been only once amputated?

When those around him became too smug about their well- being, however, or seemed too certain of their safety, his imagination broke through the mask. And he attacked. Either in open battle (outbursts of temper as sudden as a hailstorm;

dire prophecies that echoed for months in their ears), or by
more secret means (written caricatures; verbal sarcasms that
smote their vulnerable parts with subtle whiplashes slow to
scar over). Most did not know how thoroughly they had been
castigated, until his works appeared; but almost none were
spared.

One could hardly accuse him of subscribing to the dic-
tionary meaning of the word "loyalty."

Yet a strange fidelity linked him to his friends of the past
—lost, misplaced, estranged, in far lands. Carried off in the
flow of time. Years later, he would still try to uncover their
tracks, find links that would establish contact:

> Just imagine . . . my wife and I are looking for the
> traces of a tenor! a certain Sydney Rayner, tenor at the
> Metropolitan Opera in New York, 1936—He's com-
> pletely disappeared . . . a magnificent voice at that
> time—Thus I follow a certain number of destinies. . . .
> They get lost in the mist . . . reappear . . . loom up
> again. . . .[7]

Even those whom he had already demolished and re-
created in his books, were subject to such concern:

> My former boss—at the League of Nations—Dr. Lud-
> wig Rajchman—a Polish Jew—full of the highest and
> most splendid culture, as well as political skill—He's now
> at the U.N.O.—he's the Yudenzweck of *L'Eglise*—Un-
> fortunately, he didn't take it too well—and his wife even
> less so! . . . He liked me a lot, I wrote all his letters for
> him—I think, he doesn't like me anymore, too bad! Be-
> sides, he's old now. . . .[8]

It was as if they belonged to him still, and would never
stop being his creatures. No matter in what faraway places
they now hid and what dread rumors surrounded their being.
They risked being called upon to appear in his books:

Honest to God, it's him . . . talking of surprises . . .
right here, in this clown's rig . . . Le Vigan?

It's a fact, we hadn't seen each other in a long
time. . . .

(CAS, 89)

Owing to their existence to him, they could never become
totally indifferent to their procreator. Even their shades were
subject to his watchful eye:

I have a whole world of ghosts and semi-ghosts . . .
old Descaves who's 90. . . . Abel Bonnard in Portu-
gal, the dead like Brasillach and the young dead-drunks
like Gen Paul. . . .[9]

But such moments of nostalgic perusal were rare. It was
the drama which mattered above all. The world was full of
personages. Alternately, he saw fit to select and reject his
models—according to mood, to a particular need. As if they
existed only to be examined under his intimate microscope
(where, for an instant, they could perform and wriggle; only
to be laid aside after sufficient scrutiny). To fall into disuse
or be discarded; if necessary, be once again revived. Their
exits and appearances were dictated as by an omnipotent
playwright.

One might have thought they had no existence of their
own.

True, many of them did not strike one by their innate
powers of fascination. The image was not easily discernible
in its model—certainly not to the naked or untutored eye.
His coterie thus seemed far from an elite. In the Montmartre
days, he was often seen with a group that seemed quite un-
distinguished: Pepino, the local garage mechanic; a Spanish
plumber with a fine tenor voice, who preferred smoking to
an operatic career; Nocetti, the Italian violinist who hid his
face under wide, floppy hats; Gen Paul, invariably drunk and
abusive; Le Vigan the actor who—when not wearing the skin

of one of the characters he portrayed on celluloid—appeared
a dull and lifeless thing; some drifters from the underworld;
assorted pimps and their breadwinners. —The group of poets
and intellectuals who frequented the same restaurant, seemed
to hold no interest for him at all.

To the casual observer, their conversation was as banal
as its source. It consisted solely of jokes, word-challenges
that ended in banter, slang-duels (such as an hour-long exploration of the word *merde* in all its possible prolifera-
tions), street witticisms, wisecracks to pass the time of day.[10]

A neutral backdrop, adaptable to any scene. And a cast
of nonentities, with just enough touches of color to spark the
imagination; or simply tide one over, until the next act
opened.

Much less demanding and more suggestive than are true
friendships and close bonds.

There were those also. Stormy and full of heat as loves. Rarer
than ties with women. Virile; or capricious as adolescent
flings. Vehement as a sudden infatuation. They followed no
uniform pattern, but were as varied as the facets of the man
they involved: painters, businessmen, adventurers, actors, sea
captains, writers whose sensibilities differed vastly from his
own; a German sculptor and a Polish Jew; a French Resistance leader and a Danish mystic; a Flemish patriot and
an SS surgeon; an old army doctor and a young veterinarian;
a right-wing journalist and a leftist art-critic; a famous playwright and the local carpenter.

Some lasted for thirty years; others, for a few intense
months only. A few could only thrive at a distance—they
burst into hatred after a single face-to-face encounter. Still
fewer survived the years of exile and trial, the test by silence.

1951–1961

In the end, only a small number remained.

—Marcel Aymé, a friend of his early days who had no need of letters to communicate. A common calling linked them, yet there was enough distance in the forms of their art for each to see the other's worth. Céline could pay homage to Aymé, yet mock him for understanding so little of exile:

> Ah! what a magnificent friend! . . . I know no one comparable to Marc in the world of letters today! . . . Not a single rival! . . . He distills the dream like a wizard. . . . There's Maupassant and then he. . . . Therefore it's only natural that he should pamper himself, refuse himself nothing, hunting parties, yachts, mansions. . . .
>
> *(FEE, 39)*

> Marcel is a good guy—but completely corrupted by prosperity, the "good life," and probably some pretty mistress. . . . He speaks about prison the way a virgin speaks of dicks: "Oh, it's nothing at all!" . . . full of talk—about castles—and grandchildren who adore you . . . etc., all the bourgeois gab, stupid, catastrophic. . . .[11]

—Arletty the actress, his "pal" and somewhat sister (born on the same street as he). Whom he had despaired of ever seeing again, in exile:

> Kiss Arletty for me. . . . We said farewell without much hope of ever meeting again . . . but we have the spirit of our homeland to link us, the heart of things, and of *la Rampe*. . . .[12]

His female double—with her finesse and harsh laughter; the speech that so skillfully mingled slang and noble words; her outcast's lot for having loved a German; her expertise in judging the perfections of women (one of her favorite sayings being: "You can always gauge the worth of a woman from the shape of her neck").[13] A laughing amazon in her youth—one of the "children of paradise"—she now sat aging among fast-dwindling mementos of past glory.

—Jean Dubuffet, a late friend whose path had only crossed his shortly before the end. But whose piercing blue eyes so closely resembled Céline's (was it the color, or the uncanny intensity?) that it was not surprising that they produced works which bore such fundamental resemblances.

—Marcel Brochard, dividing his life between film studios and African lion hunts, whose continuing vitality was almost disconcerting (they were approximately the same age). It painfully brought back his own youthful years when he had courted Edith in Rennes, ridden horses and motorcycles with equal zest.

—André Pulicani, a man involved in the odd business of insuring insurance firms (what would his father have thought of such complexities?), whose Corsican birth may have accounted for his rare warmth and candor. Their friendship dated back to the Montmartre days and had not faltered during the years of exile. Besides, he was one of the few to be trusted by Le Vigan and bridge the gap between Paris and the pampas of the Argentine.

—Paul Marteau, Tarot card king and patron of literature, who had sheltered Céline and Lucette on his Riviera estate, upon return from exile. The pages of *Féerie pour une autre fois,* begun on the paper provided by his Danish prison-keepers and dedicated to Marteau, still lie on the shelves of the magnificent salon which overlooks the Mediterranean from terraced gardens; as does his death mask, which the Pekingese sniff delicately and examine.

—C. Bonabel, who had become the friend of a Dr. Destouches, in 1929, and remained faithful to Céline until the end of his life. A great connoisseur of music and of men.

The uncle of Eliane Bonabel who had blossomed into an artist of renown. (Her brand of gaiety fitted Céline's lighter moods and works of fantasy so well that only she could have been chosen to illustrate his *Ballets sans musique, sans personne, sans rien.*[14])

—Jean Pommery, the young veterinarian whose love of animals was matched by that of books. . . .

So many others were now far away, estranged, dead, or withdrawn from life:

—Le Vigan, who had been such an integral part of their triumvirate as they fled through Germany in its death-throes. Now he existed—some said, in a state of madness, while others periodically pronounced him dead—in a small town (Tendil) some four hundred kilometers from Buenos Aires, cultivating his Argentinian garden. A series of tortuous paths had led him through prisons and hospitals, a hideout in Spain, to his last shelter (from which he only ventured a decade later, to undergo a "delicate operation.")[15] He had lost all trust in those around him; his friends had become suspect; even his whereabouts were known only to a select few. The "man from nowhere" had finally earned his name.

—Albert Paraz was dead of tuberculosis. The medical advice that he had urged upon his friend (even from his hut on the Baltic) had been of no avail. Paraz, the "young one" —as he had always called him in his letters—was now one of the young dead. As irrevocably lost as Bébert whom Bardamu had tried to save.

—Robert Denoël, his publisher and friend (despite their fierce disputes over each manuscript), had long ago been assassinated on a Paris street. Perhaps, due to his loyalty to Céline's books; an extension of the guilt which had been attributed to his works. What good had it done for both men to be exonerated after the war, when Denoël already lay rotting in his grave and he would soon be joining him there?

—Jacques Deval, who had reached the height of his fame in the thirties with his play *Tovaritch* and whose amazing generosity to the sick had started their friendship, now lived in a shabby "den" in an old workers' section of Paris. It was a far cry from the splendors of Hollywood they had enjoyed together, and the rustle of lovely women's dresses that had always surrounded Deval, as radiance floats about the heads of painted saints. Now all that remained were some dim remnants of the past, crowded together into narrow rooms; and an aged, asthmatic dog that dragged itself across the worn oriental carpets. Nevertheless, wit still sparkled in Deval's eyes whenever he spoke of his friend—who, in turn, had said of him:

> He has an admirable heart and one of the most subtle minds I know . . . he's the French spirit in person— almost hallucinatory—he is frightening, almost monstrous in his cruel wittiness. . . .[16]

Their friendship had withstood the years of anger and accusations (which might have wounded Deval deeply, in that his own religion was involved). Even exile had not severed the bond. Now, though, the journey from the northernmost corner of Paris to Bellevue seemed endless; it kept them apart, each in his separate shelter. They might have inhabited opposite poles of the earth.[17]

—Bonabel was on the long road to dying. He weakened visibly, becoming thinner and more transparent over the years. If he survived his friend, it seemed only in order to mourn him. Years afterwards, he murmured still: "Poor Céline . . . poor Céline." And spent his last reserves of strength in writing the movingly simple homage to the man he still called "the doctor," [18] despite the fact that both were now beyond the reach of medicine.

—Henri Mahé, the painter whose frescoes had decorated so many of Europe's music halls, had long ago sold his houseboat on the Seine and now lived in a furnished studio, wedged in among the bourgeois abodes that smugly basked in the glory of the XVIth Arrondissement. The laugh-filled moments of their past (in London, Paris, Brittany ports) were wiped away. They had clashed in a bitter quarrel and no longer communicated.

—Jean Loiret, the painter (alias Bonvilliers, the actor), sometimes came from his tiny Montmartre studio, hidden behind a wall, across a courtyard, up long flights of stairs without banisters. But both men were haunted by time; each had to hoard the fragile moments that would not return.

—Perrot, his neighbor on the rue Girardon who had seen his apartment pillaged but had, by some rare chance, been able to salvage some of his manuscripts that already lay in garbage pails, remained close despite distance and age that made their meetings infrequent.

—Roger Nimier, the young novelist whom Gallimard had chosen to be the editor for his books, fought against the wall of silence that surrounded Céline's work and became his friend (only to die a few short years from then, cut off mid-path, before his talent had a chance to ripen).

Céline knew that it was too late, however, for old friendships to burst into flower, or new ones to grow.

Now and then, a spark of communication flared up. Some momentary warmth linked him to others, and them to him. Most often, though, he remained a solitary figure in his

back garden. Too weary, ill, obsessed with work, to cultivate the art of friendship or repopulate his world with characters fit to figure on his interior stage.

There were enough shadowy forms from the past that
moved there (waiting to be remembered, revamped, resusci-
tated). A little artificial respiration sufficed to make them
rise up, as if galvanized, from the dead. —Lazarus was a
sluggish dawdler compared to them; Atys and Osiris were
slow to heed the call. —His creatures obeyed instantly, as
if they lusted after resurrection.

1961
At the end, he grew weary of all such miracles.

Curtain calls were now in order. By late spring, he
bade them all farewell. He knew that both his friends and
their imagined doubles must be put away.

No one seemed to believe him, though. What use was there
in saying "I'm finished" to Marcel Brochard, when his old
crony was convinced that all it would take to bring him
back to life was a short ride through the Bois (where, in
former days, the mere sight of a "pretty pair of buttocks"
moving through the trees, could give a fresh start to their
day). How could he know that the grave pronouncement
made as they were parting at the gate ("You'll never see me
again") was any more than a skillful histrionic exit-line.
Only two weeks later, did the words reveal their prophetic
message of doom.

Even Marcel Aymé might have passed it over as a
mere theatrical phrase. Didn't his plush summer residence
sport a miniature theater where lines such as these could
have been spoken, only to be topped by a light, witty retort?

Besides, he was so ill himself, and Céline's ailing body so much resembled his own, that he could not view it with shock. Or perhaps he preferred to see the image of the bent old man before him faded out (as in a swift flashback) to focus on the Céline of younger days:[19] the "laughing wrestler" who was forever eager to engage in a struggle, knowing that he would soon have his opponents in one of many crushing holds. How could he see that this former pose was now wiped out, that so splendid a character had been diminished? Once he had cast a role of such stature, how could he admit that the old garments now hung on an empty frame, or that the mask no longer fit the player's face? It was a blindness born of affection which made Aymé impervious to the last cry of his friend. —Only when he heard the parrot scream his name, did he know that anguish had been cast into unheeding space.

The fate of old actors frequently demands dying unnoticed in one of their many roles.

And since the danse macabre had been so long part of his repertoire, it is not surprising that none had noticed when he performed it in earnest.

Only when they saw the plaster cast of his face, did the image of his death become clear and finalized. —Yet, even there, doubt entered the scene. For the two halves of the mask did not match. Creating an effect both lofty and gruesome; tragic and grotesque. Recalling the separate faces that ritually frame the stages of theaters. Here, fused into one. Stating enigma, unresolved.

The play had not ended, even with death.

1900–1961

Perhaps because its cast of characters had been assembled so long ago (as soon as he became aware of a world apart from his self) and had accompanied him through a variety of traveling shows, that ranged from one-night stands to lengthy engagements, and added a new dimension to his every act.

A versatile group of performers, as large and fanciful as those that enacted medieval mystery plays, embodying clowns, monsters, strange beasts, saints, and giants; hunchbacks, sinners, simpletons, tempters, fairies; traitors, magicians, executioners, victims, the quick, the dead, and the resurrected; even a Christ who sported pink silk pajamas.[20]

He moved among them, as actor, director, master of metamorphoses; appeared and vanished on the vast stage, controlled the action of trap doors, propelled a character to the sky (in mock ascension) and laid him low, conjured up floods or hellfire, spread the jaws of the sulfurous maw and encouraged devils to come forth, made locomotives float in the clouds and flaming chariots roar over devastated cities.

Actually, the actors were often humble creatures (without marks to distinguish them) if one but looked beneath the fantastic costumes in which he clothed them or the words that they pronounced when guided by his skill. The raw material hardly suggested what shape the perfected form could take. The most graceless creature could thus become a demigod upon his stage (although, in the next scene, he would almost certainly be reduced to the role of abject fool). Neither one nor the other had anything to do with the reality that lay beneath the mask.

(By such means, a well-intentioned though somewhat pompous academician was just as swiftly raised to the rank of Hindu prince as he was relegated to a blind bookworm's burrow.)[21]

For, as he insolently explained (when he felt inclined to do so at all):

I find my music . . . in human beings . . . but despite them, and not from the angle they wish to present, I rape them. . . .[22]

Only by such maneuvers could Courtial des Pereires have arisen from Henri de Graffigny, the magnificent madness be developed from the puny inventions born of eccentricity. And from a simple office (tritely named Eureka and located on the Place Favert near the Opéra Comique), the *Génitron* would unfold in all its delirious glory.[23] As a Japanese garden grows from folded scraps of paper housed in a lumpy gray oyster shell.

Many others were altered, or "raped," in this manner.

But none as thoroughly, and with such flourish, as Gen Paul, Le Vigan, and Louis-Ferdinand Destouches.

The scene was set in the studio of Gen Paul.[24] If one opened the curtain of the ground-floor flat, an odd setting appeared: truncated easels, paint boxes on wheels resembling the toy trucks of a child, palette knives and clotted sable brushes, primed and unprimed canvases everywhere; paintings stood, leaned, lay, dried, were stacked (unframed) in every possible inch of space. There seemed to be no place for human beings. Yet, in the center of the room, sat the one-legged creature who had produced all this:

"Ge-gen" or "Popol," as he was called by his friends. Seated at the navel of the painting world he presided, like a gruff sage whose judgments were as truculent as they were true. His mastery of Parisian slang added to their authority.

Judge of the two-legged species around him, merciless and full of mirth. Infallible in his estimates—perhaps because they were always low. Drunken oracle, devoid of the ritual three-legged stool (which could conceivably make amends for his own loss of a limb).

He worked only at night. In artificial light. The blues, greens and yellows produced by electric bulbs could alone illuminate his subjects with sufficient garishness and distort their features in the desired way. In the afternoons, he slept —disdaining the northern light that most painters seek. Only when the sun had gone down, did he come alive.

Then the studio became crowded with a steady influx of people (as though the late hour had made them come crawling out of the walls). They assembled, circulated, dispersed, gathered again. Some poked their heads in at the window merely to shout a greeting; others sent a wisecrack sailing in with a gust of spring air—to which he invariably retorted with a sharp remark of his own; many wandered in and roamed among the paintings during the entire course of the night. Arguing, laughing, swapping stories. Bouncing phrases back and forth, as in a skillful soccer game.

Mostly, they bandied about local gossip of "la Butte"— their *quartier,* which they defended against intruders and non-initiates with all the zeal of feudal lords. But the conversation also pounced on other topics, dissecting everything: politics, the current crop of leeks, history, the price of wine, love, the new barmaid on the corner, art, the legs of a starlet, Nijinsky's bones, the concierge's latest abortion. The words welled up without a stop, filling the room with scraps of phrases as rich in color as the canvases about. Here and there, a voice rose and stood out from the rest: Le Vigan's, the tranquil Pulicani's; Céline's.

Once he decided to speak, it was instantly established that he would dominate the common flow of words.

As by a natural impulse, all talk ceased as soon as his raucous voice was heard above the general chatter.

Few could match his storyteller's skill. Which could be applied to the most banal subject matter and cast its spell by virtue of the vividness of his words, and the pantomine which always accompanied them. It was impossible to forget his rendering of a visit to Maeterlinck's château (to reward the speech he had given at Médan, somewhat against his will).[25] He began to speak in drawling tones, balanced by the malicious twinkle in his eye (some said his voice—jerky, grating —resembled the great Jouvet's):

> . . . we were received by the master's gracious companion. She used language that must have been inspired by the music that Debussy had composed for *Pelléas and Mélisande*. That is, she spoke in recitatif, she chanted in a slightly discordant tone . . . "Ha-a-ve some peu-eu-ti-tis fours, dea-ear frie-ie-iends. . . ."
>
> In the room where we were seated, there was a fountain, and a door which created a draft each time it was opened. And each time, the fountain doused one of the guests. The mistress of the house rushed over and closed the door . . . but someone always opened it again, and each time another guest was sprayed. . . .
>
> As for the master (Maeterlinck) . . . well, the master himself, was busy ba-an-ter-i-ing.[26]

At other times, he spoke in a bard's rhythm, with the conviction of a preacher, or as one inspired. Then his phrases waxed almost biblical:

> "And the Cossacks shall come. . . ."

One felt a series of verbal gusts come down, as he invoked future cataclysms, depicted Europe under a hail of fire, urged his listeners to rush for shelter, flee instantly, without waiting, without thinking, even if it meant leaving with

only a bundle on one's back.[27] (One almost expected him
to say—"with unleavened bread.")

The only thing which could halt the conversation, was the
sound of a gong. It was the signal for the evening soup, given
by Gen Paul's wife Fernande, a fiery despotic woman who
ran a laundry and cleaning establishment on the floor above,
and would not be kept waiting. He hobbled off, obedient as
a lame dog, and left his friends to join her.[28] His judge's robes
(which seemed to envelop his shoulders when he made his
pronouncements on the skill of others' speech—the use of an
invective, a popular phrase, the numerous slang terms applied
to one act or thing) fell off him, as he attempted to run.

Le Vigan, who sometimes read poetry or scenes from plays in
his rich, sonorous voice, fell silent as soon as the prescribed
words ran out. He sat brooding, an ambiguous expression on
his face:

> He didn't shock us anymore . . . we were used to his
> strange airs, his fixed stare . . . especially when he was
> "looking for himself," when he was preparing a new
> role, and couldn't find himself! . . . he hesitated . . .
> for weeks . . . he was looking for himself! . . . he
> found himself . . . he composed himself . . . recom-
> posed . . . he didn't stop "composing," for one film,
> another. . . .
>
> (NOR, 321)

(He may not have realized for what roles he would
be composed, decomposed, and recomposed by Céline; or
guessed the final epic in which he was destined to play such
a major part.)

*   *   *

The observer's art was easy to cultivate in this studio where subjects of such varied interest moved, yet would soon be forgotten or lost, unless they were transposed. Even the best of them remained mere objects, without the gift of speech. Gen Paul's colors would fade; Le Vigan had only the mute face of silent films to fix his image. Neither, without him, had any power over words.

This he could give them. If they allowed themselves to be molded as he wished; abdicated from their former selves. Then he was free to endow them with an intensified existence. View them from any angle he pleased; furnish costumes and make-up, soliloquies and asides, buskins, wigs, hats, and beards; hack off a limb here, add height or volume there, shrink or distend them, have them appear in the guise of magicians, angels of the Apocalypse, or ferrymen to the underworld:

So that Gen Paul would suddenly sit astride the Moulin de la Galette, with sparks flying from his fingertips, to direct the course of a night of wrath—blow his bugle, incite a rain of fire and the splitting of the sky, cause the destruction of the world (or the bombardment of Montmartre, which comes to the same thing), as blithely as any angel of doom turned transvestite.[29]

And Le Vigan would spring up, as though from a conjurer's box—in full dress, attending a formal dinner completely alone, in a room miraculously preserved within the walls of a bombed-out house.[30] Or suddenly appear in a gaucho's disguise, as the ferryman of the dead with an old *bateau mouche* for Charon's dread bark; half boatman and half tormenting demon, whom only the word "nasturtiums" could keep at bay[31] (a formula missing from the Egyptian

Book of the Dead, which lists all useful incantations to keep the threats of the netherworld away).

The third character was as ruthlessly ruled by Céline as the rest: Ferdinand—that portion of his self which otherwise would have to remain voiceless and inert—could only come to life if subjected to the same distortions, contortions, torments as the others. He "raped" the everyday man in him as diligently (to provide the "music" he sought) as if he were a total stranger spied in the streets. Obviously, no one could be spared—not even a part of himself.

Ferdinand was shown in a variety of poses: as a sniveling masturbator; a "fellow without the least collective significance," a helpless cuckold, a downright clown; but also as a seer, a prophet, the oracle and chronicler of doom.[32] Within him lay the entire spectrum of human possibilities and impossibilities. One sweep of Céline's pen could trace the opposite poles of his double's image: from Pan with his all-powerful flute to the groveling movements of the worm, the distance was covered by a few drops of ink. The portrait swelled and shrank as if its author had drunk from Alice's magic bottle.

Evidently, the reality of his own self was no less mutable and prone to destruction, than that of the people around him.

All of them wore stage names (perhaps to shield them from attack; perhaps to accent their theatricality): Gen Paul alias Jules or Julot; Robert Coquillard alias Le Vigan alias Norbert or La Vigue; Marcel Aymé alias Marc Empième; Lucette Almanzor alias Lili or Arlette; Destouches alias Bardamu, Ferdinand, or Céline. . . . Yet, fragments of their daily doubles never ceased to adhere to them. (As do shreds of skin even in the most skillfully flayed victim or patches of old feathers to the best of phoenixes.) Not one could be so totally transfigured that some last remnant of his "real" self did not remain hanging there; the smell of life clung to his garments in even the most dreamlike poses.

*   *   *

As if to remind us that the play was a play.

That artifice (or even an "apotheosis of artifice" [33]) resembled a network of lace in which a stitch was purposely dropped, here and there, in order to allow reality to poke a dirty finger through. A construct insolently kept on the edge of peril, threatening to slip, slide, perish . . . allowed to do so. . . . Only to have us watch it arise again on shaky foundations, and soar inexplicably despite its grounded buttresses.

A play not unlike that of life.

Written, rehearsed, and performed *en permanence* during the entire span of his days.

Despite any number of curtain falls.

TWO

When I shall have inspired universal
disgust and horror, I shall have conquered solitude.

BAUDELAIRE

. . . only man can curse (it is his privilege, the primary distinction between him and other animals).

DOSTOYEVSKY

5

HOMO HOMINI LUPUS

There are still a few hatreds
I'm missing.
I am sure they exist.

(Epigraph, *Mea Culpa*)

1936–1937

It was a time of hate. Despite the seascapes of St. Malo
and Le Havre (that "haven of grace" to which he had fled).
They should have cooled his furor but instead seemed to
whip it into foam and mirror it in vicious red sunsets.

He had returned from Russia, seething with rage—
either over the loss of the proletarian paradise, or because
the Marinski Theater in Leningrad had turned down his
ballet, "La Naissance d'une fée." [1] His retort would be *Mea
Culpa:* a biting attack upon the Soviet system, its aims, its
hopes (without so much as a mention of his failure as cho-
reographer and scenario writer). The message it carried applied to both his public and private chagrin; raging against
the bitter realization that reality triumphs over the dream,
and all legends end in their own destruction (as his ballet
had more gracefully stated).

The pretention to happiness, that's the vast imposture!
That's what complicates all of life! What makes people

so venomous, rotten, impossible. There's no happiness
in life, there are only greater or lesser, more or less be-
lated, dramatic, secret, avoided, surreptitious misfortunes. . . .[2]

Illusions were the criminal harvest of hope. They must
be amputated, cut out as a poisonous growth—his own, as
well as those of others. In this, the Christian religions had
some merit, for they refused to "sugarcoat the pill." They,
at least, "grabbed Man right at the cradle and broke the
news to him, then and there." Addressing him in Célinesque
terms:

> You formless little putricle [*sic*] you'll never be any-
> thing but a piece of garbage. . . . From birth on,
> you're nothing but shit. . . . Life, you idiot, is no more
> than a bitter trial! Don't bother getting out of breath!
> Don't search for noon at two o'clock! . . .[3]

(He might have been one of the church fathers, so thoroughly
had he always castigated man.)

But the tides of anger which had launched his books in the
past, no longer seemed sufficiently high. Even *Mort à crédit*
—fresh off the press—had not sapped all his reserves of fury.
There was more, so much more still to be poured out. Besides, he had so far only explored self-punitive measures,
heaped the blame on scapegoat doubles of himself. Bardamu
and Ferdinand had borne all the stigmata he could possibly
imagine. That avenue of attack was now exhausted. Their
specters had already been laid low.

And yet, the need to snarl, pounce, rend, devour, continued.

He was about to shake off the last drop of former victims'
blood, and prepare for new prey.

It was not long in coming. The familiar scent of vulnerable flesh soon rose to his nostrils. An expert hunter, he instinctively knew the path to take and where to lie in wait. —Others had already proven the ground, tested the air, successfully struck. (In Fascist paradises, where the crime of hope was also committed, but a specific portion of mankind designated as abject "putricle," carefully distinguished from those that could aspire to *Lebensraum*.) —But then, he also had already strayed in the direction of this prey's watering places. He fondly remembered *L'Eglise* now, with its scenes at the League of Nations where Moïse, Mosaïc, and Yudenzweck had been unmasked (though still allowed to hide in the shrubbery, amongst other targets for attack).

Perhaps though, one had first to suffer the pangs of the hunted, before the skin of the *Carnivora* would fit.

Lycanthropy is only contacted through contamination. The smell of his own blood would best initiate the bloodletting. (As physicians of old cut the tail of leeches, to be applied to patients, in order to let the blood flow more freely through.)

He did not have to search too far afield. His first two books had already brought on several wounds that remained open: the slashings of the critics; the blows to his medical career.[4] Now, *Mea Culpa* was doing the rest: the Leftists railed against him;[5] he lost his job in the clinic he had spent long years in building (convinced it was due to a coalition vendetta of Communists and Jews).

The corrida had successfully begun. He wrote almost triumphantly to a friend:

Yes, Clichy is finished. The last months were a nightmare—I held out to the last—Ouf! They showed themselves as abject toward me as they were cowardly, vile,

and crooked—They gave me great pleasure. I was over-
joyed.[6]

All that was needed now, was the dismissal of his work.
—The ballet presented to the Russians had already been re-
buffed. The same might happen in France. —He would soon
report two such attempts: the first, involving the very same
ballet which had been negatively received in Leningrad (submitted to the Paris Opera by Léo Gutman, Jew); the second,
another ballet, "Voyou Paul, Brave Virginie" (proposed for
the Exposition of 1937, guaranteed to be all Jewish-con-
trolled). Both, as expected, were refused.[7]

What more could one ask now, except the wounding of one's
virile pride. Already, the memory of Elisabeth Craig festered.
(The judge who swiped her, retrospectively became a Jew.[8])
Now, the rank suspicion grew that all dancers (realizing
which side their toeshoes were laced on) were gravitating
toward the wealth and influence that Jewish patrons were
offering, considering that their future lay in the ringed palms
of Israel.[9]

The barbs were fast being gathered. It would not be long
before they could be woven into a crown to be pressed down
on his forehead (according to that old Roman custom, which
the Inquisition had so successfully revived).

The ache in his head (outgrowth of the imagined wound
and trepanation from the last great war), the sound—as of
freight cars clashing—would do the rest. He broke out in a
sweat of rage and lashed out all around him.

It was a year of violent upheaval. He knocked over the
past with a series of kicks, swift and deadly. The homage he
had paid to Zola (the defender of Dreyfus), contained the
prophecies of his own malediction:

> The great enthusiasm of the masses, the lasting frenzies
> of the crowd, are almost always stimulated, provoked,
> kept going, by stupidity and brutality. . . .
>
> Hitler is not the last word, we'll experience still greater
> epileptics, perhaps here. . . .
>
> In the game of Man, the Death Instinct, the silent In-
> stinct, is certainly well placed, perhaps right next to ego-
> tism. It takes the place of the zero in roulette. The
> Casino always wins. Death too.[10]

He too would place his chips on the zero. The inveterate
gambler's instinct had risen to such frenzy in him now, that
even his own words could not keep him from the game.

Semmelweiss (which he had Denoël republish this year)
had contained the warnings which he would not heed: Semmelweiss, having found the microbes that caused puerperal
fever, viciously attacked all those who would not follow his
preventive measures. Dr. Destouches then commented on his
hero's wild fervor:

> Although these truths were only too urgent, he was
> childish to proclaim them in this intolerable manner.
> The hate evoked by this pamphlet was the amplified
> echo of the hate whose violence he had already felt ten
> years before. . . .
>
> *(SEM,* 111)

(Just as the hate Céline would reap in 1942, was but
the amplified echo of the animosity his early works had elicited; although the microbe he denounced was of another
nature.)

Especially, since this favored son of the Left, chose the
moment of greatest triumph of the *"Front Popu,"* to throw
Mea Culpa in its face. The all too urgent truths he felt that
he must now present, were put forth in as intolerable a manner as that of Semmelweiss.

*   *   *

His restlessness increased in 1937. Not even his old haunt
in Montmartre contented him. He left the apartment on the
rue Lepic, camped at his mother's in the rue Marsollier, em-
barked as ship's doctor on a freighter that went from Bor-
deaux to Newfoundland; he also considered the Isle of Jersey
for future asylum (only to be suspected of regicide); was
dismissed from the clinic in Clichy. Which fourteen years
later still rankled:

> I was fired by the communist municipality, on the orders
> of Dr. . . .[11] a Lithuanian Jew immigrant who wasn't
> a DOCTOR at all: an impostor, whose brother was an
> editor for PRAVDA, imposed upon Clichy by Pravda
> . . . as soon as he arrived, he was named Chief Physi-
> cian, when he undertook to get everyone fired who
> wasn't Jewish, especially me! who had started the clinic
> and who represented the French, the hated French. . . .
> He won. I had to resign.[12]

He took on jobs as an itinerant doctor, replacing others,
living as a medical nomad the way he had done once before.
The years of revolt (overthrow of everything he had built
up) were beginning again. He had broken out of the mold,
destroyed all success behind him. As in 1925. Only then, it
was the bourgeois comfort of Rennes which he abandoned.
A decade later, however, it was his writer's glory: *Voyage
au bout de la nuit* had won him world acclaim and been
translated into seventeen languages; *Mort à crédit* cemented
his fame and made him "the most expensive author in
France." [13] How easy it would have been to continue on the
same path, to let oneself be rocked by success.

At the summit, however, he must descend [14]—or throw
himself off the nearest precipice.

There was no lack of chasms in the Europe of these

days. The noise of obsidian knives being whetted for the sacrifice, was everywhere.

He sharpened his pen. The flow of invectives was about to be let loose. One venomous work after another poured forth: *Bagatelles pour un massacre* (1937); *L'Ecole des cadavres* (1938), judged defamatory and prohibited; *Les Beaux Draps* (1941).

The judgments of his friends did not deter him now. What did it matter that Vlaminck wrote, deeply shocked:

> I just read Céline's book. . . . That's no longer hate in *Bagatelles pour un massacre!* it's a pogrom!! an invitation to a Saint-Barthélémy massacre! [15]

Even the lawsuit that followed the publication of his next pamphlet, left him rather indifferent:

> The suit against *L'Ecole des cadavres*—has made for a busy winter—a corrida without mercy—the dog pack.

> All this is part of the game—part of my destiny I suppose. I'm not complaining. I presume that I won't change.[16]

When friends defended his need to lash out, to attack, his response was just as categorical. He claimed the right to determine his fate; to take the leap over the cliff he had chosen. It was clear that he was doing so with eyes wide open:

> For God's sake, don't ever come to my defense! I do, and will continue to do, everything in order to be and to remain, if not the richest then at least the most unpopular man in France. At that price, I am able to retain my calm and my independence.

> The total contempt of all of humanity is extremely pleasant to me—as is total oblivion.[17]

Both wishes would soon be granted him (in more complete form perhaps than he had anticipated). But he continued to work, with frenzy, toward their realization.

Sometimes, he compared the steps he was taking, to sacred rituals of self-abnegation; the slow dissolution of the self; the path to silence:

> You know that Lamas go through various ordeals that are increasingly painful, until they have reached that stage of wisdom when they no longer speak—when they are, at last, left alone.[18]

But for him, the only road to tranquillity, to muteness, was one paved with words. Everything had to be spoken, cursed, screamed, vomited, before one would have earned the right to be still. He had long known this, although in the past it was his double who proclaimed the conviction:

> Perhaps, the only terrible things inside us, on earth and in heaven, are those that have not yet been spoken. We shall only have peace when everything has been said, once and for all, then finally we'll be able to be silent and no longer fear to shut up. It will be over.
>
> *(VOY, 323)*

At present, the need grew to throw away all shields, to put himself in the arena. Naked, without pomp or disguise—bull rather than matador.

Few others had been willing to thus enter the ring—Villon, Cervantes, Rabelais. . . .

> What's so great about Rabelais, is that he put his skin on the table, he took chances. Death was on the lookout for him, and that's what inspires, death! I know it, when it's there, right behind you! When death is angry.

> . . . I've had the same vice as Rabelais. I also spent my time getting into desperate situations. Like him. I can expect no mercy from others, like him, I regret nothing.[19]

Céline would develop a genius for placing himself in the dead center of the holocaust, at the crossroads of every hell. And in so doing, assumed the right to place the skin

of others upon the same table as his own, and death at their
backs. The risks he took were at their expense also. It was
as if he had named himself the master of annihilation. Only
later, much later, would he concede that one's own blood
must flow first, before that of all the others; and come to
know that:

> Alchemy has its rules . . . the "blood of others" never
> succeeds in pleasing the Muses. . . .[20]

Now, he fed the Muses any prey he could catch hold
of in his furor.

Nor did he have to search long in the vast charnel house
which Europe was fast becoming. Victims were plentiful in
this place. It was a surrealistic nightmare, full of gigantic
machines programmed to wipe out those whom the punched
cards designated: one wrong ancestral move could doom;
a taint of skin or eye sufficed to click shut the gates of crematoriums. Life and death became a matter of foreskins, noses,
hair texture, cheekbones, and pigmentation. —As in the
witch hunts of the past, red hair, birthmarks, insensitive
areas on the skin, blue eyes, or the docility of snakes, could
lead to the stake. —The natural selection of the "others"
proceeded, based on a set of rules worthy of witches' alma-
nacs, to weed out Slavs, Gypsies and Jews. (The identification of the latter, suggested the known anthropologist Mon-
tandon, could be assured by simple means: amputation of
the nose.)[21] The plan was for the Nordic strain alone to survive the bloody flood. And to repopulate a cleansed earth
with blond and blue-eyed robots.

The world was full of executioners.

But few willing to risk their own skin. Who recognized
that the hangman was inextricably tied to the noose; that

knife and wound were one; or that the keeper of the guillotine lives in the shadow of its blade.

Céline knew. Had always known that victim and executioner were as inseparable as the two sides of the same face. That only such alchemy could produce the delirium he needed to create, the trance where ranting took on the accents of poetry.

It was with instinctive abandon that he now plunged into this heart of darkness. The price paid did not matter. His own body, those of his lovers and friends, had already been offered up in the past. Why not then, a larger and more anonymous mass of victims (or executioners who threatened), already branded for slaughter? As long as he himself belonged to the doomed inquisitors whose head was destined to fall, whose heart would one day be rent from the living flesh.

Only in this manner could the stage be set for his most devastating ritual.

He saw the road that he must take in order to become the Stranger (outlaws were obviously superannuated); knew the procedures to be followed in the manufacture of lightning rods; what rooftops to shout from, if he were to be certain to draw the thunder.

Ferdinand had already revealed the formula; Céline would now put it to use:

> I'll tell stories that will make them come . . . to kill me, from the ends of the world. Then it will be over and that will be all right with me.

> (*DIP,* 16)

The risks were available, in abundance. They lay on all sides, just waiting to be taken. In action or by words. Left,

right, and center could be of equal danger in *this* ball game.
He would explore its demonic recesses more thoroughly even
than the masters of demonology themselves. For he could
pitch in several directions at once, run, dodge, change sides
at will. The only rule of the game which he did not shun,
was to be always the loser.

Thus, he wrote pamphlets that were certain to inflame
and attract the threat of fire; attempted to enlist when war
broke out, after all his "pacifist" rantings (as he called his
diatribes of the first two of these works); drove an ambulance
during the Exodus out of the occupied zone; became the
ship's doctor of the *Shella,* sunk in collision with a British
patrol boat on its way from Marseille to Casablanca; returned to Paris held by the Germans; was adopted by Nazi
circles as spokesman for their cause (as he had been the
foster son of the French Left and Right, before), while de-
lighting in predicting their downfall; allowed himself to be
seen with members of the dreaded *Milice* and the Resistance;
treated torture victims of the Gestapo, while befriending a
high medical official of the Reich; railed against the Jews
and hid one of them from his persecutors;[22] put himself in
danger of being lynched at an anti-Semitic rally, yet furiously
demanded to have his works included in an exhibit of anti-
Jewish literature;[23] feared for his gold (the alchemist's metal
produced by his art), yet did not place it in Europe's traditional safe—Switzerland—but in a garden hideaway in Denmark; only thought of going to Germany when its defeat was
certain; refused to escape to England, Spain, or into the
maquis of Brittany (despite repeated offers of such safe-
conduct) but turned toward the center of annihilation: Germany in its last moments of convulsive rage.[24]

His gambler's eye fixed on the zero of the roulette wheel.
Playing with deadly chips. Defying the law that the Casino

inevitably wins—which he himself had long committed to memory.

How distressed he had been at the shipwreck of the *Shella*. It was more than the horror of seeing the dead and dying; it was the loss felt over the end of a hazardous life style:

> "Where shall I go?" he mourned. "Ah, destiny is fero-cious these days. I hope they'll find me another hideout where I can earn the wages of excitement. Between you and me, I never had so much fun. The good old days were really in the XVIIIth century, one easily went through a whole life in a week. Nowadays, with all that so-called speed, we battle like slugs. . . ." [25]

Yet—like a slug seeking a shell to hide in, to protect its soft, vulnerable flesh—he made some random moves to se-cure asylum: shelters for his gold, his person, his violent dia-tribes. True, they were all badly chosen: the garden in Copen-hagen, the Isle of Jersey, the "pacifist" aim of his war cries. Almost as though he hoped to fail. But driven to disguise such need under a mask of self-preservation.

As Bardamu had done before him, he darted in and out of danger, moved into the most threatening situations, and slipped out. Mostly, however, he bought delirium and the concomitant inspiration at the highest price possible. To play his own life, risk exile, mortification of flesh and spirit, seemed a small fee, if it would feed the springs of his art. The words from *Semmelweiss* seemed to echo in his head:

> "Good as well as evil has to be paid for. . . ."

And, if other offerings failed, his own head and those of many others would have to fall. Nothing was too much, if it propitiated the fates sufficiently to give him the fire of creation. —Hadn't a thousand victims been sacrificed on high altars to effect the return of the sun at the winter solstice?

—The winter of his life needed warmth. What matter, if it fed on blood or fire.

Monstrous drives demanded the creation of monsters. (If needed, he would become chief among them.)

He soon conceived of hallucinatory fictions, crowded his pamphlets with them. Huge effigies of dread; outgrowths of inner panic turned into menacing beasts; fantastic creatures that constituted "a permanent cosmic apocalypse." [26] Though named "Jews," "Yids," or "Kikes," they encompassed a whole world of hated beings: from the Pope to Louis XVI, from Laval to Racine, from Montaigne to Stendhal, from Zola to Cézanne, from Roosevelt-Rosenfeld to Maupassant, from La Guardia to the British Intelligence Service, guilty of every form of corruption from greed to lasciviousness, from bloodthirstiness to lack of lyricism, from intellectualism to occult powers.[27] (Not unlike the horrendous effigies of Death that Moravian peasants burned to drive winter away; or beasts ritually dismembered in order to be planted in the four corners of a field to ensure a fertile harvest.)

All reason was lost; delirium allowed free reign in a time of delirious evil. He had cut the thread between reality and monstrous dream, or so knotted and distorted it that there was no longer any path that could lead out of the labyrinth. The only move left was that which led to the Minotaur: the beast of darkness, the anomaly of human drives which, in more placid times, is skillfully disguised, or hidden out of sight.

How could an angry modern Daedalus shield it from view? No meandering walls would harbor it. There was no hero to slay the monster. Then he must be led into the light of day, dance like a performing bear who maintains constant

terror by threatening to break through his chains. Only by
such continual menace, could one prevent the drying up of
panic, the loss of potency that has its roots in terror.

A sense of history, political morals, even the most elementary human pity, seemed puny stopgaps when compared
to this instinctive need to scream, for fear of stifling or falling
silent too soon.

Then also, the victims stopped mattering. Or became hateful.[28] As if their sufferings were an affront, their bowed necks,
waiting to receive the blow, an outrage. Even his own victim-
double revolted him now. In the past, he had exorcized this
demon—cast him out of himself by the rite of creation—
propelled him into his books and watched him writhe there.
Bardamu, Robinson, Ferdinand, Semmelweiss had served this
way. Now the scapegoats must be of a different order, for the
nature of the terror had changed. The "hateful self" (which
Pascal had already known) was no longer alone. "Auto-
phobia" was joined by "aliophobia," the dread of the "other."
Especially when this otherness recalled the traits of the guilty
self.

> Hybrids frighten me. . . .
> 　　　(*CAS,* 206)

he would admit, unconsciously revealing his fear of their
strangeness, and of the many-faceted nature of his own being. Thus, it could not matter whether these hybrids were
the lieutenants of the Führer, named Laval, Nasser, Louis
XVI, or "the Jew." His attacks upon them had to be of equal
violence. It was their devious, variegated strain that caused
him such unease (too reminiscent of his own dual nature).
He had to lash out at them, whether they represented power
or were subject to persecution, whether they happened to

be kings or lepers, slave-keepers or slaves. Even his own country, he counseled, would best be cut in two, with the hated hybrid portion amputated like a gangrened limb.

> It was at the end of 1942 or the beginning of 1943. Suddenly, our Bardamu [Céline] violently deplored the fact that the line of demarkation between the north and south zones had disappeared, since the latter was populated by bastard Mediterraneans, by degenerate, dwarfed, feverish, senile "Narbonnoids," arabic parasites, which France should have thrown overboard. Below the Loire, nothing but putrefaction, sham, disgusting half-breeds.[29]

It was a private terror, too hard to contain. So he struck out against it, as one would do with a mirror that reflects too well.

Once the mirror is shattered, however, the images can no longer come from an individual source. The private vision is obscured, obliterated, and runs the risk of being submerged in the general outlook of the times, the clichés of horror which are being commonly propagated. The path leads from authenticity to falsehood and even forgery.

(How else could one explain Céline's stooping to the use of such source material as *Israël, son passé, son avenir;* not even disdaining *Le Règne des Juifs,* and *La Prochaine Révolution des travailleurs*—leaflets such as are often sold at Paris subway exits, with racing sheets and pornographic postcards? [30] And then, to bowdlerize even such rags, in order to make the statistics appear more horrendous still? True, he had long ago mocked reason and "ide-as" as being the tools of the impotent, and celebrated the irrational drives that underlay creation. But now, he would fall into the trap of cliché ideologies, content himself with unoriginal notions, and subscribe blindly to a variety of political borrowings[31] (as hybrid as those of the worst half-breeds of the intelligence).

He had abdicated the right to look into the mirror which his own genius had allowed him to turn upon the world, as probing as a surgeon's lens, and fallen into the error of gazing into the common glass. The deformations seen there were ready-made, as coarse as those caused by bubbles in cheap windowpanes, as monstrous as the reflections in deforming mirrors that catch the movements of the passing Sunday crowd in fun houses.

The result was the monstrous outpour of his pamphlets.

Monstrous, because they grew side by side with the real nightmare world (that sprouted with mushroom-like speed to explode in Hiroshima skies). Because they no longer pitted the strength of individual creation against the destruction all around; or images of personal hallucination against the general insanity. Finally, monstrous in that reality no longer intruded at all: works encapsulated in their own venom; creations based upon a void, floating adrift on an ocean of blood and unaware of their wake; constructs of hate that never cast anchor into the abjectness of suffering around them, nor ventured to sound the depth of its misery.

Half humorous, half devastating, they mingled light fantasy and scenarios for ballets, with madness and choreographic studies for annihilation.

And always turned about a central figure, his "dada," [32] the Jew. Who appeared sometimes as the most dreaded of men (more terrifying than the human crocodiles, sharks, and carnivorous apes of the early works), to be approached only with this warning:

> One must always beware of Jews, even dead ones.
>
> (*BAM*, 70)

Sometimes described as a quasi-mythological beast (furtive, nomadic, elusive—in the best tradition of Bardamu and his author):

> Run! . . . Run! . . . Disappear. . . . He was indefatigable in his pirouettes, fast escapes, trapeze work

. . . his furtive colloquia and international sleight-of-
hand tricks. . . . Always throwing himself a little further into the fight, unearthing still other deals, more
tangled threads, knotting it all into an enigma, and then
protecting all these intrigues with the help of a lot of
little occult trapdoors. He never stopped. . . . Now you
saw him . . . now you didn't. . . . He reminded me
of that extravagant animal in the London zoo, the ornithorynx, which is so agile, that incredible fake beaver,
which has an enormous bird's beak and also never stops
diving, digging, coming back. . . . He disappeared in
the same unpredictable way, this Yubelblat. . . . Plaf!
he plunges, dives down into India . . . you don't see
him anymore! Another time it's China . . . the Bal-
kans . . . into the shadows of the world . . . into the
depths. . . . He was infinitely supple . . . extraordinary to watch, but at the end of his mitts, watch out, he
had claws . . . and poisonous ones too, just like the
ornithorynx. . . .

(BAM, 77)

(Yubelblat far outstripped his earlier double Yudenzweck,
that rather harmless intriguer of *L'Eglise*.)

It was not the Jew alone, but also his black, brown, and
yellow brothers that gave rise to terror. The war, which was
rapidly spreading, seemed actually

An implacable combat of different species. Ants against
caterpillars. To the death . . . no holds barred. Negroid Jews against Whites.

(EC, 25)

In this onslaught, only the Nordic race—pure, white, implacable caterpillar—could provide a bulwark against the
occult terror, the claws of the ornithorynx, the warriors of the
dark continent (cradle of Negroid and Semitic horrors),
the yellow peril, the contaminated Slavs who dared to suggest that Prague should be voted "Miss Martyr 1938" (*EC,*
42).

*   *   *

He soon concluded that it had become necessary to practice "biological racism." (His expertise in medicine could lend itself to such ends also.) The conclusions seemed obvious, if only one accepted the basic hypotheses:

> Racially, Jews are monsters, goofed-up, twisted hybrids who must disappear. . . .
>
> The Jew must vanish. . . . He won't allow anything to exist, outside himself. . . . He's a delirious impostor, an insane dying man, a condemned tyrant, beside himself with rage, in a world that is his prison. . . .
>
> (*EC*, 109)

The danger always existed that, in order to hide his tainted heredity, he would resort to violent means:

> If it took floods of the perfumes of Arabia to wipe out the traces of some puny little crime, if Madame Macbeth had a tough time of it, several wars and all our blood won't be too much to ask, to wipe out the stains on the chromosomes of Israel.
>
> (*EC*, 112)

Only racial selection could prevent disaster. Practiced with rigorous measures of elimination, it could result in a species less abject and not nearly so terrifying. For he had become convinced that, "to track down the devil in man, to exorcise him," it sufficed to breed him right. He reasoned (or ranted) thus:

> All the vegetables, all the animals have undergone selection. Why not man? Why can't one do for man, what has been done for the beet, the pig, the fowl?
>
> (*EC*, 135)

As though the world were a gigantic barnyard. (Besides, the Teutonic "farmers" were already at work. Their practices

evoked the castration of capons, or the nailing down of ducks'
feet to fatten them for the knife.)

If biology and "biological selection" did not suffice, it was
always possible to resort to Shakespeare. And to insist that
if Hamlet were to reappear on the contemporary scene, his
meditation would have culminated in such words as these:

> "To be or not to be" Aryan? That is the question.
> (EC, 222)

A variant of the dilemma might also be phrased thus:

> To jewefy or to die. . . .

He knew full well, however, that, by his prescriptions and
remedies containing such poisonous ingredients, he put a
price upon his head. He even announced the terms of the
vengeance which would one day be exacted from him:

> I open my big mouth how, where, and when I want
> to. . . .

> I can't be bought. Haughty as thirty-six peacocks. . . .

> That's Ferdinand, in the flesh. He'll have to be killed.
> I see no other way.
> (EC, 299)

(Just as he provoked German persecution by making appearances among the Nazis and their sympathizers, to assure them
maliciously that they would inevitably lose the war.)[33]

At the moment, however, another hunt was on. France was
at the height of confusion, torn in two by dissent, faced with

the almost insoluble dilemma of military collaboration or threatened "polonization," led by a doddering, broken old man. The toll of hostages was constantly rising; the persecutions of Communists, Freemasons, and Jews increased rapidly. The Vichy government's only reaction was weak protest, appeals dictated by senility (Pétain was almost eighty-five), or even complicity.

At this juncture, Céline published his only article in *La Gerbe* (encouraging such persecutions),[34] and *Les Beaux Draps,* which attacked the despairing French in their most vulnerable parts (citing their cowardice, duplicity, and degenerate naïveté) and attributed all their (deserved) misfortunes once more to racial impurity. The course of action to be followed was drastic:

> To inform on the Jew[1] isn't enough, let me tell you, it's going around in a circle, it becomes a joke, a way of sounding off, unless one grabs the strings he pulls and uses them to strangle him.
>
> [1] By Jew, I mean any man who has a Jewish grand-parent, even a single one!
>
> *(BD,* 116)

Systematic elimination (based on exactly such rules) had become a reality in his country.

(For purposes of selective breeding, it was preferable to nip corruption in the bud: to weed out the undesirable children, as one destroys an imperfect pup—one that is not blue-eyed—in a litter of Weimaraners.)

By August 1942, such practice became a cold fact. Four thousand children (whose error was to have been born of foreign Jews) were separated from their parents and interned at Drancy, before being shipped off.

The children were from 2 to 12 years old. . . . They
were put 100 in a barracks. Buckets were placed on
the landings, since many could not climb down the long,
rickety staircase to go to the latrines. The smallest, in-
capable of going alone, waited desperately for help
of some volunteer or an older child. It was during the
era of cabbage soup at Drancy. This soup wasn't bad,
but totally unadapted to children's stomachs. Very soon,
all the children began to suffer from terrible diarrhea.
They soiled their clothes, they soiled the mattresses on
which they lay day and night. For lack of soap, their
laundry was rinsed in cold water and the almost naked
child had to wait until it dried. A few hours later,
another accident occurred, and it started all over
again. . . .

. . . every night, from the other side of the camp, you
could hear the weeping of desperate children and, from
time to time, the calls and screams of those who could
no longer contain themselves.

. . . on the day of deportation, the children were
awakened at five o'clock in the morning. . . . It sometimes happened that a whole barracks of children,
seized by uncontrollable panic and insane fear, would
no longer heed the words of appeasement of the adults
in charge. . . . So, the police had to be called in to
carry the children downstairs, howling with terror. . . .[35]

Only a year before that, however, Céline had written:

Childhood is magical. . . .

(*BD*, 178)

(Aryan childhood that is.)

The orgy of fear and hate was far from over. Layer upon
layer of dread had to be explored. The panic could not stop

at the Jew. Even after this "insane parasite" had destroyed all Europe, there were other dangers that lurked behind him. He screamed of peril upon peril (an apocalypse of human origin), which would not end until the earth was uninhabited, a wasteland in which original chaos reigned, and evolution proceeded in reverse. For the black man's shadow hovered larger than the Jew's:

> When everything is reduced to ruins, the Negro will arrive, it will be his hour, his turn, together with the Tartar maybe. The Negro, the real papa of the Jew, whose phallus is even bigger, is the only one who will win out in the end, at the far end of decadence. . . . It's the forest that will claim everything, the gigantic, the tropical one. . . .
>
> (*BD*, 195–196)

It was a long orgasm of fury—more intense than those "instants of delirium" that coitus could usually provide—which lasted him for four years. It only spent itself when artifice and reality too closely began to resemble each other. How could the hallucinatory constructs of terror continue to remain standing apart, when in 1942, twelve thousand Jews awaiting deportation to concentration camps were crowded into the Vel' d'Hiv',[36] where the annual circus was otherwise held?

The road of creation, paved with flayed skins, strewn with bone-meal and ashes, seemed suddenly worn out. He turned to the past once more and began work on *Guignol's Band* (a fairy-tale subject of another time; a flashback setting that took him to the London of World War I days).

1943–1944

> . . . he howl'd fearfully:
> Said he was a wolffe,: onely the difference
> Was, a wolffe's skinne was hairy on the outside,
> His on the inside: bade them take their swords,
> Rip up his flesh, and trie. . . .[37]

Lycanthropy is not so easily shaken off. He could not climb out of the abyss that reeked of blood. No longer content to explore and describe, he had added to the stench that reigned there. The skin of the beast clung to him, chafed against his flesh. Words had been turned into murderous weapons.

(In 1943, he allowed Denoël to republish *L'Ecole des cadavres*. When persecutions in his country reached their most hideous toll.)

He, who was so well aware of the danger of words, their threatening potency, that he had long ago issued this warning:

> One can never beware enough of words, they look like nothing, words, naturally they don't appear dangerous, they resemble little gusts of wind, mouth sounds, neither warm nor cold, easily taken back. . . . One is never suspicious of words, and misfortunes happen.

> There are some words, hidden among the others like pebbles. One doesn't especially recognize them, and suddenly there they are, making you tremble in every fiber of your life. . . . Then there's a panic, an avalanche . . . you're there, like a hanged man, dangling above the emotions aroused . . . it's a tempest . . . much too powerful for you, so violent you would never

have believed it possible, born only of emotions. . . .
Therefore, one can never beware enough of words.

(VOY, 476–477)

Just as he would admit, a decade later, that

All misfortunes happen because of one superfluous
word.

(FEE, 81)

The need to liberate the monster in man was too great;
he did not heed his own insights. But gave his myths the name
of realities, and continued to lose his way in a morass of
ready-made symbols (scapegoats and archangels, Nordic gods
and swarthy demons). Even his new apartment—on the rue
Girardon in Montmartre—reflected the penchant. Gone were
the African masks of Clichy days, and the slight preciosity
of the décor on rue Lepic. The new setting was of rustic
Breton style, such as a petty employee might choose if he
came into some money from an inheritance. Everything was
polished, waxed, carefully shined. There was no trace of
artistic or intellectual life; the books were hidden or disguised,
as in the houses of old peasants who read but do not wish to
let on, for fear of giving away their secret tastes.[38] (There
could obviously be no chance, in such a décor, of being associated with the "Narbonnoid" bastards, the suspect Mediterranean hybrids below the Loire valley.)

He continued to bellow, to affirm in the most belligerent
manner, his "right to be wrong to the very last." [39]

His red motorcycle was filled with gasoline from suspect
sources. His books were printed on paper which Germans
must have supplied. Yet, he assured his friends that he would
"prove that Hitler was a Jew" [40] and almost succeeded in
getting himself lynched for patent Judaism. It was during a
meeting at the Institute for Jewish Affairs (on rue de la
Boëtie, in the former Rosenberg Gallery, now transformed

into a lecture hall), which, some people thought, Céline
should have joined as one of the directors:[41]

> Céline, incognito, was in a corner all the way back,
> buried in his sheepskin and his filthy muffler, his gaze
> dimly filtering through sleepy eyelids. . . .
>
> The speaker droned on, and I heard some grumbling
> from Ferdinand's corner. . . . As the clumsy, intermi-
> nable reading continued, Céline's bass voice became
> more distinct.
>
> —The Judeo . . . Judeo-Marxist . . . tyran . . . tyr-
> anny. . . .
>
> —And what about the Aryan imbecility, how about
> mentioning that?
>
> Fifty pairs of amateur policemen's eyes turned all
> around, tried to identify the author of such sacrilege.
> Suddenly, the shrill cry of a female:
>
> —That's him! A Jew! A Jew! Over there!

(Another man was seized. He objected that he was a
publisher whom Radio London had condemned to death for
collaboration. A fight followed, however. The meeting had
been sabotaged by Céline, and broke up.)

> "I got to the door," the witness states, "in the midst of ir-
> reparable confusion. Céline hadn't moved. . . ."[42]

The danger games continued to amuse him. No detour seemed
too risky to take. Not even the one which led into the midst
of total madness.

To some, it seemed as if he had inadvertently ventured
into a world which closely resembled that of his books. As if,
by chance, he was plunged into one of his own creations,
or had

. . . suddenly been dragged into the canvas he had
painted; as if Michelangelo, while working on the Sis-
tine ceiling, had all at once found himself falling amongst
the naked bodies of his *Last Judgment.*[43]

It was a much more lucid venture, however. The fore-
knowledge of his fate had long been with him. Almost a
decade ago, he had already mused about its possible outcome:

> Perhaps they'll shoot me, either in one camp or the
> other. The Nazis execrate me, just as much as the So-
> cialists and the Commies. . . . They all agree when it
> comes to ejecting me. . . .
>
> I ask nothing of anyone. One must deliberately place
> oneself into a nightmare state. . . .[44]

When it was all over, he would summarize his exploit as
though he had plotted its every move, acted to carry out his
own prophecy (a sly Cassandra, almost destroyed by the
doom she had foreseen for herself):

> . . . one puny success I have achieved during my life
> is to have, after all, managed the tour de force of having
> them all agree for an instant, Left, Right, Center, Sacris-
> ties, Lodges, cells, charnel-houses, the Count of Paris,
> Josephine, my aunt Odile, Kroukroubezeff, the Abbé
> Piggy-Bank, that I'm the biggest bastard alive!
>
> (*NO,* 363–364)

It was evident that devious path must be followed to arrive
at such ends.

If he read John Donne, he would have agreed that he,
too, was "ready with loathsome vomiting to spew his soul
out of one hell into a new." But he needed no literary en-
couragement from an outsider to spur him on. For he had
already begun to prepare his next move by a gesture that was
as extravagant as poetry, as irrational as the impulses to
which he attributed creation.

1944–1945

The gold,[45] which lay in a Danish vault since 1938, was to furnish the impetus for his *Nibelungenlied*.

The first journey was to Berlin. In 1942, he decided that it was time to give the key of the treasure to a Danish ballerina (who had crossed his path at several strategic points in life), so that she might bury it in her garden.[46] While some were led to think that he had put it into the hands of a court photographer.[47] Officially, he disguised his trip as a visit (undertaken in the company of several other French doctors) to inspect various hospitals in the German capital.[48]

Two years later, he took the final plunge.

In July 1944 (coinciding with the Allied drive into Europe), when Germany's fall began to appear inevitable, he felt impelled to reach Denmark. And if direct routes were shut off—if the last train to Copenhagen had left Paris—he would proceed by detours, along tortuous paths. By crossing the falling empire of the Germans.

It was an exodus no less dramatic than the one he had participated in some years before, when he drove an ambulance to La Rochelle on roads crowded with his frantic countrymen fleeing from the conquering German. —Now, the movement was reversed. He ran from the menaces of his own people into the midst of the retreating Germans. Exchanging one hell for another—the "little coffins" sent by the Resistance to those who would be purged, the smashing of his IHP motorcycle[49] (as if it were his effigy), the announcements of the B.B.C. that broadcast his condemnation and invited to the kill, or predicted that: "the *Monster of Montmartre will be chopped into little pieces!"* [50]—for the menacing German countryside.

Others were taking a parallel path (but for more clear-cut reasons): Laval, Pétain, and their cortege of ministers including Brinon, Marion, Bichelonne, Déat, Bonnard. They also were on their way to Sigmaringen, where they and Céline would eventually meet. Some, such as his friend Bonnard, went into exile in a style that resembled Céline's most grotesque fictions: dressed in a lilac-colored suit with a brilliant series of ties, he rode in the midst of bedlam created by the reflux of a conquered army, complaining of three things only —that some of his precious Chinese knickknacks had disappeared; that Marion, not he, had a driver "as handsome as a god" (when his own special tastes were so much better suited to the appreciation of male beauty); that someone had stolen his last jar of "irreplaceable, perfumed cream." [51]

Meanwhile, Céline was ready for flight. Lucette, Le Vigan ("the man from nowhere"),[52] and Bébert the cat, were preparing for departure. They put Bébert in an old gamebag, collected money, identification papers, and poison for emergency use.

(Laval, en route to the same destination, was not as methodical. The cape in which he carried his cyanide since 1942, was left behind and had to be fetched by special messenger.)[53]

July heat beat down on the rue Girardon. The heat of panic was also in the streets. The Allies were almost in Paris; the

torture chambers in the middle of the city resounded with re-
doubled cries, as victims were more frantically tortured by
Gestapo and *Milice*. Elsewhere, the Germans razed villages,
burned inhabitants alive; the *maquis,* in retaliation, accelerated its executions. Death without trial, without question, was
the order of the day. A final paroxysm of rage held the entire
country in convulsions.

Panic seized him also now. The corrida was general.
There was no telling where the arena ended. He turned in
circles, like a dazed beast, unable to decide which way to flee.
Spain . . . Brittany . . . Italy? It seemed safest to follow
up a tale which he had already spread: the medical congress
in Baden-Baden.

"A strange medical congress," a friend would muse, "for
which Dr. Destouches was leaving with about 20 trunks, a
dozen of which were said to be stuffed full of horseshoes, pick-
axes, barbed wire, hatchets, scythes, harnesses, and copper
for purposes of trading with the Teutonic farmers. . . ." [54]

A month after the Normandy beachhead, they were on
their way. With the unerring instinct of homing pigeons
trained to fly into the center of the holocaust—a far cry from
the olive-bearing dove.

For him, it was a return to the country where he had been
exiled in adolescence. Now, in climacteric years, he would go
back to the starting point of a circle whose circumference had
stretched to the far ends of the earth.

> I don't think much of the country . . . a sandy plain,
> poor soil with huge forests all around! . . . potato,
> hog, and mercenary country . . . and the storms on
> those plains! . . . no tourist country! . . . dismal lit-
> tle lakes, still more funereal forests. . . .
>
> (*CAS,* 231)

The Prussia of pubescent days where he had learned to feel like a stranger, a hated outcast, would now receive him with arms no more outstretched in welcome than before.

They landed in Baden-Baden, where the sumptuous Park Hotel, with its pastry shop, Casino, and rose gardens still functioning in the manner of reflexes that continue after death, became their first shelter. They wandered among destitute aristocrats who treasured their faded fans and formed an elite whose hierarchy was based upon the number of ration cards each managed to hold. To pass the time, the inmates devised small vendettas amongst themselves, or denounced each other to the Germans.

From there, the journey led to Berlin—the very center of this grandiose Guignol show. A city that smelled of cadavers and where bombs fell continuously, like rain. There were no linden trees to be found Unter den Linden. Even the river had an ominous look. One of the few floors left in the only remaining department store, contained a counter where canes, crutches, and other devices for the maimed were sold by mutilated store clerks.[55]

Only a few names gave any direction to this wilderness: Epting, a sculptor who was a member of the German Cultural Institute in Paris; Dr. Hauboldt (alias Harras in his novels), an important medical officer of the Reich, whom he had met during a film lecture on typhoid along the Champs-Elysées. But it seemed that Hauboldt was somewhat taken aback by the strange trio. And judged that it was best to send them off to Kränzlin—where they could remain in a small castle, not at all an unpleasant place. (Céline would treat it in his characteristic fashion: rename it Zornhof ("Court of Anger") and enlarge upon its absurd horrors in his best hallucinatory manner when he wrote of it many years later, in *Nord*.)

It was a time of repeated leave-taking. Epting saw them

vanish around a bend of the road, after they had met in a somber little restaurant thus far spared by the bombs:

> Céline went off, slightly bent, with Bébert on his arm, Lili [Lucette] and Vig [Le Vigan] at his side, across the rubble of caved-in houses. . . . Ferdinand en route without respite, like Ahasuerus wandering among the ruins of the earth.[56]

Departures were rapidly succeeded by arrivals, as the stages of the journey grew more hectic. One day at the beginning of November, 1944, they landed at Sigmaringen.[57]

Céline made quite an impression. His appearance was indeed memorable:

> He wore a blue canvas cap resembling those that locomotive drivers wore around 1905, two or three battle jackets with all their grime and tatters superimposed upon each other; a pair of moth-eaten gloves hung around his neck on a string and, in a gamebag on his chest, there was the cat Bébert showing us his typical, phlegmatic Parisian snoot which seemed to say that he'd seen everything under the sun.[58]

The assembled company (consisting of members of the deposed Vichy government, a motley crew of sundry Nazi sympathizers and collaborators) looked with surprise at this grotesque apparition. Asking themselves if this could be the "great Fascist writer" they had heard so many stories about; the prophetic genius come to join the dispossessed.

Irony was utterly fitting to this place. An outlandish spot (so ill-suited to their delusion of grandeur) and nowhere near their idea of a noble refuge, some island dwelling where exile could proceed with dignity:

> The little town . . . was one of the places in Germany which had remained most anti-Nazi and faithful to the old traditions. It is dominated by the Hohenzollern-

Sigmaringen castle, an old romantic outpost to which
each generation of princes had added excrescences of
stone that were complicated and colossal . . . a gigantic castle constructed on a steep cliff, above a bend in
the Danube. . . .

On October 1, 1944, the French flag was hoisted above
the castle.[59]

The fluttering banner was the final outrage. They objected,
but to no avail, that it made their captivity and exile seem
voluntary (and their heroic position a mere joke).

Into this setting of pseudo-melodrama Céline made his entry.
It could not have been better chosen, for here was just the
kind of world he thrived on: full of "laughs and cemeteries."
It hardly needed embroidery or efforts to transpose. A few
touches here and there, might suffice to make it into the kind
of macabre Disneyland he would have delighted in.

The inhabitants were as grotesque as the place. Some
flattered themselves into thinking that this "Elba" was a tem-
porary abode, from which they would return triumphant and
be acclaimed the liberators of the French nation; others
dreamt of being treated as heroes and martyrs to their cause
by a grateful German populace. Mostly, however, they were
reduced to hunting for rooms. It was a Kafkaesque task: for,
in order to have employment, one needed a domicile; and in
order to be assigned a room, one had to have proof of employment. The vicious circle in which they were trapped, gave
the populace the joyful opportunity to make sport of them.[60]

Among the higher-ups, the game took on an even more
hallucinatory character: Bonnard spent his time inventing
malicious epithets for the leading figures of the deposed Vichy
regime (it was one of his favorite sports and had delighted
the sharp-tongued wits of Paris and Vichy, in better days):

Laval became the "Auvergnat of the Danube"; Pétain, "the Invisible Man"; Chateaubriant, the "Magus of the Black Forest"; and dread Darnand, "Jojo, the Mover." Doriot paradoxically imitated every move that de Gaulle was making in London: he considered himself a dissident too, who had left France for the same reasons, i.e., the better to reconquer it; organized parachute landings into France, etc. The others spent all their time conjuring up a list of Germany's secret weapons which would assure her an all-out victory without delay: freeze-bombs; incandescent bombs that could create heat of millions of degrees; mauve gas; orange gas; human anti-aircraft missiles; pink clouds; death rays.[61]

An alternating current of exaltation and despair swept through the castle and its environs. When panic reached the highest voltage, it led to the inevitable short-circuiting of their hate. The familiar phenomenon of interior bloodletting was the outcome. The need arose to institute purges within the circle of French emigrants in Sigmaringen. Some recommended the elimination of two-thirds of their own men. Those who subscribed most eagerly to such violent means were the same men who had relished shedding the blood of others—the leaders of the *Milice* and the chiefs of the French SS.[62]

Inside this arena of maddened bulls and senile matadors, Céline undoubtedly circulated with some relish. But also remembered that his double calling must be put to use. The doctor undertook to heal what the writer noted. The grotesque creatures were often in need of care; their abject writhings demanded treatment in both medical and literary terms. His role as physician had often led him into the darkest corners of life. Now it permitted him access to every recess of this gigantic stage, and opened numberless curtains upon ridiculous and dolorous scenes.

Seen from one angle, he was the good Samaritan, come to rescue his countrymen from disease and certain death:

> Upon his arrival in Sigmaringen, Céline and his wife moved into a tiny room without the slightest comfort. One of the windowpanes was broken; it was freezing cold. It was in this room and on his own bed, that he received his patients, examined them, nursed them. . . . At night, if he was called, he went forth in heavy snow, often very far, on foot of course, without even the help of a flashlight. . . . He told me that, touched by so much misery, he went himself to buy the medicines he prescribed, convinced that otherwise his patients couldn't procure them for lack of money.[63]

From another vantage point, however, his doctor's satchel and special *Ausweis* were as useful to his voyeur's predilections as the *Tarnkappe* used by Teutonic heroes of old to render them invisible. His ambiguous figure could insinuate itself into every recess of the labyrinth. The double nature of his calling made for the most perfect disguise.

He might have passed unseen, but he could not remain mute. He began railing against the Germans. Accused Hitler of having brought him to this end. Reminisced loudly about his exploits (on the other side of the fence) during the Flanders campaign. The only thing which saved him from the wrath of the Germans (whom he mocked even during state dinners) was the fact that they knew him as a trickster, the court jester whose traditional role it is to make sport of his great masters. Besides, they had heard of his literary fame and chalked many of his outrageous remarks up to the use of poetic license.[64]

One would have thought that he had now found an ideal domain for the exercise of his craft. Yet, he soon grew testy, and suspicious of those around. He seemed as though he were hunted, or:

> . . . constantly pursued by the demon of persecution; this inspired him to create fantastic schemes and devious paths in order to defeat the maneuvers of countless imaginary enemies. He meditated endlessly on omens that were perceptible only to him, and arrived at solutions that were equally erroneous and full of cunning.[65]

Sometimes, the two tendencies would merge. As in the case of the strange death of Doriot (voted most likely to succeed in pleasing Hitler at this time). He had been killed by machine-gun fire from a mysterious plane, as he was riding—unsuspectingly—to a meeting at Sigmaringen.

Doriot's funeral was a mixture of sincerity and imposture. Just the kind Céline appreciated; material for literary transposition that was just what *this* doctor would have ordered: Almost all of the major figures of the "pseudo-governmental microcosm" were present, plus actors, journalists, soldiers, and members of the *Milice*—a whole "fictitious society," that would soon be dispersed. Luchaire (Doriot's worst enemy) pronounced the funeral oration in eloquent and tearful tones. The village bell tolled feebly. The cemetery gates were flanked by immobile *Hitlerjugend*. A French priest officiated. Some unknown soldier threw a few clumps of dry black French earth (which he had carried into exile with him in a little bag), unto the coffin.[66]

It seemed an evil omen.

A few months later, all those assembled would be running in every direction, like rats.

The first to smell the coming catastrophe and to get out, was Céline.

By the end of February, he had received the almost

mythical *Ausweis* for Denmark. The trip toward his gold could now begin. (Though no one knew whether this treasure existed, was recouped or had been lost from its hiding place under a tree.)

Ferdinand's triumph was undeniable. Two or three days later, for the first time during his stay at Sigmaringen, he offered a round of beer to his friends (for which he allowed his colleague, Dr. Jacquot, to pay).[67] Before leaving, he pronounced a monologue in his inimitable style (full of venom, humor, and the smugness of those that have escaped the executioner):

> It has been written. The situation is in the bag. The Germans are completely screwed, wrap up the bones and plant a weeping willow, the guts on one side, the shins on the other. . . . The French at Sig . . . those guys with their ears stuffed, blind. . . . They can't see that the Americans and the British will pick them like flowers and put them against the wall . . . Waltz, you ghosts, to the ballad of the firing squad. . . . As for me, I'm not crazy, I'm getting the hell out! Let them croak if they want, those revolutionary office clerks . . . me, I'm leaving this dump. . . . Adieu, Sigmaringen . . . I've had enough; for me, it's the end of the ballet of the crabs . . . I'm leaving for Norway. . . . Good-bye, Kollabo . . . I'm off to the land of lakes. . . .[68]

His instinct did not fail him. In another month it would have been too late. By April, the nets had tightened around Sigmaringen; they thrashed around frantically, looking for a hiding place, a hole to escape through. Violent and abject scenes accompanied the leave-taking of those who succeeded in buying, begging, usurping a form of exit from the trap.

Ferdinand's departure, though dramatic, had all the markings of a gala performance: the audience, the setting, and the costumes. It was a scene which remained engraved on one's memory:

> We met on the quai . . . Abel Bonnard, Paul Marion
> . . . La Vigue, now reconciled with Ferdine after their
> twelfth quarrel this winter, and several other close
> friends. There was the Destouches household: Lucette,
> always impeccable, serene, acquiescent, who carried
> about 500 lbs. of luggage by hand, undoubtedly the
> relics of those famous trunks, now sewn into duffle bags
> and attached to poles, a veritable accoutrement for a sa-
> fari. . . . Céline, with Bébert on his belly, beamed, a
> little too broadly. Finished, the bombings, the resigned
> waiting for the kill at the bottom of the mousetrap. We
> would not weigh on his memory. The train got on the
> track, one of those miserable trains of a Germany in its
> death-agony, driven by wood. We embraced for a long
> time; the sacks were laboriously hoisted aboard. Ferdi-
> nand unfurled his incredible passport and waved it for
> the last time. . . . And we remained there, with heavy
> hearts, in that hellish cauldron.[69]

Now, however, began a journey which did not reflect the triumph of his leave-taking. It was more like an infernal dance—performed on shattered railroad tracks, bombed-out bridges, in smoke-filled tunnels that seemed to have no end; a grotesque rigadoon, in which any steps forward were immediately nullified by the same number of steps in the opposite direction. The sound of freight cars clashing was no longer just in his head, but all around him. The trains zigzagged across a countryside in ruins, hacked apart by spearheads of invasion and the craters of bombs; they detoured, advanced, backtracked, side-stepped, picked up companions along the way only to lose them.

Even Le Vigan soon decided that it was time for a parting of the ways.[70]

Their incredible load of baggage vanished, piece by piece. It could not survive this jungle trip.

Long lines, swarms, maddened hordes of people crossed their paths; in total confusion of country, race, and uniform. They swept all around the pair, moved them as in a sea swell. Cries and silent looks of horror alternated. Everything was falling apart, fragmented, reversed, or slipping—houses, rail-road tracks, bridges, tunnels, skies, all seemed askew. Even the trees seemed to have lost the sense of which way to grow, their roots and trunk thrown out of kilter by the shattering throbs that shook the earth.

Yet there were still those who believed in "natural selection." They heard tales of a German doctor who applied such theories to wounded soldiers (believing that Nietzschean concepts now found their truest application):

> . . . the cold, the snow, the nudity fortify them . . . especially the wounded! . . . the weak succumb, they are buried . . . the technique . . . is to empty the railroad cars, all of them, they put the bodies down on the ground . . . just as they are . . . they're left there . . . two . . . three days . . . in the cold, the snow, all naked . . . those that can get up make an effort . . . even on one leg . . . they go to Rostock . . . where they are separated! . . . those that'll go to the hospital, into surgery . . . and those that'll remain . . . to dig the ditches . . . for the dead, the ones who don't move anymore after two . . . three days. . . .
>
> (*RIG,* 58–59)

The icy stretches often gave way to panoramas of flame. Luxury editions of the *Inferno* could not have been more skillfully illustrated. For there were colors such as no cactus button could produce; visions of locomotives floating upside down among the clouds; mines bursting into gigantic flowers.

Strange fragments of languages filled the air—phrases in rags, words that were as twisted and splintered as the countryside—which might have passed for ersatz German or Apocalypse-Esperanto.

But they were effaced by even weirder conglomerations of objects—melted into each other, inexplicably intact, haphazardly merged: ships' cables and soup tureens; rakes and oxen; bricks and ocarinas.

Even the ports had not escaped reversal in the topsy-turvy wind of disaster. For there were

> lots of boats . . . but all these boats had their ass up in the air and the propellers sticking out . . . their noses stuck in the mud! . . . it was funny, buffoonish!
>
> (*RIG*, 203)

The water boiled and burst into strange growths; submarines thrashed beneath the surface in dying convulsions, like Leviathans.

Most hideous, however, were the herds of lost children. (As pitiful as those interned at Drancy, or Biessen—alias Cissen, that "Grand Guignol nursery" where he had seen them die.) What hope was there for those who should have been "eliminated," who were anomalies of breeding: the cretins, mongoloids, and such runts of the litter?

It seemed a long time ago, when he would have abstractly condemned them—or their like. Now he could understand that

> Slaughterhouses could no longer exist, if the officials in charge looked at the eyes of the subnormal. . . .
>
> These snot-noses of ours weren't meant to live, but they had gotten this far and they were hungry. . . .
>
> (*RIG*, 208–209)

There was nothing for it, but to become the Pied Piper of this "debilitated, slobbering" crew which could not ask for

anything and had no stake in any claim at all. He led them
to the sea where they would end their journey—not by drown-
ing—but in the protective arms of Danish nurses.

For them, the voyage lasted over three weeks. The landmarks
passed. The country dissolved as they went by: Ulm, Leipzig,
Oddort, Berlin, Hanover, Hamburg[71] (cities in a dream of
destruction). Hamburg recalled Pompeii: the tar still burned
underfoot; they saw domes like gigantic bells, formed by the
action of liquid sulfur. Inside, preserved intact in clay, they
found entire warehouses stacked with canned milk and meat;
groceries with their keepers still seated at the till, disem-
boweled; apothecaries who bent over their flasks, mummified.
Outside these bubbles, everything had been devastated by
fire:

> The houses, the streets, the asphalt, the people running
> in every direction . . . even the sea gulls on the roofs!
> (*RIG,* 232)

It became evident now that the sea and its inhabitants
had not escaped the holocaust. Not even the sea!

They must increase their frenzied pace. Speed up the
choppy rhythm of the rigadoon.

Waiting rooms, heaps of cadavers, rubble, bombs, railway tunnels, docks, freight cars, mines, fields, truncated
church steeples, shreds of armored battalions, supply depots,
derailed trains passed by with jagged and ever-increasing
rapidity.

There was nothing left of their baggage. And only a
shred of the impressive passport which he had waved at his
receding friends at Sigmaringen. They were but shadows of
their former selves. Death by hunger, fatigue, or exposure
seemed more than likely. All sense of direction and distance
had gone, in the mad dance they had been performing along

so many railroad tracks. All that was left was the feeling of total loss.

The roulette wheel had swung around to zero.

Suddenly—as in a mirage—a Swedish Red Cross train approached. It moved very slowly. But as they reached out toward it, threatened to pass them by.

In one swift motion of despair, Lucette threw herself at the mirage, across its very tracks.

The train slowed down and halted. Arms hauled them aboard. Cups of hot liquid were thrust into their hands and towels wrapped around them.

The dream materialized among red faces, and the strange lilting sounds of a Nordic tongue. Phrases of English intruded now and then (transporting him suddenly into the far-off past—to London Hospital on Mile-End Road).[72]

It was the end of their journey.

But by no means, the end of night. The long silent winters, the sunless days of exile, were stretching before them.

At this still point, one could almost hear the howling of white wolves.

Oh keep the dog far hence, that's friend to men

Or with his nails he'll dig it up again.

T. S. ELIOT

6

BESTIARY

To Animals
To the Sick
To Prisoners
—Epigraph[1]

To Animals
—Epigraph[2]

DENMARK—THE LATE 1940s.

It was in the north country where the animals gathered. By the side of the silent Baltic Sea, where miles of wind-swept fields separated the pair from the nearest human habitation.

In exile, they attracted other exiled creatures: dogs from the local pound, or abandoned by retreating Germans; wild cats roaming the woods, or strays the Danish farmers had neglected to drown at birth; birds that nets and lime could not capture; a number of porcupines.

Often, the only voices heard in this wilderness were those of beasts.

He looked at them all with a wry smile.

"A real circus," he muttered, "the whole show—a dancer and trained animal acts." [3] As he bent to set down a dish of milk for the porcupines, or repaired the perches of

the birds. And Lucette patiently coaxed a frightened dog
into the hut.

The creatures were becoming slowly habituated to the
human smell, the hands that fed, lips that called, commanded,
soothed.

In their midst, Bébert reigned. About thirty felines
deferred to him; even the dogs knew how to keep their distance. He ruled them all with his indifferent eyes (which had
seen half of Europe and the almost total ruin of a world).
His superiority, however, resided also in a victory over his
cat's nature—the abdication of his ancient seat at the hearth
for a ragged gamebag, in which he accompanied his master.
The proof was in his passport, which certified that:

> The cat, known as "Bébert," owned by Dr. Destouches
> of 4, rue Girardon, does not appear to have any commu-
> nicable diseases. . . .

(His photo was attached. There was no mention made of
his inability to reproduce, nor the uncertain nature of his
race.)[4]

It was an indisputable distinction, which none of the
others could share. He occupied a place as secure as that of
any feudal lord. Only he could mirror the prevailing mood
of his master, bound to him by links as close as those of human doubles.

> "His life is a tragedy" in numberless episodes. . . . All
> of them indescribable. . . . At one point in Sigma-
> ringen we thought we might escape across the Swiss
> border. . . . He trained with us, like a dog. . . . He
> followed us at night in three feet of snow . . . for sev-
> eral miles. . . . And froze two of his paws. When we
> had to cross all of Germany in March 1945, in the midst
> of four armies engaged in a furious battle . . . you can
> imagine what hell it was . . . and it took us 18 days to
> get to Denmark, across the flames and chaos . . . the

bombs flying . . . Lucette put him in a gamebag. He traveled that way, without drinking, eating, pissing, or anything, for eighteen days and eighteen nights. He didn't move or meow once. He understood the entire tragedy. We changed trains twenty-seven times. Everything burned en route, except the cat. We did 25 miles on foot going from one army to another, under fire. . . . Lucette was thrown under a train, by a bomb, with Bébert. He didn't make a move. We know all about animal intelligence! While I was in prison, he developed a cancer. I had him operated on when I got out. He understood perfectly.[5]

The bonds of pain and exile. Which few could share. And none could break.

On the long walks across the fields, however, the dogs predominated. They formed a pack around the man as he moved (hidden under several capes and armed with a staff), forged ahead, sniffed the underbrush, passed, herded, led the way. Warding off nonexistent forms of ambush in the deserted winter plains.

Bessy was soon established as Céline's favorite among them. Perhaps because of her resemblance to him—her flightiness, the need to remain instinctive, unhampered by human law. When he spoke of her, the tenderness rang through the words:

She'd run away . . . I'd call her . . . blue in the face . . . she didn't hear me . . . off on a binge . . . away she'd go around the trees so fast you couldn't see her legs! bat out of hell! . . . her animal life came first. . . . I didn't count . . . this was one of her escapades . . . wild in the animal world . . . woods, meadows, rabbits, deer, ducks . . . she came back with bleeding paws, affectionate. . . .

I really loved her with her crazy escapades. . . . She had a bad time of it up there . . . the cold . . . ten below . . . and no kennel . . . and not just for days

. . . for months . . . years . . . the Baltic frozen
over. . . .

We forgave her everything . . . she'd take a powder
. . . she'd come back . . . never a word of reproach
. . . the worse the world treated us, the more we
spoiled her. . . .

                                        (*CAS,* 138–139)

The world seemed to have forgotten them. The long
years of cold and silence continued. The sea was frozen over,
for them also. In such climes, only the simplest forms of life
could survive: the search for food, fuel, words, feelings. Reduced to the barest essentials.

When all other means of communication had revealed
their futility, howls, barks, cat calls, and mute gestures, retained some meaning. And rendered the ice-locked wilderness
somewhat less desolate.

When the glacial stillness was finally broken, when exile
was over, their homecoming had quite a different aspect than
their leave-taking. They returned, not with a countless array
of trunks that held implements for survival in a jungle of
war, but with a collection of beasts that had made the wilds
they inhabited more endurable. The plane could hardly contain the odd menagerie which they refused to leave behind
—more precious than buried gold, cyanide, or ax-heads
destined for trade with Teutonic farmers. The only remaining link with life.

IN THE 1930s.

It had not always seemed thus.

The descent to the basic pulse of living things (the
fragile beauty of the bird, the dog's intuition, the aloof gaze
of the cat that harbored depths of meaning) had only come
about during the later stages of his journey.

In the beginning, he had been alone. There were no animal companions sharing the road. His feelings toward them had to be divined—or extricated from his books—so hidden were they under a mask of harshness, of disavowal. Even their torment seemed to leave him unmoved.

As on the day when he and Lucette witnessed a harrowing scene in a small village where they had stopped in their travels:

They stood at the edge of a river at evening time. A barge came floating toward them. Filled with strange, moaning sounds such as she had never heard before and could not identify. His face, however, lifted and became intent.

Soon they were able to distinguish dark shapes bound to the deck. It was a herd of old horses destined for the slaughterhouse. Their necks strained forward or bent in terror. Dank manes stuck to their bodies.

As the barge approached the banks of the river, one still-powerful stallion tore loose from his rope, struggled into the water, slipped, staggered, gained the rocky incline, limped toward the dark countryside. The other horses watched with wild eyes, quite silent now.

Men shouted, leaped from the barge, in hot pursuit. The stallion ran toward a thicket, was almost out of sight. Only his strained breathing gave him away. The knackers were soon at his heels. They screamed from all sides, beat the branches, threw ropes to fell him, to bind his thundering feet. He crashed heavily to the ground, legs flailing; was tied and dragged back over the stones. His terrified eyes looked up at them.

Lucette was sobbing. Céline turned roughly away, making no effort to console her. Nor would he ever speak of the incident again.

She only noticed that he made a large detour around the village, each time they passed it in their travels.[6]

She could not fathom how he, who had loved horses and their fierce grace since earliest cavalry days, would refuse to acknowledge pain at their suffering. She did not yet know that she would have to turn to his books for verbal utterance of such compassion. There, one could read all that he had been unable to say:

> My horse . . . didn't have a back anymore, that poor beggar, nothing but two patches of raw flesh in its stead, under the saddle, the size of my two hands, that oozed large streams of pus along the edges of the blanket all the way down to his fetlocks. Yet, one nevertheless had to ride on that, one, two. . . . He writhed as you trotted. But horses are even more patient than men. You could only keep him out in the open. In a stable, due to the stench that rose from his wounds, you would have choked. When you got on his back, it hurt him so that he bent down, gently, until his belly was level with his knees.
>
> (*VOY,* 28)

Not only horses aroused his pity. But any animal, tormented, baited for the amusement of men, before being led to the slaughter. Even the lowly pig who suffered. As grotesquely as (but with greater helplessness than) men.

> It was a fat . . . enormous one. It moaned, there in the center of the circle, just like a man upset, but enormously. They didn't stop torturing him. People twisted his ears, just to hear him scream. He writhed and twisted around, his feet got caught in the rope that pulled when he tried to get away, as others whipped him so hard that he screamed still louder with pain. And everyone laughed even harder.

He didn't know where to hide, that big pig, in the little
bit of straw left, which flew into the air each time he
grunted and snuffled into it. He didn't know how to escape from men. He understood that. He tried to urinate
as hard as he could, but that didn't help either. Nor did
grunting, or screaming. There was nothing to be done.
They were having fun. The butcher . . . exchanged
jokes and signs with the customers and gestured with his
big knife. . . .

(*VOY,* 286–287)

Human torments were hardly ever described with such force
in his works. And seldom with such evident compassion.

Yet, animals had not become part of his life at this time.

1937–1951

Only after the advent of Lucette did they begin to arrive
on the scene. At first, by accident. Bébert made his appearance via Le Vigan (who had bought the cat at La Sa-
maritaine[7] in 1932, only to find that he could not keep him).
His entry into their lives resembled that of an unplanned-for
child who grows into the consolation of one's old age. Céline
grumbled at the intrusion. Lucette accepted it with animal
candor, as naturally as she moved and expressed unspoken
things with her body. It was only fitting for her to become
the guardian of his bestiary, to open the door to joys otherwise unknown. Was it of her he thought, when describing
Virginia who introduced Ferdinand to the domain of animal
delights?

It was she who made me move . . . come to the
window . . . she wanted to show me something . . .
there, through the Venetian blind . . . in the ivy.
. . . Ah, yes! I see, in the light . . . between the
slats . . . the tiny eye of a sparrow. . . . Ah! he
was watching us . . . *couii!* . . . *coui!* . . . How ex-

traordinary it was, really! a fat, ruffled sparrow, as sturdy
as she! . . . he waited . . . he spied around . . .
looked at us out of his little round eye, through the
blinds . . . tiny eye head of a pin . . . all black and
shiny. . . . Whenever I see a Venetian blind, or some
ivy, I always think of that small eye. . . .

(*PL,* 29–30)

Such insights would remain with him. Later, much later, they
would still serve him well. And sustain him in moments of
great despair.

During very difficult times when sleep won't come anymore, it's best to think of really lovable small creatures
. . . like that robin red-breast . . . which the rats
didn't get!

(*NO,* 269)

Or rejoice with the fox who had succeeded in getting out of
the trap and had escaped on his remaining three legs[8] (just
as he would flee Sigmaringen on his canes).

But he also became the chronicler of their suffering
which paralleled and exceeded that of human kind. Tracing
the long death-agony of a dog named Iago (victim of a
German cavalry officer whose senile delights combined flagel-
lation sessions with enforced hunger-artistry) as faithfully as
the deterioration of the world of men.[9] Only with far more
compassion. Describing the massacre of a horse by a band
of modern bacchantes in terms of much greater horror than
the same treatment inflicted on his master.[10] (In the same
manner as Raskolnikov's dream of the old mare's killing is
much more moving than the account of Alyona Ivanovna's
murder.)

The cry against pain rose much more poignantly for beasts
—for the mute prey, recipient of all the reasoned viciousness

of men, exposed to their laughter at the kill. Their moment of truth.

Animals knew no such laughter.[11]

Ravens circled to devour cadavers, wolves responded to hunger, leopards pounced on their prey, in gravity. Led by necessity. According to need.

Man was by far more hideous.

(It was the Ninth Marvel of the World that the dog should have chosen to make him his friend.)

When human contact had become abhorrent, only a few still uncontaminated domains seemed tolerable. Animals; the sea. Exile was mitigated by these presences. To lie low, in the silence, and listen to their slow, unending pulse that evolution, machines, humanization (and dehumanization) had never succeeded in altering, sufficed to keep a flicker of life aglow.

Perhaps the beast could best effect a rebirth of the human. The lowest level of being, renew one out of nothingness.

1951–1961

The return did not bring resurrection. Exile gave way only to reclusion, the icy plains to a landlocked terrain.

Only a few of the animals were able to survive. —Many had to be buried in the back garden, their graves marked by poplar, ash, and pine. Bébert and Bessy now lay there. The cat had lived to the legendary age of twenty-one. Spry, graceful, alert until the morning of his death. Silent in his dying. The dog had pined for the northern woods, the icy freedom now denied her; grown weak and listless. Until:

. . . one morning she wanted to go out . . . I tried to
lay her down in the straw . . . right after daybreak
. . . she didn't like the place I put her . . . she
wanted a different spot . . . on the cold side of the
house, on the pebbles . . . she lay down very prettily
. . . she began to rattle . . . she was pointed in the
direction of her memory . . . the place she had come
from, the North, Denmark, her muzzle turned toward
the North . . . she died with two, three little rattles
. . . oh, very discreet . . . practically no complaining
. . . and in a beautiful position, as though in mid-
leap . . . her nose toward the forests of the chase. . . .
    Oh, I've seen plenty of death-agonies . . . here
. . . there . . . everywhere . . . but none by far so
beautiful . . . so discreet . . . so faithful. . . .

                                        (*CAS,* 140)

His own approaching death was best envisaged in such
terms. He also would point his face toward the domain which
held the final meaning for him, which had not failed him in
his faith.

When I finish myself off, let me tell you: it'll be while
thinking of animals, not of men! of "Tête de Chou," of
"Nana," of "Sarah" my cat who left one night and was
never seen again, of farm horses, of the animal companions who have suffered a thousand times more than
men! rabbits, owls, blackbirds! who spent so many winters with us! at the ends of the earth! . . .

                                        (*FEE,* 309)

He often thought of the sea gulls, those wanderers he
loved and who seldom strayed now into his garden. And
shuddered at a story someone had once told (of executions in
the gas chambers at Alcatraz which felled the birds that flew
over the chimneys from which the deadly fumes escaped).
Thinking that even they were not free from the viciousness
of man to man.

The exotic birds of reclusion multiplied around him now

—a rare Abyssinian breed, reputed never to reproduce in captivity, but which soon numbered several dozen; Japanese nightingales; weaver-birds; and grackles that have the fatal habit of falling in love with humans (the only species of their kind). Finally, there was the parrot.

Toto (or Tototte, if sex roles of parrots are to be faithfully established) at first did not arouse his interest at all. Irritated him rather. The bird seemed hardly fit to mitigate the loss of old fur-bearing companions. How could this absurd creature—whose greatest accomplishment was to ape humans—compensate for Bébert's sagacity or Bessy's magnificent abandon? It sat there, a grayish ball of malice, trying to mimic the sounds of his voice.

"Take this filthy beast away," he would cry. Lucette obeyed, but remained nearby. A few minutes later, Céline would shout: "Get him back here!" [12] And their confrontation began anew.

Slowly, the mass of colorless feathers revealed its cunning and fidelity. As they sat for hours, side by side. An old man and a gray bird. Master and disciple. One vociferating; the other echoing what he had acquired—a heritage to be passed on through the crooked beak of the bird, as though he were the last scion of a dying lineage.

Toto soon enacted tricks that revealed the nature of his trainer: he expertly pinched intruders in the tender part of the calf; screeched into the telephone to deafen unwelcome callers; ordered the dogs sternly to heel; indulged in catcalls; cursed traffic police in perfect slang. Even engaged in word-duels:

> "Just imagine," Céline said, full of admiration yet scandalized, "each time Coco [alternate for Toto] got a little fresh air in his cage on the terrace—and naturally showed off his little repertoire, or whistled and cooed—the neighbor became furious and put a record on his

record-player. Ah, but what a record! . . . An unbeat-
able selection of vociferations and noises, which would
have disgusted a tribe of Zulus. It never varied: parrot?
loud-speaker! Perfect automation . . . Coco, infuri-
ated, screamed even louder. Then, the record rose an
octave. One could have sworn one was at Charenton
Asylum, in the wing of violent cases. . . ." [13]

But he had also been taught to sing. Céline felt that he should
know "On the Steppes of Central Asia" (in case he was ever
sent to Siberia), as well as sailors' ditties and other bawdy
tunes.

The man had begun to delight in watching memory
dawn in the minute brain of the bird.

Soon he was allowed to be present while his master
worked. Toto alone could touch the yellow sheets or hobble
across pages with scraping noises. Sometimes, he perched on
Céline's shoulder, blinking his red eyes as he watched the
gnarled hand move. Or created further disarray among the
clothespins that lay all about. The washlines on which
the manuscripts hung, served him as perches; from which he
surveyed the proceedings and commented from time to time
in his raucous voice.

An almost human presence. Which never became sufficiently human to be obtrusive.

It was a different matter, though, when battles among the
other animals broke out. When the survivors from exile raged
at each other, as though the outer world had intruded upon
the otherwise inviolate domain. Sometimes, it was a visitor
who caused the unrest; but it could just as easily be the
neighbor's bitch in heat. —The cats were generally quiet. At
most, Flute had a moment of rebellion against the collar
around her throat (which warned the birds that she pursued,

away); or Thomine, of a more lascivious nature, required
some human intervention as she bore her unending litters
(Lucette had to massage her belly to make the young come
forth, and Balou the Great Dane assisted by licking them to
life).[14] —It was the hounds (Agar, Totom, and Balou) or
their bitches (Frida and Ingeborg) that caused all the furor.

The great fatigue of his last years made him suspect the
worst: that the vices of men had somehow invaded his bestiary. He grew frantic. Began imagining that his beasts had
been transformed into monsters. And addressed them in terms
he had always reserved for humans:

> "You're a bunch of hoodlums, you rotten bastards! . . .
>
> Half-breeds, mongrels, as ugly and as vicious as
> men. . . ." [15]

He even thought of desperate and violent remedies.
Such as resorting to the surgeon's knife.

It must have been such frenzy which made him reach for
the telephone on that rainy afternoon in the fall of 1957.

A startled young veterinarian heard a voice rant into
the mouthpiece:

> "Destouches here [he was using his medical name, for
> this occasion]. . . . It's about my dogs . . . a bunch
> of monsters . . . dangerous monsters. . . . You have
> to castrate them for me. . . . Come and get them. . . .
> No, I don't have a car. . . . I have a horror of
> cars. . . ."

When he stood in Céline's garden looking at the victims
designated for mutilation, the tirade continued:

> "You can't imagine . . . with two bitches . . . al-
> ways trying to separate them . . . giving away the
> pups. . . . And the neighbors. . . . Balou, that big

jerk . . . climbs the trees to get at the bitch next door.
. . . I have too many troubles . . . I don't want any
more."

The dogs were piled into the car. Soon, the first was stretched,
anesthetized, across the veterinarian's table. Surgery was
about to begin.

Instantly, Céline became transformed into Dr. Destouches: He was now acting as though in an amphitheater,
judging the performance of a student, operating techniques,
sutures, instruments. Observing. Questioning. Alert to each
detail.

Agar . . . Totom . . . Balou. The incredible bout of
sacrifice continued, until all three were neutered.[16] Céline
rode back to his garden with a carload of sleeping castrati.

1961

At his death, however, the same dogs remained motionless in his room. Without food. With lusterless eyes.

One of them did not survive his loss.

In a letter his widow wrote, "Louis is dead." And a
few sentences later, "Balou is dead too."[17] As though the
two had now been joined.

(Some "primitives"—in their wisdom—bury a man's
most beloved animals within the same tomb.)

His grave must remain unvisited by dogs.

(French cemeteries are run according to customs of a
very different nature. Designed perhaps to guard against
canine fidelity, which so outlandishly surpasses that of humankind that it knows nothing of the sanctity of the dead
or the hallowed earth of burial grounds. But only the terrible
yearning to reclaim what has been lost—which men term
necrophilia, the most dreaded of all perversions.)

* * *

In our age, animals are condemned to mere survival.

Which, in the parrot, is a sentence of several lifetimes. All they can do to mourn, is to fall silent.

Toto has done so. On the rare occasions when he does speak, it is evident that he has sunk to the level of an aged clown, who mimics weakly but no longer creates new acts.

The voice of Céline is now locked in his brain (as securely contrived as any stone mausoleum). The fragile bird-skull houses the "small music" which the man had spent his entire life in creating. But nothing escapes from his beak. The feather armor hides feelings as hard to divine as those which boiled beneath the old man's capes. A veil descends over the parrot's eye, at each attempt of strangers to stare into his face. Betraying nothing.

Perhaps, all has been said and done. And he has acquired the wisdom of silence his master worked to attain. Though human longevity had proven inferior to that of birds; and the most longed-for achievement been limited by the failings of the all-too-human beast.

If he boasts, I abase him; if he
abases himself, I extol and contradict him, until he comprehends that
he is an incomprehensible monster.

PASCAL

7

LOUIS-FERDINAND, JUDGE OF CÉLINE

*J was struck by this terrible
thought of Chateaubriand:
"Only misfortune can judge
misfortune. . . ."* [1]

1945–1947

The prison cell was without light. A damp shaft into
which a little air filtered from a high, barred hole. More like
a dungeon than a cell. Another passageway. In the K Pavilion
—where the condemned were lodged—at the far end of the
labyrinthine Vesterfangsel in Copenhagen.

It was impossible to measure time, but he sensed that
he had already been here for months. His body told him so:
the shreds of skin that peeled from scurvy; pellagra which
made him blink like a mole if ever he moved into the light;
the sound of his voice, flattened by interminable monologues,
devoid of the inflections of those who had not been stunted
by solitary confinement.

His eyes troubled him most. He could barely write. Unless he pried them open. . . .

The rest was just bearable: the oozing walls; the puddles

collecting on the slanted stone floor; the roaches that scurried over one's shoes, one's lips during sleep (their light touch sometimes creating erotic sensations); the wooden stool, on which he sat for hours, stuck to patches of skin.

Bearable, as long as daytime lasted. In these northern parts, light faded so quickly.

It was at night that the real terrors began: laments, mad outcries, howls, menaces, the barking of the bloodhounds outside. And apparitions that screamed through his Judas window, of crimes and betrayals, of lampshades and bars of soap, of crematoriums and the fall of the Maginot line. "Spy, pimp, assassin, traitor, mad dog," they called. It may have been his fellow prisoners, itching for a kill. Having heard of the foreigner among them. Leper of lepers.

He saw mouths drooling, like those of rabid dogs. A thousand tongues that uttered calumnies. Teeth bared, whetted into sharpness of knives.

Night, the real night was falling. And with it, the chorus of voices rose . . . accusing . . . calling to the hunt . . . singling him out for slaughter. The monster! The human beast! Mad dog!

(An old French proverb echoed through his mind, vindicating, exonerating: "A man who wishes to kill his dog, goes around proclaiming that it's rabid.")

It did not still the voices.

He let himself drop from the stool onto the straw mattress; covered his head with the stiff blanket (lid of coffin); waited. For the dark of dreams. The drunken sleep of misery. The voices continued. Threatening. Promising the whole gamut of deadly torments: the stake, the rack, petroleum, sulfur, brine; head, balls, and manuscripts destined for the garbage pail, the sewer; license to loot, pillage, sell the wind, pawn his ghosts.

Perhaps he would despair. Do the job himself, with the belt left in his cell, as if by chance. The bars were strong enough to hold his weight. —Besides, he had recently lost over fifty pounds. —Wasn't it preferable to being publicly executed in France? And not the easy way either (like De-noël, by machine-gun fire in the street), but in the fashion befitting a traitor:

> Place de la Concorde, for example . . . the crowd is already tearing up the trees . . . to get a better look at his face when, slowly, very slowly they cut off his head, with a very small penknife. . . .
>
> (*EPY*, 9)

When the screams (in his head, and outside) became unbearable, he began to scream back. First, invectives hurled at the voices. Then songs: violent street-cries, full of curses and harsh laughter, that both charmed and terrified the listener.

His hoarse voice rang out among the stones.

> I'll get you, you filthy carrion!
> one foul night!
>
> I'll put two big black holes!
> in your eyes' site!
>
> Your bitch of a soul . . .
> will take wing!
>
> You'll meet a lovely bunch you'll dig!
> You'll see how well they do their jig!
>
> In that Bone-Yard Palace!
> Where they do their thing!
>
> (*FEE*, 70–71)

Sometimes, for a quarter of an hour, the song created silence
in those walls. Then it began again—the screams rose once
more. Even louder than before.

His insides began to knot up. The simplest functions seemed
to have been suspended. Peristalsis itself no longer obeyed
the natural rhythm. Functioned backwards. Backing up
waste products, until his body became a sewer. A polluted
thing.

(Surely, self-respect could not be salvaged in such
straits.)

His methods of survival had to be suited to the mean
nature of the case. Shame, as well as pride, was a luxury of
those who lived in the sun. Here, only reduction functioned.
Low life called for low means.

> When I really can't stand it any longer, when I suffer
> too much, when I haven't been able to shit, for example,
> for ten, twelve . . . thirteen days at a time! when they
> refuse to give me relief, I bark! They administer it ter-
> ribly hot . . . on purpose! I don't give a damn! at
> least it's an enema! . . . if I bark, I'm sure they'll
> come! . . . I drown out all the screams! I'm a power-
> ful dog when it comes to barking! . . . the watchdogs
> answer me . . . three or four packs . . . the guards
> arrive, with four machine guns, I signal to them: I'm
> glued to my seat! can't get up anymore! can't even rock
> any longer! . . . *finish!* [2] they leave and get the ladies!
> . . . the stretcher! . . . There! . . .
>
> (*FEE,* 73)

Into the hospital. They dosed him up with vitamins, cleaned
out his innards, returned him to prison once more. In and
out. For nearly two years.

*   *   *

The months were punctuated by few events—Lucette's illness; her visits; an attack published by one of his fellow
writers in France—hardly enough to mark time which ebbed
away around him, as though he were marooned on a growing island of solitude.

It was a time of doubt and bitter remorse. Touching
everything: writing, actions; people.

> My friend, I said to myself, look where you've landed!
> . . . you played your flute backwards! . . . you didn't
> attract the true rats . . . if you had modulated right
> . . . you'd have your own hole in the iron curtain!
> you'd go in and out, just as you pleased! . . . you
> didn't modulate in the right direction!
>
> *(FEE, 121)*

Past neglects, abandons, ingratitudes began to haunt him
in the dark and silence that were pierced only by inhuman
noises:

> One always sabotages the living . . . one understands
> life badly. . . . I have my personal collection of re-
> morse! . . . Courtial . . . Follet . . . Elisabeth . . .
> Edith. . . .
>
> *(FEE, 130)*

and his mother—dead on that park bench in Paris. She was
buried in the Père Lachaise Cemetery, that was all he knew
beside the mechanical location of her grave (Row 14, Section 20). It was uncertain that he would ever visit it. Surely
it was unmarked—they would have purged her name that
he had covered with shame. He mused for a long time on
that matter.

> She didn't even know what had become of me . . . I'll
> bring her a pot of daisies [Fr. marguerites] . . . that
> was her flower. . . . Marguerite Louise Céline Guillou.

> . . . She died of sorrow and exhaustion, heart strain
> . . . palpitations, worries . . . of everything "they"
> were saying about me . . . just imagine those people in
> Clichy! . . . the benches! . . . public opinion! . . .
> And she never knew what had become of me . . .
> we watched her leave one day . . . it was forever . . .
> she hadn't been able to sleep for months . . . she never
> slept much. . . . Now she sleeps. . . .
>
> (*FEE,* 87)

And remembered that her weapon had been laughter.

It was high time that he, her son, her larger double, called upon this barbed spear to force the prison walls. Or else went under.

> She was like me, anxious. . . . Still, she had a small
> laugh inside her, while mine is enormous. . . . The
> proof . . . even at this bottom of a pit, I can laugh if
> I want to . . . there's laughter inside a man or there is
> nothing. . . .
>
> (*FEE,* 87)

The laugh must rise out of nothingness. Despite the "Article 75," [3] hung around his neck in deadly albatross fashion; despite the constant threat of extradition that made his life dangle by a single hair.

It was a talent which the prison keepers soon discovered. And found ways of exploiting. In the hospital wards where the condemned exasperated the staff by refusing food. The hospital superintendent grew anxious; the guards tried force, in vain. It was a matter for grave concern. Public opinion demanded fatted victims for the scaffold. "No skeletons for the executioner!" was the motto of the enlightened crowd. Then, they discovered Céline's "psycho-persuasive method," brought to perfection by use in many desperate places. Suddenly, the condemned began to devour bread, margarine, and the delectable Baltic herring. He obviously knew the business of despair.

For his own uses also. Where, by some personal alchemy, he could turn the infernal winter and the solitude
into creation.

> When I'm cold, when I have the shivers . . . I start to
> laugh! . . . independent of my will . . . a personal
> peculiarity. . . .
>
> All I need is to be left alone, and right away, a little an-
> ecdote comes to mind . . . I work it over and have a
> good laugh . . . I grab my wooden board and go to
> work! . . .
>
> *(FEE,* 132–133)

And the yellow sheets that the guard threw to him each
morning (as raw meat into the cage of a ravenous beast)
were covered with the black marks of his pencil by the time
they were collected each night. His mind's outgrowths fixed,
for an unknown destination (posterity? the rubbish heap?
the tribunal?), despite all mockery. The stub of a pencil; his
laugh; the bark *in extremis;* these were the only possessions,
the last unctions he could still lay claim to. All the rest was
now a lost inheritance.

When night fell, however, the pencil was of no avail. Laughs,
barks, or cries were drowned out in the chorus of voices that
echoed through steel doors. All that was left then, was the
stage lodged in his head. The stories he could fabricate; the
characters that came to life there. As the gates of the world
were shut more tightly still, the inward journey began. He
knew the progressive stages that preceded the departure for
these ports unknown, knew them as if they were part of an
unholy ritual:

> The bells, the barking of the dogs at the top of the walls,
> the cemetery closing, the gaffs, the exchange of key
> rings on five stories of steel . . . ! twice, and twice
> three thousand doors, triple-locked! the whole height of

the building! *crac! crrac!* the sixteen bridges! . . . we're locked in the cemetery! the ship, hermetically sealed now, enters into night. . . . A prison is a sort of vessel, it travels. . . .

(FEE, 141)

Into the imagination. Landscapes, apparitions from the past glide into view. Laments, regrets, menaces rise from the deep, assail the traveler.

He knew that his ship might have to float on oceans of hate. And uttered his cry of defiance (as brazen as a sailor's call astride a swaying mast):

Here I come! with my avenging verses! . . . Judge me! and my acrid lyre!

(FEE, 152)

The judges were not long in coming. His own words turned against him; his inventions surrounded him in menacing poses. Danced an infernal round inside his head. They tore him from his chair. Spilled him in the dust and leapt at him. His voice was failing. The song came out in snatches, retched up from his innards. Which only increased their fury.

They seized him.

. . . my poet's body! . . . they throw it into their wheelbarrow! . . . flatten it out! . . . With their work tools, shovels! picks! brooms! . . . They are infernal! . . . They prod pieces of my flesh, turn it over! . . . They shove me in again! and *vlof!* into the wheelbarrow! . . . En route! . . . They carry me off, it's extraordinary! . . . They move out of the prison! . . . The giant portals open! . . . Magic! . . . The guards, the dogs just look at them! . . . Not a single "woof!" not a whistle! . . .

(FEE, 168–169)

As if they had been the Eumenides.

The journey led further and further along a road of jeers, threats, hideous mimicry of his songs, among crowds of accusers—a relay race of hate, a gallop of cannibals—until the place of final abasement had been reached: a cesspool. They threw him in, urinated vigorously on him, left him to drown. While chanting: "He has gotten his! He's got his due!" [4]

The Furies suddenly vanished. He found himself back in his cell. Glued to his chair. Fixed . . . fixed. And screaming in chorus with all the inmates of the prison. Giving way to madness. Covered with the combined shame of dream and reality.

At other times, he saw himself before a military tribunal. Accused of having defiled his medals, his citations, his pension, his comrades, even his wounds.

(He knew that Lucette also had been urged to confess to crimes chalked up to him: the procuring of newspapers for enemy use; the betrayal of the Maginot line, of the Auvergne, of Toulon; the performing of abortions; pederasty; pimping; the sale of military plans; the dynamiting of the dike at St. Malo; the sale of morphine, cocaine, the Alps, the Eiffel Tower; the invention of infanticide and sneezing gas.) [5]

His behavior before the tribunal vacillated. From abject postures to superhuman wrath.

He saw himself on all fours, gagged, writhing, imploring for pity. The high judge, impassible at first, soon grew impatient with his antics. Demanded a verdict. And immediate expiation; the beginning of the feast of purges.

Suddenly, a "cosmomediumological storm" was unleashed. It lifted the obelisk on the vast square, and brought it crashing down on the tribunal. In a dreadful, exhilarating turnabout of fate. For which he immediately disclaimed responsibility:

Ah, not through my fault! None of it is my fault! I did
not want to liberate these forces! . . .

(*FEE,* 193–196)

Yet, he knew that the unleashing of the forces of destruction
had always been one of his favorite diversions (needs):

The devil is not born of himself, he is born of indiscre-
tion! . . . And all misfortunes arise from one superfluous word! . . .

(*FEE,* 81)

Words . . . words had been his downfall and his glory. Now
they echoed in his mind. In the form of accusations and de-
nials, judgment and vindication. Within this narrow cell,
this silent trap, these last concentric circles of stone and bone.
Hate lashed out and bounced back, a deadly tennis ball glancing off the confining walls.

He heard a wail rise. It was his own. Demanding recognition, glory (a score of love–nothing in this solipsistic
game), the erection of a statue, a square, a city named after
him (Célinegrad),[6] or perhaps even two, a mausoleum where
worshipers could file past to pay him homage; the option of
life-in-death, in a coffin illuminated all night, where he might
listen to the varied sounds of life, its festivities, its crowds.
Not solitude among the dead—not the Panthéon, that "impeccable, but dreary place"—but a grave rocked by the exclamations of the living:

Is it he? . . . he? . . . dead? . . . alive? . . . buried?
. . . in this mausoleum? . . . Is it he? . . . He? . . .

(*FEE,* 224–232)

The murmurs stopped. He was once more back in his cell.
Where death-in-life prevailed. And a traitor's fate awaited
him. No glory, but spittle, howls of execration; no mausoleum, but burial in some potter's field. A cadaver left to be
defiled, unburied. For scavengers, or to enrich a cesspool.

He sensed their watchfulness. Knew that the other prisoners, the guards, the judges, his countrymen were waiting for him to die.

The end seemed very close.

I have no more skin! No more shirts! No more teeth!

My shirt! my skin! my years! . . . my virility! . . . everything went down the drain. . . .

(FEE, 299–300)

He felt their anger at his refusal to come to an end.

The judges of the Highest Court have my hourglass in their hands . . . they are saying: "Filthy puppet! Another month gone by! He still isn't dead! That piece of trash!"

(FEE, 302)

"I am immaculate!" he screamed at the judges of other, even higher courts. But his defiance shrank to a whimper, as he saw himself reflected in the tin surface of his prison plate. He had become unrecognizable, a clod of filth. If the magistrates of the Hourglass left him to rot here much longer, there would be nothing left to identify him by. His guts were stagnating poison; half his buttocks had rotted away; teeth fell out of his mouth, like seeds spit out after they have been sucked from a pomegranate; his red eyes could not bear the light.

(Perhaps it was best, though, to have become unrecognizable. For surely, otherwise, they would begin to torture him anew. The wheelbarrow was always waiting at the door. The Furies were ever ready to recommence their gallop.)

He lay down on the floor. Listening. His ear to the tiles as if they were a heart, a pair of lungs. The auscultation yielded all the sounds of suffering—shame, despair, dying; but also the echoes of boat horns outside, the owls in the cemetery, the howling of dogs. When all the other senses had failed, and his body become almost extinct, only the ear remained. Nothing but an ear glued to the ground, that recorded the vibrations of pain—that of others, and his own.

The endless thirst to search the darkness, which had pursued him all his life, was not yet quenched:

> What I regret most, there, flat on the ground, listening
> to the stone, is not having experienced enough! . . .
>
> *(FEE,* 326)

COPENHAGEN, 1945

Then, they thought that they had experienced everything. The rage of France; Germany in flames; the progressive pulverization of the world, as they fled north, the deluge of corpses behind them; the dread of any backward look; the cold retreat before them.

Their golden egg of six million francs buried there, was subject to many questions.[7] According to some it had shrunken; others maintained it was intact. It could not buy them ease, even if it doubled in weight and size.

The Germans would not retreat until the summer of the year. While they remained, in hiding from their former host, at the apartment of Karen Marie Jensen (to whom he had, once upon a very different time, dedicated *L'Eglise*). The house at 20 Ved Stranden overlooked some lovely grounds. Bébert could roam there. It would have been a moment of respite from their journeys, except for the heavy atmosphere that prevailed in the country still occupied by enemy troops. Karen was away in Spain.

The loss of his mother was announced in one of the first letters he received from France.

Together with the news that his country had issued orders for his arrest.

His reflex was almost automatic. He took up his pen, wrote a rebuttal to the accusations of treason; and a ballet ("Foudres et flèches") which he submitted to the Royal Theater of Copenhagen.[8] —Its refusal would undoubtedly have unleashed diatribes as violent as those written on similar occasions in the past. But there was no time to see.

A matter of far greater consequence was brewing.

Without Céline's knowledge, prison was being urged against him: the French attaché G. de Girard de Charbonnière had asked the Danish Minister of Foreign Affairs for his "arrest and extradition." [9] At the same time also, a fellow-writer who was swiftly rising to fame had published "Portrait of an Anti-Semite." [10] (Sartre had singled Céline out for attack and left no doubt about his supposedly monstrous nature.)

The storm was about to strike.

Christmas of 1945 dawned with icy clearness in the city. The winter solstice had arrived.

They had slept badly, having been plagued by strange noises in the night. The whole apartment was filled with ominous creaking sounds. The very wood seemed to have come alive; as if the house were responding to an unknown warning:

> One would have thought that the furniture was being crushed. It lasted for several minutes. Occultists call it the *Raps*.[11]

(Sounds known to be the psychic effects of disintegration.) [12] It was as though they heard minute echoes of the cracking of the macrocosm; a private storm in their teacup, which reflected the approaching holocaust.

By morning, the police had arrived at the house.

They fled to the roof.[13] Up the small ladder that led

from their floor through a trap door; up to the snowy inclines, high above the streets of Copenhagen. Lucette was armed. There was no way of knowing whom she might shoot—the pursuers or herself.[14] She clung to a chimney. With the desperate eyes of a hunted beast turned towards the trap door, which slowly opened. He screamed at her to stop where she was. Not to move. Knowing that she considered this the end. Was ready to spring (the trigger or the icy abyss below?). At the sound of his voice she froze. And waited.

They were soon taken. Handcuffed. Led separately away. At the end of the street, she turned and watched his limping figure recede.

She would not see him again. Of this she was certain. It was truly the end.

It was then also, that she remembered the tubes of aspirin. —Someone had told her how efficiently this commonplace remedy worked to bring about death. —If only she could find the right dosage.

But irony had not yet exhausted itself in their lives. Instead of gauging the lethal number, she only succeeded in damaging her kidneys in the attempt. And, long after his death, continued to suffer from the grotesque affliction which was a vestige of her desperate move.[15]

The prison doors opened. Each was swallowed by different walls.

A road of solitude. Lapidation by silence. The fatal crack in the wall of being.

1946–1948

The wolf dies without howling. But not I!
(*FEE,* 43)

When death seemed imminent, his cry regained all its venom. He seized the hourglass and violently turned it over.

In defiance of all reason. In denial of every expectation.

A year after his incarceration, he had formulated an answer to his accusers. As categorical as their attacks. Refuting charges, point by point. Denying all crimes charged to him. Offering proof of his innocence. Reminding his judges of his glorious past. Depicting himself as a victim of his rivals, of the crowd's delirium. Inviting all to share his self-portrait's conclusion:

> In truth, I find myself quite innocent.[16]

But Sartre's portrait still rankled. It must be answered in kind. He chuckled with delight, as his own brand of viciousness emerged again, gave him back his old powers. Hate would sustain him. Better than any other prison fare. It was the food which his thoughts and creations thrived on. The bread and wine of his communion.

> An enormous hatred keeps me alive. I'd live a million years if I could be sure that I would see the world croak. . . .[17]

What cut his pride most to the quick, was Sartre's smug assertion: "If Céline supported the theories of the Nazis, it's because he was paid to do so." [18]

It was a challenge to a duel. A verbal slap that could only be answered by a crossing of weapons.

His sword-thrust was a vicious one: *A L'Agité du bocal*,[19] missile of attack below the belt, full of furious obscenities, which parried his opponent's "rational" style. Accused him of rising to power, not by his own talent (which, Céline affirmed, was sadly lacking), but through the betrayal of friends and literary rivals—by the common means of calling them "collaborators"—while he himself was only too happy to have his play *Les Mouches* performed under the "German boot."

Almost ten years later, Céline would still defend him-

self against accusations similar to Sartre's, and rage in a
letter to a friend:

> . . . they'd like to hang me, just like all the intellectuals
> of Siegmaringen [*sic*] . . . they execrate me for being
> absolutely free . . . "a woman of the world" and not a
> whore . . . I never touched a cent and will never touch
> anything from anybody . . . I never had any dealings
> with the Staffel and the German censorship. . . .[20]

Jean-Baptiste Sartre (as he had renamed him) had cut
him to the quick in other ways also. These rankled perhaps
even more. For he had painted the anti-Semite as

> A man who is afraid. Certainly not of the Jews, but of
> himself, his conscience, his liberty, his instincts, his re-
> sponsibilities; afraid of solitude, of change, of society, of
> the world . . . in a word, of the human condition.[21]

The thrust was too close to the heart to be allowed to
go unanswered. He parried with the most familiar weapons
he knew (those which fear had always honed to a perfect
edge): obscenity, and thrusts to the vulnerable parts of the
opponent. In Céline's former disciple, these lay in his works.
With biting irony, he gave Sartre a lesson in successful play-
writing, filled with ideas that would ensure his advent to the
company of "sacred monsters" the literary world of France
revered. He counseled a work of the bloodiest kind: with
music by the "Builders of the Wall" (of lamentation?); a
chorus of the "Hangmen of Nürnberg"; sound effects of
death-rattles, colic, weeping, chains; intermission entertainment assured by a "Futurist Bar" and a "Blood Fountain,"
where real blood would be available in steins, "fresh blood,
guaranteed to have come from hospitals . . . aorta blood,
foetal blood, blood from the hymen, from the firing-squad
. . . blood to everybody's taste!" [22] And predicted a great
future for "little J.-B. S." when he had finally blossomed into
a "Real Monster!"

top
Le Passage
Choiseuil, ca. 1911.

right
Le Passage
Choiseuil, 1969.

left
Céline, ca. 1934.

right
Denoël & Steele
(Céline's publisher),
19, rue Amélie.

center
Home of Céline's
parents, 11, rue
Marsollier (5th floor).

bottom
98, rue Lepic (where
*Voyage au bout de la
nuit* was written).

top
Studio of the painter Gen Paul, 1969.

bottom
Rue Lepic, with the Moulin de Galette.

top right
Marcel Brochard, friend of Céline, photographed
during an elephant hunt in Tchad.

bottom right
Henri Mahé, friend of Céline, photographed beneath
a dolmen in Brittany.

1959

à Erika

L U C I E N N E
DELFORGE

top left
The young pianist who
was Céline's companion
at the time of *Mort à
crédit*.

bottom far left
4, rue Girardon, Céline's
abode until his departure
for Germany in 1944.

bottom left
The hut on the Baltic
(Klarskovgaard), where
Céline lived in exile.

top
Céline during his exile in
Denmark.

right
Céline, his wife Lucette,
and the Great Dane
"Bonzo" in 1952, after
return from Denmark.

top left
Entrance view of Céline's house in Bellevue where the writer spent the last decade of his life.

top right
Back garden

above left
View of the house

above right
Céline's study (after his death)

top left
Back garden (bordering on Yveline Forest), with one of Céline's dogs, "Cri-Cri."

top right
"Toto," Céline's parrot, and Mme. Agnès, housekeeper.

bottom
Lucette Almanzor-Destouches-Céline.
                All photos of the house and its occupants: 1967.

top left
The house of Céline after its destruction by fire in May 1968: Front view

top right
Back view

above left
Terrace and reflected garden

above right
Céline's study

far right,top
1969: reconstruction of the house of Céline, with window (top story) showing the apartments of Lucette.

far right, bottom
Card advertising the dance courses of Lucette Almanzor.

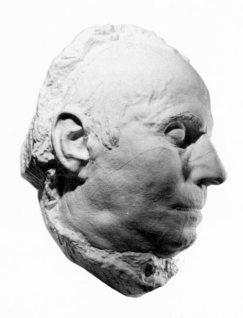

Arthur!

Ça dépend des goûts... Londres c'est pas Paris!..... ~~Versailles~~
~~~~ ~~étaient crêchés~~?.... Moi dis je l'ai vu le Louvre!....

Moi j'y tenais au Louvre! il me
ferait pas démordre!

— ah! Dis un peu! je le connais!

J'y énumère

— ah! alors. pardon les tableaux! des
millions Dis la queue leu leu!

— comment. qu'il s'appelait nom de
dernier? il me pose la question. Je
me rappelle jamais!

— Louis XVI!

Je me gratte pas.

— T'as de l'instruction ~~total!~~ qu'il me rétorque

mais Tout de Suite ça le vexe

— ~~~~ ~~~~
~~~~

— C'est pas tout, ~~petit-père~~, apprend ça! Ce qui compte tu vois dans
la vie c'est l'intelligence naturelle!....Moi j'en ai, voilà le

retiens l'instruction!

Ça te ~~~~

dis _____ qui savaient des cinq

Various signatures of the author.

*   *   *

There was some relief in such bloodletting. The anger would have choked him, without it, as he sat in his prison cell. Not only his own. The whole world seemed to be suffering from hate—a vast case of eczema that would not stop itching, and must be scratched, scratched, until the blood showed. It was a gigantic horror show, with continuous performances, in which the spectators never seemed to get their fill.

Duels incited other duels. Vendettas engendered vendettas without end.

Judges sprung up in every field, as though the whole earth had been sown with dragons' teeth.

His mind paced the confines of the cell. While his body remained glued to the wooden stool. His board, the paper, and the pencil stub, were puny weapons of attack. Words aimed at judges or duelists came back at him, with the deadly accuracy of boomerangs. Which he had no power to dodge.

Perhaps confession was an avenue of escape, a means toward quietus. Not to judges or assailants (against whom one then became powerless), but to those whom he could hold under his spell: readers and correspondents.

Each had his function to fulfill. The reader, mesmerized by his verbal skill, could be counted on to watch him perform. Any number of roles could be played out before him: of martyr, penitent, judge, lawyer, witness, criminal, judge-penitent. The tone could be modulated at will: noble, pathetic, virulent, righteous, tragic, defiant, dejected, boastful, despairing. —A whole panorama to which he would willingly submit, controlled by the emotions that Céline had long learned to manipulate more expertly than Javanese puppeteers.

While disavowing the exhilaration of this maneuver:

In truth, I dislike writing. I have a horror of that game.
. . . Creation is always a disgusting battle. . . .[23]

and hiding a sword-play under a skillful swirl of his cape.

Such as the title given to the work in which his prison-voice was to be heard: *Féerie pour une autre fois*. Which was far from a fairy tale for another age; but the account of his bitterest hours, full of the nightmares, jealousies, accusations, reprieves, vindications, menaces that plagued him.

Or the ballet written at this time. "Scandale aux abysses" [24] which, on the surface, resembled a lovely bubble that rose and bounced along the dank prison walls; whose form and controlled content were pitted against despair or the falling apart of his own being. Beneath the frothy appearance, however, lay all the sorrows of his old age—the pathetic pirouettes of an impotent king. All uttered in a swan song among the howling of the prison dogs; and by means of the soft, gliding sounds of perfect bodies that screened the hideous noises of his, and other cells.

The paper accumulated with regularity. The yellow sheets, thrown into his cell each morning, were collected each night.

Just as the months passed, cut into rhythmic intervals of mechanical precision, predictable almost to madness. Cell —hospital—cell—hospital. The pattern never varied. It was only his own being that progressively diminished. Yet, he was carefully maintained at the edge of life, suspended above nonexistence by lawful means. The food, the vitamins injected intramuscularly, the airings prescribed in exact doses, all had been calculated to that end. Life was ladled out in spoonfuls, too small to give one strength, but just large enough to keep one from dying.

Even feelings were correctly rationed. Lucette was put before him for prescribed periods each week. Allowed to speak to him, but only in English and in the presence of a guard. Which resulted in the most meager interchange, on the borders of nothingness. The gifts she could bring him were limited to a carrot, several lemons, some cakes made without butter or eggs.[25]

Back in his cell, the day passed with awful accuracy: bells, meals, guard shifts, outings; searchlights passing at night at precise intervals. Even the air was carefully measured and confined to a determinate space:

> During my 17 months of solitary confinement . . . they took me out for 12 minutes each day, into a sort of cage, 6 feet square . . . to have me breathe the air. A fence 2 feet away shut out the view, so that I could see nothing from this cage. . . . I've heard some prisoners say that in Antwerp, "collaborators" had been put in the animal cages at the Zoo . . . is it true? . . . I've often envied them, I often thought of them. . . . At least they saw people! . . . I would not even have minded the spittle, the stones. . . . I remember visiting that zoo with you, it's very centrally located. . . . Better to be a hated beast in Antwerp, than caged in Copenhagen. . . .[26]

When madness seemed ready to claim him, when he felt sure the end had come, he was suddenly released. The prison doors inexplicably swung open.

On February 26, 1947, a dazed Céline stood in the streets.

(He did not know that his own work had accomplished this turn of events. The Danish Minister of Justice, after having read *Les Beaux Draps* and finding nothing there to justify the writer's incarceration, had ordered his release.)

It was a brilliantly lit, clear icy day.

*   *   *

He wandered through the city. And found himself suddenly in the corridors of the plush Hôtel d'Angleterre, where they had stopped (ages ago) upon their arrival in Copenhagen. Now, his pockets were empty; his eyes unseeing. He watched constantly over his left shoulder for pursuers.

As he turned back to the lobby, stealthily looking around, he noticed a small man who seemed to be behaving in similar fashion. He guessed him to be a Jew, probably of Lithuanian or related origin. The man came closer. Almost as though he recognized Céline. Then he bent forward and whispered to him, in confidential tones that one prisoner employs with another, having recognized the marks of captivity still engraved on body and face. "It was all because I'm Jewish," he murmured. "It was all because I'm Céline," the other confessed in low tones. And they continued talking, their voices held to a whisper, while one or the other looked furtively about.[27]

Guilt hung about him like a mantle. As he climbed the stairs to the wretched attic where Lucette slept and gave lessons to survive, ironically located on the Kronprinsessegade. As he took to his bed at the Ryshospitalet, where he was to be interned and nursed to recovery. The interval of freedom was a respite, not a liberation. He had to sign a declaration that he would not leave from the hospital without permission from the Security Police of Copenhagen.

He was marked forever. Once designated as a criminal, he could not hope to rub out the stains. (If Lady Macbeth did not succeed, then how should he?)

> I have been so betrayed, attacked, and insulted, so covered with all forms of garbage and shit—that a thousand

tons of all the perfumes of Arabia could not make me smell clean again! [28]

Judgment had fallen upon his head, but no death sentence carried out. Reprieve upon dull reprieve stretched before him. With no hope of exoneration.

True, he found himself outside the prison gates. But in the form of a wrecked and wretched creature: a skeleton, toothless and bent over with scurvy, on the verge of blindness, turned in upon itself like a half-crushed hedgehog too weak to erect its quills.

Slowly, very slowly, though, he began to recover. The sore gums gnashed together once again; the bitter grimace of the skull showed through the skin. Anger started to filter through the inflamed lids. And he already plotted his next fight.

It had to be done through letters. In which his correspondents would become his confidants, his accomplices, his messengers. He needed listeners.

Which he gathered wherever they could be found. Irrespective of their circumstances, convictions, or intrinsic interest. Lawyers, priests, professors—Mikkelsen, Pastor Löchen, Hindus. Old friends, capable of being roused, awakened—Paraz, Aymé, Perrot, Descaves, Monnier, Canavaggia, Bonabel, Eveline Pollet. He bombarded them with letters. Encouraged them to act. To visit, defend, vindicate, urge clemency, but mostly, not to forsake him.

He uttered some of his intimate hopes to almost total strangers:

> I must make a smashing literary comeback, or perish, this time without appeal. . . . I accept the challenge, but I need time and sufficient health to do it.[29]

And confided his fears to most recently acquired sympathizers:

If I went back to France, I'd be instantly assassinated,
just as surely as the women's dresses are long now,
whereas they were so short two years ago! That's fashion
for you! Who can fight against fashion?

"A shallow and hard nation," Voltaire has said. I
didn't share their shallowness. They turned that into my
crime. I have no wish to share their hardness.[30]

His epistolary activities increased with a kind of frenzy.
All correspondents were good, if the exchange could accomplish the vindication of his works—which mattered more
than the salvation of his body.

He invented epithets for himself. Almost as if these
could spawn slogans for publicity campaigns or prize-awarding juries—at worst, epitaphs to snare posthumous glory.
His letters bristled with titles which he accorded himself to
this end: "Martyr of a too-furious pen";[31] "A Breton . . .
mystical, messianic";[32] "The author of the only communist
novel of the soul";[33] the *Résistant par excellence.*" [34]

Even the Jews now seemed a possible source of consolation. His own struggle against them in the past, seemed
merely an archetypal battle of generations. It was even conceivable that one day their causes would merge, their paths
converge for greater glory!

Which of us hasn't bitched about the Jews! they are the
fathers of our civilization—one always curses one's father at a given moment. . . . Anti-Semitism no longer
means a thing—we'll get back to racism, surely, but at a
later date—and indubitably under the leadership of the
Jews, if they haven't become too decadent, empoverished, besotted—or too decimated by wars. . . .[35]

The fight at present was not against them but against illness, despair, old age; the menaces that sprung up from all sides, from nowhere.

Spring, and advancing years assailed him.

> 54 years old yesterday! The decline is here!—*I feel 200 years* [*sic*]!
>
> May 29, 1947 [36]

Otherwise, nothing had changed. It was as though time had forgotten him (except when it came to aging). The constant horror of his days knew no alleviation.

> I'm still in the hospital and surrounded by nightmares, threats from every side. . . . Your letters seem to come from a world of the living . . . here, everything is dying—nevertheless, one exists—but one frequently has to rewind one's music—The nights especially, are hideous—And the monsters nothing to joke about. . . . Assassination, prison, hunger, never vanish from our horizon. . . .
>
> June 11, 1947 [37]

By autumn, hope seemed to stand completely still. A sense of exile had gripped him. The silence was beginning to descend.

> Yes, this is the time of harvests . . . of homecomings. . . . Not for us, alas! The situation is hopeless! . . . It will soon be night here, the Nordic night. . . .
>
> September 5, 1947 [38]

Doubts began to creep into everything. Not only the future, but even the right to speak of literature—the right to speak at all.

"I look great, trying to play judge!" [39] he chortled bitterly. Seeing the clown's pose in every one of his moves.

Later, much later, he would pass judgment upon himself in the high court of his ironic imagination:

I have suffered like no other man and am suffering still.
I shall die in shame, infamy and poverty, all because of
my stupidity. The complex from which I suffer, is to
have been such an ass.[40]

Now, however, he bore the burden of expiation. It was
a long road still, until the price was paid in full. Prisons and
hospital wards were only the beginning. He would know
other menaces, other silences, before the harvest of his furor
was gathered. Before his meager homecoming.

In prison, he had considered that they were living on a
knife's edge.

Not knowing that the blade continued to be honed.
That the cutting winds of the Baltic were preparing to whit-
tle away what was left of his strength.

That exile had other, more insidious torments in store.

What can a poor voice do against the Flood?
who hears it? How absurd to think that a
voice can be heard! . . .

When the flood has passed, the voice is
dead. . . . And the world goes on to other
things. . . .

CÉLINE

8

THE MUTE SEA

The inner Man has no language,
he is mute. Man must be put
before this mute panorama.[1]

The ferryboat blew its horn, faint and slow; then edged
into the nearly deserted port. After a moment's halt, it continued on its way, to the island of Fionnie.

Few voyagers descended. Korsør in winter was not an
inviting place: stubble fields swept by an icy wind, stretching
into the distance; trees divested of all life, loomed up like
eastern crosses in some ghostly calvary; salt and sea-spray
covered the branches of dwarfed shrubs. The circumpolar
stars that never set, shone bleakly in the northern sky. Now
and then, a bird shrieked from a sparse thicket. Otherwise,
complete silence reigned.

Denmark is a bald land. The wind gallops, charges without any respite. . . . It rages continually. Six months
of the year.[2]

It was a long way to Klarsgovgaard. The path led along
roads whose ruts had frozen into a permanent pattern, forcing one to walk in the narrow central portion as treacherous
as an ice bridge across a glacier. Past houses so tightly shut

against the cold that they might be mistaken for mausoleums. And forests that creaked under their burden of snow.

The village inn had damp sheets. The traveler's only comfort was found in heated bricks placed at his feet. The food was as inhospitable as the land: smoked fish encrusted with salt, and steaming liquid in glazed mugs, tasting vaguely of roots. The nights were full of a silence so great that the throb of one's blood became obtrusive. And sleep lay swaddled in layers of nothingness.

A white sun arose in the morning. Warming no part of the landscape, but glaring on the icy surfaces about.

> Obscure province, mute sea, wooden people. . . . the
> sun is a kind of tepid moon.[3]

The smell of the sea was harsh in these surroundings. One sensed that there would be no relief at its sight; no softening of contours. Only greater expanses of desolation.

The blood-red cottage[4] (which the natives pointed out as the habitat of "the Frenchman who writes") stood near the water. In front of the door, there was the figure of a man. It was wrapped in a complex array of garments superimposed upon each other; the hair was agitated by the wind; the odd stance was the result of its leaning on a cane. The face was sharply outlined against the sky, and turned toward a woman jumping rope on a flat space of earth in front of the hut (like a boxer in training).

It was Céline.

Lucette had just finished her exercise. Throwing down the rope—flushed from the effort—she ran off toward the shore.

> The sea is vicious and freezing cold. Lucette swims in it,
> two or three times a day. That's her affair.[5]

It was obvious that she was determined to keep herself in shape, as rigorously as if she were still appearing nightly on the stage of the Opéra-Comique.

Her leotards hung stiffly on clotheslines, like black scarecrows trapped in ice. Her dancing shoes were caked with mud.

"It's a good idea to marry circus girls, if one is going to live a hazardous life," [6] Céline grumbled, and went inside. It was barely warmer there. Some peat burned feebly in the stove, giving off acrid fumes and a great deal of smoke. The water had frozen in the basin which served as a sink; moisture seeped along the walls. The dirt floor sent up the cold.

He tried to light an oil lamp, bending over with difficulty to strike the match. The wick sputtered and went out. In disgust, he turned to the window and watched the trees blowing in the high wind.

"The country . . ." he muttered. "That bitch, always out to get you!" He had hated nature all of his life. Even in his youth. It was a rotten place, under the best of circumstances.

I've never been able to stomach the country. It always struck me as sad, with its mud holes, the houses where no one is ever home, and its paths that lead nowhere.
(*VOY*, 16–17)

Exile only reinforced all its loathsome traits.

I find the country tragic, above all. . . . Nothing but the cries of birds cutting each other's throats, a thousand murders a minute! What savagery! And soon, the hunt. Rapid, full of anguish, bloody.[7]

The sea had always been a different matter. But here, even the ocean had turned against him, in its gloomy silence:

The Baltic is an enigmatic sea—The "mute" sea, the Ancients used to call it—[8]

None of its aspects had the power to calm him. The waves here rolled sullenly onto the gravel. As far as the eye could see, only leaden gray waters carrying ice floes that ground against each other with a screeching sound. No sail; no mast nor smokestack ever appeared on the horizon. Sometimes, the waves threw up the skeleton of a fish—calcinated and broken; or a fragment of driftwood—white as a specter. And always, the colorless mists gathered, swept over everything, made it impossible to distinguish between rock and water. Landmarks vanished. The loss of orientation was nearly complete.

Time also became undecipherable. The far past rose up, at the mere turn of a path. The mist swirled to reveal forgotten altars and impenetrable signs.

> Two steps from my house in the forest there are menhirs and a small druidic stone circle. . . . Three thousand years old, it seems! And an upright cutting stone for doing in the ritual sacrifice. I go there often, it's more beautiful than the Milan cathedral. Would that humanity had ended there! [9]

He felt as though he had been swallowed up in this vast panorama of muteness. The echoes of the world were so feeble, so faint that one began to doubt its existence. As though the ferryboat that brought him had crossed Lethe to arrive at these shores. It was a forsaken place—out of time, out of mind.

Sometimes, it seemed as though his very self was beginning to dissolve, fade into oblivion. As if in response to a secret yearning for the void.

> I would like to end, the way Turner did. Vanish, one
> fine day. Forget everything, even my own name. . . .[10]

he wrote. Or said. For he had long developed the art of the
monologue.

His work had begun to resemble an endless series of
ruminations, turned inward upon the self.

He sat—almost without moving—at a rude table in his
attic retreat. As under a spell of hibernation. In the suspen-
sion of life, the only incongruity was his moving hand (traveling slowly across the damp paper). It alone had power to
continue his tale begun in prison, with the halting voice of
exile. The fairy tale which spoke, not of snow queens and
deforming mirrors whose fragments would dissolve when
touched by innocent tears, but of executioners and prison
cells, and visions conjured up by hatred, infidelity, and guilty
laughter. A tale told by a recluse, full of mute sounds and
fury.[11]

A monologue on the borders of extinction.

For no one spoke any longer of his books. His very name
seemed to have passed out of existence. No editor inquired
after him in his leper colony. (Perhaps they were waiting for
him to be posthumously exonerated, like Denoël,[12] before
they decided that he was no longer one of the untouchables.)
If a spark of interest flared up for an instant, it was always
coupled with an imbecilic disregard of his state:

> Here, everything consists of cold—and night . . . of
> humiliation and nightmare—Publishers tell me a lot of
> nonsense—and do nothing—the house is falling to pieces
> —but they demand a new book! That's easily said! the
> only trouble is that in my attic *it's raining!* Mushrooms
> are sprouting on my table—I have a hard time defend-
> ing my manuscripts against nature! Oblivion is nothing
> —but mushrooms! [13]

The ludicrous grew side by side with the dread. The silent signs of decay appeared on everything that he touched or felt. In the fungus that spotted the sheets; the sweet taste of frozen potatoes; the snowdrifts that smothered all life beneath them.

He might as well have pricked his finger on an old woman's spindle, so completely was his life grown over and his voice now stilled. An enormous weariness crept over him.

Even the visits of friends (which he had craved, prompted, even arranged) were almost a burden. For he had become as touchy and easily offended as a neglected child. Pity humiliated him; optimism and consolations seemed ridiculously out of keeping. Even laughter irritated him now. A huge sense of exasperation countered almost all expressions of feeling.

> All my patience is worn out—all foolishness too! the only qualities that make happiness possible . . . small talk . . . and all those futile things. . . .[14]

It was as though his nerves were frayed from overuse. And he could only grimace in response to effusions.

The old Parisian cronies could still be tolerated—Monnier, Perrot, Daragnès. . . . Nordling, the Swedish Consul General to France, at least brought the prospect of legal help for the coming trial which his friends hoped might bring him exoneration.

The worst error was to invite Hindus. Their frequent correspondence had been a solace to Céline (the nearest thing to a dialogue), creating a feeling of growing understanding, mixed with the sly conjectures that in the U.S., markets for books and other offers might be arranged.[15] But he sensed that Hindus' stay would turn out badly; that the confrontation would not fulfill their expectations.

The visit was a decided flop. Céline was at his most sullen. Constantly incited to anger. Irritated by his guest's every move. Hindus was obviously surprised and angered by the developments. When he left, his cap remained, not as a memento but probably from his excessive haste to be gone.

Céline was now filled with misgivings. Hindus' transatlantic crossing—storm-tossed—seemed a bad omen. As was the name of the book in which he described their encounter in Denmark—reported to be *The Monstrous Giant*.[16]

Another betrayal, he concluded. A further proof of his aberration. Anger boiled up for an instant, but was replaced by a defensive gesture. He wrote to Hindus—for the last time —in terms that betrayed his weariness, his preference for oblivion instead of further infamy:

> Oh no, don't send me your account of the Journey to Denmark! I have quite enough sinister surprises every day! You are among the *fortunate* of this earth, respect the plight of the *unfortunate*—Leave them in peace.
> . . . No sinister news, Hindus! I beg of you! It is only the spoiled children of fortune who need the spice of polemics and tragedy. . . . We are dying of horror! [17]

All of which did not stop the book from appearing. Its title softened to *The Crippled Giant*.

There seemed no future in asking for clemency. "You see where the artist's life leads!" he said with a wry grimace to Monnier who had come to visit, as they stood together on the devastated, wintry heath. But Monnier gave him some hope for his books. He would work for their publication on his return to France.[18]

A crack in the ice of oblivion. The muffled sound of his own voice, instead of the ramblings of others.

But the wilderness closed over them once more. Their lives continued, snowbound. In a long series of repetitious tribulations. Until they were sick even of their lamentations:

no water, no electricity, no toilet, no change in sight. It seemed to him that he had been condemned to an endless bout of sleep. A hundred years out of the world. An embittered Rip Van Winkle of the North. With no reality other than the maddening prospect of continuation:

> It's exactly as if we had left the world. . . . In this state, one becomes cracked and abusive! seven years of lousy persecution, plus illness and old age . . . ! [19]

France was so far off, it seemed impossible to imagine even its contours. Nor could he see himself walking once more in his birthplace. He would be outlawed to this alien soil until the end of his days.

> No, I don't believe in my return to France . . . never.
> . . . I'll croak in some faraway place, of poverty, fatigue, and age. . . .[20]

The rumors of an amnesty (which his friends were working to obtain for him) were a hope as grotesque as the various forms of paradise he had denounced in the past. True, he sometimes let himself be drawn into schemes of appeal, with the vague promise of obtaining exoneration.[21] But it all seemed so slow, so feebly pitted against overpowering odds that time would pass over them . . . ten . . . twenty years . . . and it would be too late. Even success would have become ludicrous by then.

> A good joke! What shall we have died of by that time? Hunger? Cold? Poverty? The Tartars? [22]

Sometimes, it struck him as surprising that he had been allowed to remain alive even this long. It must be attributed to the almost total oblivion into which he had sunk. The mantle of silence which descended on them like falling snow. Perhaps it was best not to create a stir. To lie low. Feign death, the way small beasts do when the hunter approaches.

Even overzealous friends must be kept at bay.

From time immemorial, Calvary has included spittle, in-
sults, vinegar. None of them were spared me. . . .

I think that I'm already doing well to avoid the stake.
But one mustn't speak too much of me. . . . Thus, I
beg you to leave me as I am, "forgotten and taboo." I
don't mind dying but, if possible, without too much torture, in oblivion. That is my only remaining wish.[23]

Their lives were at such a low ebb that there was no
effort in "playing dead." All actions had been reduced to a
minimum: speech, warmth, food, travel. A terrible lethargy
made the slightest move an intolerable burden. And any
extraneous gesture an outrage.

It was ludicrous enough to procure the merest survival
rations:

We live on nothing but coffee and smoked fish—but
even so, one has to trek 12 kilometers to get the mack-
erel! . . . Above all, though, we're weary of the slightest efforts, making the fire—doing the dishes—even
those two plates! What's the use of it all—. . . . We're
living at the end of hell . . . a frozen hell, which is a
rare thing. . . .[24]

They seemed to have reached the lowest circle of Hell,
where everything is fixed, unmoving. Congealed in ice. Where
Dante had already placed the betrayers.

Existence stood still. In an isolation which even prison
could not produce. As the jagged stalks of frost-flowers thickened their growth on the windowpanes, the world grew each
day more indistinct. The past slipped away. Becoming meaningless and devoid of color. And the future without light.

1924

Was it a quarter of a century ago, when he had en-
visioned the state in which he found himself now? The exile

of Semmelweiss, so strangely prophetic (or reminiscent) of his own. Past, present and future merged, as he dimly recalled the words he had written then—in the midst of freedom and opulence, but might have uttered now.

> The fire whose carrier he had been, is covered by ashes, has almost gone out.

> His past no longer speaks to him.

> A past too rich in enthusiasms for his worn-out heart. His forces are no longer equal to such a burning flame. He is dying of hunger.

> . . . his life remained somnolent, his dreams without power. For this man who must dream in order to live, the void has almost triumphed. Nothing interests him, he no longer writes. . . .

> Almost seven years of silence. . . .[25]

1950

The middle of the century.

The still point of exile.

The needle of the compass pointed north. Dead center. To zero.

Each day dawned, cracking across the windowpane with the sound of icicles breaking. Only to form anew. Break again. In an unending cycle that could only end with the final void.

As he sat, immobile before his hut, a scene flashed dimly into his mind. Before the curtain of apathy fell, he thought he saw the ramparts once more; the slow sweep of birds; the enigmatic stretches of the sea. —It must have been at Elsinore. —A group of five figures outlined against the sky. Once upon a time; on an unimaginable autumn day:

Ferdinand . . . got out at Elsinore and went with us to the terrace where the ancient cannons sleep. The slightly yellow fog lying on the . . . coastline of Sweden, the sea gulls screaming as they circle, produce an agonizing shock. One gazes, wanting to encompass more than the eye can see, yearns to hear a key-phrase. After a long look, Céline said in his hollow voice: "A sea for fishing souls!" [26]

(His own had long been hooked and pulled from his body. It wriggled on the ground for quite some time. Then lay still, no longer even gasping for air.)

Yet, it was not enough. The blows continued. As thick as hailstones. The lifted hand could not avert them. It was no use to put a moat of silence around his body. The assailants had found ways to pursue him, despite his protestations that a world of difference lay between them:

Between me and my accusers, there lies an abyss that cannot be crossed. My accusers are all hired servants —not I—and servants change masters. . . . I've lost everything in this dreadful adventure, where all was lost beforehand. I did not play the poet's card, the losing number. I didn't play at all, I consider it low to play. I threw everything away, I sacrificed everything to the imbecility of my contemporaries—except my honor which, thank God, is still intact.[27]

An intactness which would not for long prevail.

In February of that year, the French courts ruled upon his case. Their judgment read:

We condemn Destouches, Louis-Ferdinand, also known as Céline, to one year's imprisonment and a fine of fifty thousand francs.
We declare him to be in a state of national indignity.

And order the confiscation of one half of all his present
and future possessions.[28]

It was a blow that could be partially parried by irony:
An influential Jewish association[29] had risen to his defense,
and asked the court for his pardon. Besides, hilarity was
aroused in the courtroom when the prosecutor read passages
from his works (even the inflammatory pamphlets). The
reaction was thought to have been more efficacious in bringing about a relatively light sentence, than the testimonies of
Céline's famous friends (Mondor of the Academy, Arletty,
Henry Miller, Marcel Aymé . . .). For it reminded the
French of the existence of one of its greatest comic writers.

And proved the old notion that clowns are never punished to the utmost limits of severity.

His own retort to the matter was full of bravado—but
ended on a note of authentic despair:

> Isn't that minister of justice nice! . . . I can make him
> laugh even harder—so hard he'll end up under the table.
> Thank God, I still have quite a rich palette of laughter.
> . . . Every possible kind: sincere, painful, cuckoo and
> cuckold laughter, laughter-such-as-you've-never-known.
> . . . But eighteen months in prison, four years of exile,
> being hunted by the entire world is too much, even for a
> comic writer . . . the laugh freezes. . . .[30]

Beneath the frozen grimace, a cry of anguish festered. For
he was convinced that they were out for his life. That they
would have his skin, while allowing him to continue performing for their amusement. A flayed clown—what could
be funnier?

> We're living in a universe à la Hieronymus Bosch. Tor-
> ture and fun! Not to speak of lies! There is no more
> truth! [31]

For what else but lies were the cheerful assertions that he
was saved; that the sentence passed upon him was a mere

formality and really amounted to exoneration? As though "national indignity" were a title to be worn as gaily as motley; or fines and seizures of his property had the merry tinkle of a fool's-cap's bells. And they expected him to perform a dance of joy for having—with his jester's tricks—won a benign condemnation.

The second blow was far more grave.

Lucette was taken ill and transported to a hospital in Copenhagen for a serious operation.[32]

Neither pride nor talent could exert any power now. Uncontrollable fear gripped his innards, as she was carried away. Delivered into alien doctors' hands. While he stood by, inert and helpless; reduced to waiting.

Solitude was complete now. He saw no exit from the black tunnel of exile. Even she had abandoned him. Who, in her former health and youthful buoyancy, had been a living guarantee that all was not lost. How fragile a shield against despair her body had proven to be. How easily pierced by decay!

Even when she recovered, he could not regain his former belief in her invulnerability which had sustained him. It had been one of the few remaining certainties. Now that it was shattered, he felt like a lame man whose crutch has suddenly been whisked away.

The hopes he had momentarily harbored in the past seemed absurd to him now. What an exorbitant lie, for example, to have written:

> Lucette is holding up well. She does her two hours of dancing each day. . . .[33]

when now she lay, hardly able to move, back in their seaside hermitage.

*   *   *

Summer came and passed. Bringing hardly any change. And autumn did not signify harvest, but only the gradual passing into the cold. For others, the seasons, the sowing, reaping and homecoming.

> We who are shut off from the habitable world, whose every hour is further anguish, who do not dare see anyone, or be recognized by people. . . . For us, the seasons no longer have a meaning. Our season is hate.[34]

But hate was still tolerable. It was the pity which he could not bear. Their destitution must have somehow become known, for an avalanche of gifts began to come their way. Parcels of alms flooded the post office in the village nearby. The clerks watched him slyly as he received them. Alms for the lepers. Care packages, full of smug benevolence, for the ghetto-dwellers. Spelling out their shame.

His pride roused him to seething anger.

"They want to insult me by sending their lousy presents," he fumed as he threw the bundles down on the floor of the hut.

Other humiliations followed: donations collected by well-meaning physicians, a newly created society of "The Friends of Céline"—reminiscent of the "gracious gifts" (in the form of boxes of chocolate) which one of his old lady friends had thought would console him in exile! [35]

He protested against them all. Returned the money. Refused the packages. Let the foodstuffs rot in the post office. Raging that he wasn't a beggar yet.

Even a box of bananas had to be carefully disguised as a gift from Lucette's parents.[36] Or he would surely have screamed that he was being put on the level of apes.

A remnant of dignity distinguished him from them. He

clung to it, the way a dying man does to the grim determination not to soil his sheets.

Or seafarers reserve the right to signal their ultimate distress only when shipwreck is imminent; a custom that even prison could not break:

> You know that ships, according to traditions of valor, only accept aid in moments of final distress. . . . I haven't come to that point—not yet. . . . I'll inform you . . . when the waves have submerged the decks.[37]

Now when everything seemed on the point of being washed away, he insisted on remaining at the helm. If necessary, to sink with his ship.

But, as by reflex, refusing yet to go under. He went feverishly to work—stopping up holes, caulking, mending the masts—to put his vessel into shape to weather the ice. His book would pierce the blockade of silence, laughter, and pity. The prow would once again rise out of the water, its fierce masthead inspiring terror in merchant ships and all lesser vessels.

The attic room began to resemble that of a shipbuilder. Parts of the completed construct hung on pegs driven into the walls; tools covered the worktable. —The rain and fungus growths that sprouted on the wood, seemed suddenly in keeping. —The skeletal outline of the structure on which he worked, was growing more defined. Determined by a yearning as mysterious as the burgeoning of mushroom seeds. To which the only clues were provided by the pictures hung over the table: the "Moulin de la Galette," last seen from his window in Montmartre;[38] the "Sacré-Coeur," [39] high above Paris like some absurd, delightful wedding cake; other, secretly coveted spots of his city (probably cut out of a guidebook "full of lots of photos," like the one he had asked a bookseller friend to procure).[40]

*   *   *

The book would re-create the city. Superimpose an imaginary
outline on the real streets. Splice the sites of his invention
onto the places he had known. Until there lay before him a
series of Paris landscapes: fantastic photos of Montmartre
illuminated by falling bombs; the fall of the city captured in
an album full of apocalyptic snapshots.[41]

> Oh, my phantom is haunting those places . . . my next
> book *Féerie* is located on the spot of the crime. . . .[42]

If these were to be his only rights of visitation, he would
use them in the manner that he knew best. Shipwrecked on
an island of alien rock, the only way of return was through
the images of his homeland, and the mastery of its language.
Both of which he was able to call up on command.

(Not without props, however: photos cut from visitors'
guides; Lucette's chatter which he encouraged, demanded
even.)

He knew that, for him, the most painful deprivation was
not the loss of freedom, ease, or fame—but that of language.
He craved the sound of French as others lust after alcohol,
the thighs of women, drugs. The hollow syllables of Danish,
the nasal whine of English, were hateful to him. He could
not bear to be cut off from his tongue. The bonds with the
language of his origins were too powerful to be broken, even
by hate:

> Despite all that France has done to me, I can't detach
> myself from its language. It has a hold over me. I can't
> free myself of it.[43]

(Perhaps it was this bondage which led him to prefer France
to other, more advantageous retreats where he might spend
the last years of his life; to prefer the fate of the outcast in his

own land to the prestige of the expatriot in such places as North Africa, Switzerland, Alaska,[44] Greenland,[45] or Spain.)

Now he thought only of forging his word-fetters into creation. They crowded together, were hammered into weapons of language. Piled up around him; lined the walls. Defending him in the siege of silence, against the babel of foreign voices outside. As he erected an intimate fortress whose passwords were coined in argot (as the cathedral builders of his country had long ago guarded their secrets from all outsiders).[46]

Perhaps in this citadel, he would be able to bide his time. And await the passing of the flood.

Amnesty suddenly became a reality.[47] On April 26, 1951, it was announced:

> The Paris Military Tribunal has decided that the Amnesty Law of August 1947 applies to Louis-Ferdinand Céline, recipient of the Military Medal and disabled veteran of the First World War. Thus, the author is exonerated of all charges that have been brought against him.[48]

The return was now imminent. But he could no longer feel any joy. The seven years which had gone by, since he had passed the frontiers of France, had made him too embittered to rejoice.

Besides, it was a meager reprieve. Of this he was certain. A little space of time, to return—half-living among the living —for some declining years. Perhaps only to be once again hunted and defiled.

He had grown as reticent as a burnt child:

> Oh, it's all very pretty, this amnesty. But hatreds abide . . . stand vigil . . . and our fatigue makes it impossible to cope with any more idiotic, debilitating battles.[49]

In their diminished state, every move was made with misgivings. As snails venture out of their shells, trembling, because they know the full vulnerability of their flesh.

It occurred to him that the whole maneuver might have been done in sport: to spare them momentarily, in order to fatten them for future slaughter. (He remembered that even bulls are sometimes awarded mercy in a corrida, only to be later pole-axed by the butcher's lackey.) The hunt had probably been halted, so that the huntsmen might water their horses, refresh themselves, reload their rifles; and give the prey a headstart to make the chase more exciting. To add the spice of struggle to the kill.

> It wasn't a matter of meting out justice, it was a hunting party. . . . It's rare for an animal to escape, even in such a sorry state as ours! [50]

And it was far from finished. They would attack once more; surround him; beat the underbrush; set mongrels snapping at his sides.

Until the weariness became even greater than now. And weighed upon him far more heavily than convicts' chains.

"How heavy they are!" [51] he would groan, as he passed his last judgment upon the world of men.

His own being, however, had grown lighter in exile. Everything seemed to have dropped off him—titles, pounds, possessions, teeth, illusions, skin, affections. Everything had been pared away. Sometimes he felt almost transparent.

Invisibility would have been most to his liking. Insensibility also. He had arrived at the point of asking NOTHING; seeing NO ONE; affirming only his horror of EVERY CONTACT with his fellow-men. [52] The feeling of alienation was so great that even the sound of the human voice had become intolerable.

I seem to feel the vocation for becoming a Trappist! [53]

The most severe of monastic orders seemed like a noisy social club in comparison to his thirst for isolation. To sleep in coffins and take a vow of silence would be mere redundancies.

The mute sea had long claimed him. Even far from its shores, he walked enveloped in its shroud.

I rise out of the egg in the hidden
land. May my mouth be given unto
me that I may speak therewith. . . .
According to the desire of my heart,
I have come from the Pool of Fire,
and I have quenched the Fire.

THE BOOK OF THE
DEAD, II, xxii

9

THROUGH THE LAST GATE

Summer.

The brilliant light of the Mediterranean streamed through the iron portals of the villa, illuminated clusters of flowers so that they glowed with the intensity of stained glass, lifted the clay urns from their background of foliage until they floated forward like amphoras among thickets of seaweed.

The next turn of the road led to Italy. Across the sea lay the North African shore. Creating the feeling that one was seated at the gateway to the center of the world.

Yet, the sudden heat, the urgent vibrancy of life which thrust itself upon one here, were almost painful in their unavoidable presence. He shielded his weak eyes from the sun, lay back in the garden chair and abandoned himself to the torpor which gradually enveloped him. Nevertheless, the sounds continued to intrude: the purring flight of bumblebees; the splash of hidden fountains; the rasp of the cicada in a mimosa tree.

And in the distance, voices rising and falling in gracious undulations—speaking in a tongue . . . his tongue . . . so long forsaken or drowned by other, foreign voices.

Only then, did he suddenly feel that he had returned.

(Otherwise, the return had only made him smart with

a series of absurd frustrations, all the more ironic because
they were so petty: the incessant chatter of relatives, their
squabbles, gossip, avarice, and concerns that seemed to apply
to another planet—all the dribble of those who have remained among the living, half-alive, during an entire lifetime.)

Animal cunning told him that this was a time to lie low,
recover his strength while ruminating on plans for escape.

He waited, in the long, heavy afternoons, for the cold to
thaw out of his bones, the skin to be renewed, the remaining
reserves of energy to well up in him. And for his voice to
grow sharp enough to be heard once more.

All this was best achieved through withdrawal. He fled
from all contact, from every vestige of the past that might
reopen sores only recently scarred over. Even the telephone
—that half-forgotten instrument out of another world—might
spell intrusion. He hardly spoke at all. Fearing that his utterances might be too violent. Remembering that he must step
softly, as becomes a trespasser.

Even his letters had the tone of warnings. He wrote as if
he were muttering through clenched teeth:

> I'm worn out by many worries and the imbecility of my
> surroundings. I'm not hard to please, but I would have
> liked a little less hysterical gabbing . . . worn-out
> tricks, miserliness, greed, etc. . . . all this, just be-
> tween you and me, of course. Careful, super careful! one
> more word and they'll throw me out. *The hideous com-
> edy continues*. The refugee stinks.
>
> Don't phone me, it creates dramas. Why? I'll be damned
> if I know! . . . I've withdrawn into my lair, like a
> bear, you know my style! I run from everyone and
> everything—so SHUT UP!—TOTALLY. Write me,
> that's all. . . . If I can get my hands on some money
> . . . we'll get the hell out! Without fanfares! There
> won't be any tears shed! . . . I'm an experimentalist

> as you well know, one fright after the other. . . . But
> in this house of hysterics and illiterate fools my system
> is to smile and pass on. . . .[1]

All he could hope for now was to pass unnoticed. Dissemble his whereabouts. If not invisible, at least unseen, unheard.

(A fake obituary notice would have been most welcome.)

> If they thought us dead, quite simply dead, it would be
> very pleasant indeed . . . I have nothing to say. Noth-
> ing I want to see. My worries, although tragic, concern
> no one. . . . Let them just leave us in peace! [2]

Perhaps the best maneuver was to move on, zigzag, wait in another hiding place. Accept shelter in the blossoming bower —"La Fleurière"—of Marteau, the Tarot card king of France.

There, the gardens stretched in an unending succession down to the sea. A pool of blue, surrounded by slim Grecian columns, created an obvious link of water to water. Cannes lay hidden behind chains of roses draped over the trunks of old trees. Grape arbors further obscured signs of civilization. The whole was carefully planned to give the impression of carefree luxuriance. All in all, it was meant to convey the message that the owners could well afford this improvement upon Eden.

He sat surrounded by oriental carpets and vases on pedestals, while several lapdogs waddled about. Their bulging eyes questioned his presence; shrill barks rose in a chorus of unwelcome.

A butler wheeled the teacart onto the terrace which extruded from the room, brushing against the inlaid table on which a bundle of yellow pages lay. —An early draft of *Féerie,* written on prison paper, which he had dedicated to his host Marteau. Incongruous now, in the midst of all this cautious well-being. —Céline winced as the Pekingese announced the arrival of his benefactors.

He preferred the guest quarters at the end of the garden, where he could flee from such encounters, and mundane conversation did not increase the pall of heavy summer afternoons.

The climate weighed upon him as much as the rest of his supplicant's pose. These southern shores did not correspond to his temperament at all. It was the rugged coasts of Brittany, with their cool winds that smelt of brine, and villages of fretted stone where fishermen enacted rituals as ancient as the painted boats in which they sailed, that were his home.

PARIS, AUGUST 1951

So that he was almost frightened, when finally they passed through what had once been the southern gate of the city and found themselves assailed by sounds, sights, and smells as familiar as a dream, as haunting as vestiges of a previous incarnation: inverted double cones of red glass (enigmatically signaling the presence of tobacconists); the golden heads of horses lifted above the striped awnings of certain butcher shops; a herd of goats on one of the major boulevards, around the cheese seller who played a flute; the sudden miracle of the Seine; the intricate dams that street cleaners built out of rags, and their brooms still fashioned of stripped branches; the odor of chicory and crushed grapes; the sound of milk being heated by steam; the deep fragrance of ripening chestnuts; the trickle of urinals.

High up above the city, Montmartre and the Sacré-Coeur as unreal as a bubble blown into the sky.

It all whisked past, as the car turned toward the elegant

suburb of Paris which Céline had so often alluded to with mockery, in the past.

The feeling of intrusion continued. And the stance of polite gratitude he found so difficult to maintain. Especially among the Pekingese, and the society ladies who thronged to the home of the Marteaus. Their scrutiny of him was unabashed. As though his function was to be shown (at specified hours, preferably after meals) and examined like a rare new breed in a menagerie.

Kept women must feel as free as unharnessed mares by comparison.

He began to despair of ever being anything else than a recaptured fugitive, a prize anomaly, or a paid fool. And most emphatically, of ever finding his own voice once more.

When suddenly, two events changed all his black prognoses: the biggest publishers in France included him among their authors; a house overlooking the Seine, in Meudon, was vacant and at their disposal.[3]

By September (in harvest time) they moved into their last dwelling. Shutting the rusty gates against the world, they walked up the unweeded path lined with rubble.

He had found the hilltop from which his voice would thunder its final prophecies. And once again break the tables of literary commandments.

MEUDON, 1951

I have a taste . . . an animal taste for retreats . . .
countries where nobody ever goes. . . .[4]

The house lacked many things, but certainly not remoteness. Located between two small towns, on a path that served only the two adjacent dwellings, it was set back from the gates and separated by a long stretch of hilly ground. It must have stood uninhabited for some time. The boarded-up

windows, the overgrown garden, the holes in the roof—all
spoke of abandon. Bombardments had damaged its frame-
work during the war. Electrical lines hung, like severed
nerves, or trailed along the walls; the plumbing and water
pipes were in bad repair.

But in September, the splendor of the trees and colored
splotches of flowers that had been allowed to sprout un-
hindered, gave a sense of majesty and wanton ease to the
sprawling retreat.

Then the rains came. The leaves fell, choking the paths.
They had to plaster, patch the roof, prop up the rotting
beams, clear the staircase, carry the water in pails from the
back garden. And perform all these labors in an atmosphere
of growing hostility. The neighbors must have been informed
of their identity, for vague threats and clear warnings appeared on their gates. Injurious posters were glued to the
entranceway. All excursions out of their shelter were accompanied by sneers, whispers, looks of suspicion. Children were
whisked out of their paths; dogs barked in chorus at their
approach. As they descended, they almost expected the winding path to the town to be lined with swastikas, hammers and
sickles, obscenities. Once, a stillborn pig was put on top of
their garbage pail. And always, as they passed, some bitten
face peered at them from the swiftly drawn shutters of a
house.

He soon refused to go out in the daylight hours.

> I only go to do the shopping at night: it's torture to drag
> the potatoes, the carrots, the meat for the animals up
> from Billancourt, 5 pounds of stuff, going uphill, is
> tough, at 61 the ticker doesn't want to work anymore.
> . . . Then too, I've got the Renault plant right under
> my nose, their rubber factory.[5]

The stench was intolerable. Not only that of the factories
below—but also his own, which they constantly pointed out

to him: the sour smell of the outcast, the pauper, the traitor to an endless number of causes. It made them move off as he approached, and grumble about the "filth" (which seemed indiscriminately to apply to him, his house, his works, his clothes). And refuse to deliver heavy loads, boycott the simplest of requests.

A quarantine of hate had been imposed.

Besides this shame, there was the disgrace of his own body. It would no longer obey, grew weaker, often collapsed under the slightest strain—a walking ruin on canes. He sat helplessly leaning against a wall, while Lucette labored like some hired hand. He knew that she hid most of her work from him, performing all the arduous tasks at night. While he slept fitfully in a corner of his den.

The winter was fast approaching. They had to secure their shelter against the cold. It was a losing battle, for it meant fighting nature, decay, poverty, infamy, and old age.

> It was 15 below zero on the Baltic! Here, only zero! . . . miserable! . . . I'm so ashamed. We have no more coal, for example, than on the Baltic. . . . Have you ever tried working in zero weather? The dump where I live . . . is enormous . . . holes everywhere . . . impossible to heat . . . grotesque.
>
> Fortunately we go to bed at 8 in the evening and get up at 9 in the morning. Economy, warmth . . . but sleep won't come. It'll come in time and for a long time! ouf! [6]

It seemed strange now to think that he had yearned so for his country (during the long northern nights); or felt that the view from his sofa (of the Seine, his river, flowing below) would content him endlessly. How simplistic, his firm belief that exile could ever end!

His past hopes became ludicrous. A bunch of empty

phrases pronounced by a braggard. Who flaunted his inviolable ability to write, no matter how inhuman his condition:

> No, nothing bothers me when it comes to work, not even tragedy—people of my generation (2 wars) are blasé in this respect—even in my prison cell, I fooled around with some little sketches—I won't go as far as saying I can write immortal verses beneath the guillotine, like Chénier! But we all do what we can, right? [7]

A lesser doom hung over him now. The small forms of death, the ugly shadow of exile. There was nothing grandiose in this puny fight for survival—the furtive groveling in the dark, the cold; it was only the old struggle of the disinherited. (Which did not lack its ironies. After being pillaged and having lost several important manuscripts, he found himself one day, the recipient of a note:

> . . . they even came to present me with (hold on to your chair) a bill from a warehouse where the last of my pillagers (there were about 15 of them) had stored the carcass of an armchair. . . . All that's left. . . .) [8]

Lucette, however, now raised her head in defiance. And fixed her placard on the gate. Reclaiming her right to teach the dance by the bright red sign. Students began gradually to arrive. Hesitant at first, as if contact might prove contaminating. They surveyed the grounds, the dogs, the equipment of bars and mats she had, somehow, accumulated. And looked furtively around—as if they expected the monster to show his head, at any instant. But Lucette won them over with her smiling ways and quickly commanded their respect by her undiminished craft.

*   *   *

Perhaps his old profession could also be reclaimed. Medicine could not have gone completely out of style.

The bureaucratic harangue began. His license had expired (although, everyone assured him, it was never revoked) during his seven years' absence. It was only renewed after a series of fatiguing, repetitive requests. His plaque now paralleled hers at the gates. Smaller, gray, weathered by many journeys.

The patients were few. They did not often come out of choice. Most of them (he noticed) consisted of the local poor, who could not afford the trip to another town and (probably sensing his position) hoped to be treated for a modest fee or without any payment at all. Perhaps they also sensed his anguish at the loss of his title (had they overheard him cry: "People have stopped calling me 'Doctor'!"?). And with the sly instinct of the deprived, knew that in return for being addressed in this way, he would be willing to examine, prescribe syrups, urge hospitalization and welfare payments. They soon formed a shabby following and gave a semblance of purpose to his presence on the hill.

But he could not long deceive himself. His gift of lucidity and laughter touched everything he saw—even his own condition. It was an absurd role he played. Within a ludicrous drama:

> [I] feel . . . lower, much lower than a chiropractor
> . . . somewhere between a herborist and a condom
> . . . lower than Bovary . . . a coolie . . . coolie of
> the Occident! . . . bearer of packages, crates, shop-
> ping bags . . . there's more to it than my age and the
> wall inscriptions . . . the state of our house. . . .
> "What keeps it standing?" . . . and my opening the
> gate in person . . . unlocking . . . locking up again
> . . . that's the end . . . it does look bad, I admit . . .

and the location . . . in the middle of the hill! . . .
really an impossible place to live! . . . the path!
. . . the muck! . . . my poor patients in the winter
. . . climbing, sloshing, breaking their necks . . . naturally they don't come up . . . the few chronic cases
who risk it are questioned at the bar . . . am I really
as crummy as people say? . . . did they see any pieces
of victims? . . . ovens for torturing the patients? . . .
etc. etc. . . .

(*CAS*, 64–65)

Obviously, this was not the road back from exile. Only
a muddy sidepath which momentarily preoccupied him with
other sufferings than his own. In curing them, he seemed to
effect a partial faith-cure in himself. Only enough to make
him realize that the worst of his symptoms was a choking
sensation. As though his voice was stuck in his throat. Caus-
ing a terrible lump of stagnation, a toxic condition of his
insides. For the noises in his head had never been stilled.
They continued to rage, clamor, crash with the sound of
derailed freight trains. Demanding liberation. A release of all
the pent-up utterances that lay festering, and would not die.

Groaning like a galley slave, he went to his worktable.

A room was already set aside for him on the ground
floor. He did not need to climb the stairs. (Those were reserved for younger, lighter feet—of dancers who flitted, birdlike, upwards in the direction of Lucette's airy retreat). The
table faced downhill, toward the valley of the Seine. No
longer did he have to content himself with photos of Paris.
The city lay just beyond the bend of the river. His past hung
on the walls behind him now—the hut on the Baltic Sea, the
coasts of Brittany.

All that remained now, was to gather the courage to do
what he had once—long ago—described:

> I think I'll have the time to finish everything before I'm
> finished myself. . . . The essential thing is to have a
> kind of freedom and a tolerable situation, in order to
> fight my last battle. . . . To make my debut once again,
> before an infinitely hostile public. . . . I know the mu-
> sic at the heart of things—If need be, I can make alliga-
> tors dance on the flute of Pan—But it takes time to
> carve the flute and strength to blow it—Often, as light as
> the flute is, it slips out of my fingers. . . .[10]

His twisted fingers gripped the pen tightly. Although
paralysis had begun to deform his hand, and often rendered
his writing painful, almost illegible.

He had the annoying experience of having old friends
complain that they could not recognize his signature or the
scrawls that came in the mail. Sometimes they suspected a
series of hidden causes for the change. He had to explain, by
means of reassuring medical terms—almost the way he spoke
to his patients:

> I am writing to you with my right hand, paralyzed by a
> radical nerve-section on October 28, 1914. That's all.
> Nothing mysterious.
>
> So much for all the enigmas.[11]

Other ailments, however, managed to serve him well.
—His insomnia, for instance. —True, he spent long nights
tormented by the buzzing in his ears, the impression that the
roof of his skull rose and fell rhythmically, the sound of
twenty belfries ringing in his head. But in those bouts of
sleeplessness (when his hatred for drugs would not let him
resort to another dose of Veronal), images, phrases, word
patterns formed, were stored up. And, in the hours just after
daybreak, were communicated to paper.

Pages began once again to fill his room. And words lined
up, in combat formation, for his last battle.

1952–1961

From then on, his voice continued to ring out. At times it faltered, became almost extinct, sank to a whisper. But always, it gathered strength again and cunning, and hammered on death's gates until they closed upon it—unable to silence it completely even then.

Work after work was wrenched from his body. As he induced labor, prevented stillbirth; conceived, nurtured, bore down, and expelled his creations with a drive as relentless as that of the wasp, the spider or the sea turtle, who plant their eggs in hideous and arid places, neglecting the most elementary elements of their own or other creatures' survival.

Each book took its toll. He grew grayer, drier, lighter, and less accessible with every one. Until he resembled some brittle leaf. And those who saw him sitting in a crude shelter, while the rain poured down, or without moving, beside the parrot's cage, were never sure whether he was quite alive. He seemed to have removed himself to some other sphere, leaving only an empty shell, a gray cocoon in his place to create an illusion of presence. A shabby double for the world to ponder.

The words of others would glide off him. Their actions were shut out by a veil which closed (in reptilian fashion) over his eyes. The sounds of life began to grow dim, as though heard through several thicknesses of wall.

It was as if some blinding inner source of illumination had made all other lighting grow feeble by comparison. Artificial. A mere string of electric bulbs of low voltage, giving off a thin yellow glow that dies before the intense rays of the sun.

His own person had become indifferent to him now. The stares that followed him wherever he passed, did not appear to touch him at all. He walked, like some inspired tramp, on roads that did not converge with those of others. But moved along an invisible line toward a place where none could join him. Toward a last, grandiose assignation.

On a quest for silence. That led into a world where cries and aphasia were joined, and the inaudible affirmed its rights. Where the unspoken prevailed as full of authority as utterance. And pauses became tunnels of darkness from which one emerged, more stunned, into the blinding light. Or holes that let one plunge into suspense, doubt, terror, meditation.[12]

Unstated things grew into a mysterious lacework of their own. Poignant reminders of continual loss, of all that is irremediable, irredeemable, never to be unearthed again. Arraying themselves into a soliloquy that became more hermetic as the years went by. Unmitigated by the interjections of others. More lonely than a tightrope solo in an empty circus tent.

It was a downward thrust into the hollows of language. He skimmed the crests but plunged more deeply into the troughs of the waves, touched the abyss of silence; coming up long enough only to take a breath, before descending once more. The descents grew longer and longer; the links between phrases and the fragments of thoughts more difficult to seize. The thrusts into silence (marked by series of dots, or breaks in the continuity of mood, of image) became more numerous. Until the page was covered with patterns resembling Morse code, or an agitated sea whose surface is intermittently broken by the rush of white horses crowning the waves.

Of course, the path he was taking was prone to attacks, ambush, ridicule, smug condemnations. For some it became proof that he had lost his potency of style; to others, that the conspiracy of silence which made him an almost forgotten author, was justified; there were even those who considered him finished, no longer able to create his music, because he now contented himself with painting "landscapes without a sky, without anyone, or anything, just to be left in peace." [13] But he was able to laugh—now that his voice had returned —and make a royal jest of his isolation:

> It would be a gas to create a literary prize for the *Unnamables,* for our boycotted species, for us lepers. . . .[14]

His self-engendered leprosy was worth cultivating. It entailed the progressive loss of various extraneous parts, the lopping off of extremities, means constantly diminished, a mastery based mostly on absence.

Out of it would grow his final trilogy that plunged author and reader, his mute confidant, into a universe reduced almost to nothingness: a deserted eternity, where one described an infinity of circles and encountered only one's own phantom; a place where life and death existed on the same plane, had the same vividness of tone and image, could hardly be distinguished; a realm in which reality and myth were no longer opposed.[15] And he himself, throned like some old king in this domain of white feudality.

> I feel . . . a sort of detachment, of hate, for everything that moves . . . an absolute weariness. . . .[16]

Only his hand stirred. But with great effort. It dragged, lying on its side, across the sheet of paper. Like some felled animal that strives towards a secret destination—the place of its birth or the burial ground of the species.

Relentless in its progression toward the void. Which nothing seemed able to arrest.

Only once did its rhythm falter:

1956

He had suffered from a strange attack—perhaps a stroke, which prefigured the end of half a decade later. The illness left him confused, childlike, incoherent. Behind the closed doors of his room, one could hear a weird, fluttering sound. As of birds' wings when they suddenly take flight. When Lucette entered, she saw him stand in the middle of the floor, throwing up handfuls of his work, the pages flying into the air and sinking slowly to the ground. A whole manuscript rained down upon his shoulders, his head, his table.[17]

He recovered as suddenly as he had been stricken. And never spoke of the incident again.

One of the few remaining truths he knew, was that the path of nothingness was paved with words. One could travel toward death and silence by no other means. Only this vessel could attain those dread and desired shores.

During the last months of his life, lost in a reverie, a trance that nullified the observer—when the unnamables had had almost all been named—he murmured:

> To write as I do, looks like nothing . . . but it's unimaginably difficult . . . horrible . . . superhuman . . . it's a trick that will kill a man. . . .[18]

The void was almost within reach.

THREE

The last act is bloody, no matter how
beautiful the rest of the comedy : in
the end, some earth is thrown upon the
head and that's that, forever.

PASCAL

All lives end badly. . . .

CÉLINE

The fourth horseman . . . was Death.
And hell followed with him.

APOCALYPSE, VI :8

10

THE APOCALYPSE ACCORDING TO ST. FERDINAND

*The road of Man is a one-way
street, death runs all the
cafés, and the "blood-poker"
draws and keeps us there.*[1]

He knew that time was running out. A few more years
and the end would be here. Either induced, provoked, or due
to natural causes. There was no use in denying it, or shutting
out its omnipresence. It would be as ludicrous as an aging
woman posing admiringly before a mirror, without seeing the
decay that it reflected. Or pretending that termite paths were
ornamental scrollwork that embellished the beams of a crum-
bling house.

> The living-dead despair or go crazy. Sobs, revolt, or an
> even more ridiculous "lust for life"—an absurd ballet of
> recalcitrant cadavers, gripping the edge of their coffins!
> . . . Me, I'm inhabited by death. And *it makes me
> laugh!* [2]

But only if he could laugh last. The end must not come
before he was finished, without his having spoken.

(But then, it had always been a frenetic race against

time. Which—in the past—had manifested itself in that nervous tic of consulting his watch constantly, but now was measured by the ticking away of his body clock, the growing fear that the master spring was wound to the breaking point.)

Everything that he had gathered during his last voyage must be recounted. By recollection in non-tranquillity.

And be transmuted into vast panoramas that told of the grotesque ending of the world. A new apocalypse according to a latter-day saint. In a manuscript illuminated with his own visions.

> Every creation carries inside it, with it, together with its birth, its own end, its assassination!
>
> (*RIG,* 8)

He sat in his uneasy chair. And began to formulate the final act of the dread and hilarious drama.

1953–1961

The rhythm of creation must be accelerated (in accord with the pace of his own approaching end). In less than a decade, five works emerged: a quartet of novels and an odd pamphlet—*art poétique*-defense-and-illustration of his style. Only in the equivalent span of time, before the war, had he labored with such energy though driven on by a quite different despair—where horror was still mitigated by triumph, abjectness by vigor, death by eroticism, and weariness by youth. Now, the the life forces were gone. All that remained to balance the black sun that shone upon his world, was laughter. But one that came from another side of his mouth than before: the last grimace of defiance which man uses to confront the fates.

"I feel the Weird Sisters scraping my thread . . ." he cried.[3]

As he felt himself sink, ever more quickly, into the

quicksand, his gasps were reserved only for the stories still to be told. All other efforts were meaningless in this diminishing circle—food, sleep, friendships, even attacks against enemies. He had no strength to spare for such dalliance.

> At a certain age, getting angry is futile . . . we're all going to take the train, that's that: the murderers and the murdered . . . the same train! *choo!* . . . *choo! !* the machine . . . any hour, any minute. . . .
>
> (*RIG,* 38)

His gaze was directed toward a far bloodier horizon. Besides, the sun might vanish in a flash, as though a light-cord had been pulled.

His cry could not freeze in midair.

With one sweep of his large, gnarled hand, he pushed aside all other considerations.

The empty table awaited the inscriptions of doom.

1952–1954

It began with a tale of the end of his city.[4]

The story of an infernal night in which all possible horrors were unleashed against Montmartre, Céline's homeground. By Jules, the avenging angel (disguised as a crippled satyr) who sat atop the great windmill, as in a crow's nest, and raised his flaming hands to the sky in invitation to disaster. Houses trembled. The clouds poured forth a rain of fire. The skies split open. A great earthquake rocked the foundation of the hill (of martyrs from which it had gotten its name). The basilica of the Sacré-Coeur turned upside down; its egg-shaped dome pointed into the ground instead of aspiring to the stars. The rising tempest carried off the enormous bell which it had taken sixty-five horses to carry uphill.[5]

Everything was ripped apart by the cataclysm, blown pell-mell into the clouds:

> . . . souls, bodies, cobblestones, gas meters, railroad stations . . . everything into the air! bottom up! in the clouds! get those crazy sights! the Opera! . . . the Panthéon, the Aqueduct! the Bois de Boulogne! . . . Ah, the Arc de Triomphe . . . completely upside down! the Unknown Soldier? Who's that Unknown? a skeleton suspended in the sky! by one foot! . . .
>
> (*NOR,* 99)

There followed the unleashing of all the elements. Floods rose, in red, green, blue torrents. Lava gushed from the depths of the earth. The water boiled and bubbled fiercely in the lakes and rivers; banks and fishermen flew up to the chimneys. Surely, the Deluge had come.[6]

Jules, "the king of horrors . . . their master," continued to conduct the various movements of the doomsday symphony. Sailing above Paris in a gondola, he directed the flying fortresses with his fiery hands, untouched by the blades of their propellers. Until the sky melted. And lay suddenly beneath their feet, like a gigantic quilt.[7]

He raised the trumpet to his lips. The sound brought down rains, floods, avalanches of even hotter fire. Lava flowed over the sides of the highest hill. The entire city was burning:

> Twenty *quartiers* were sizzling! the Luxembourg was reduced to a rose! a burning rosebush! . . . the Académie melted . . . beige . . . green . . . dripped down to the Quai . . . to the Seine . . . its cupola floats for a moment . . . turns over! . . . sinks! . . . Ah, and the Madeleine and Chamber of Deputies are flying away . . . swollen balloons . . . they rise a little . . . get their balance . . . pass by, all blue! red! white! explode! . . . Other artifices follow! tracing bullets, far away . . . with the most original trajectories . . . spi-

rals! . . . they look as if they were sewing the clouds
. . . sewing them together . . . hemming them! . . .
with blue! . . . mauve! canary yellow!

(*NOR,* 110–111)

And sounds followed, no less phantasmagorical than the sights:

An enormity of cymbals . . . as if the Sky, the Earth
were struck against each other! . . .

(*NOR,* 111)

Volcanoes and earthquakes created dread thunder. Mines, underground vaults, crypts, edifices caved in. A whole hill was rent asunder. A gigantic chasm opened before them. No escape seemed possible. Only two choices of doom: to be catapulted up to the stars, or sucked into the void below.[8]

Jules raised his trumpet once more. The Last Judgment seemed imminent.[9]

Yet, in the midst of this world about to end, syncopated with the music of annihilation, there rose the grotesque chorus of imbecilic voices—the tender imprecations of a wife to her elephantine mate: "Don't budge, André, don't budge!"; the cruel invectives of a child toward her absurdly faithful dog; the cajoling cries of women to their sadistic lovers; the exclamations of hatred for one's neighbors; the sentimental strains of popular songs hummed *in extremis*.

The first note had been struck. The initial chapter of the Apocalypse according to St. Ferdinand was written.

It remained to be seen whether it would be classed among the apocrypha.

1954

Its apparition was greeted with derision. Many proclaimed that Céline had lost his powers, his high-voltage tension, the mastery over words. Seeing some just retribution in the fact that he dragged his wings like a land-bound albatross. And that his voice was broken. —An impotent beast of the Apocalypse whose cry need not be heeded.

For a moment, he was stunned. It seemed impossible to recover from such attacks, or retort as in the past (when even prison could not break his defiance):

> I don't give a bloody damn what an editor thinks of my books—I wouldn't even think of asking his opinion— his taste has to be bad—otherwise he wouldn't hold that job of semi-grocer, semi-pimp—anything that sur- passes him, he execrates . . . just like an ape who mas- sacres everything he can't comprehend. . . .[10]

Perhaps the battle was lost. The odds appeared overwhelm- ing. He could not stand up against the defeat of his work, when everything else was also failing. At least in exile, the hope of a literary comeback had sustained him. Or the illusion.

Now there was no corner into which his pride could retreat.

Shameful suggestions—disguised as sanctimonious coun- sel—came at him from every side: to give publicity inter- views; republish old works to cater to the growing crop of cinemaphiles;[11] to attend literary cocktails where he might ingratiate himself to editors—in a word, to become an ac- commodating clown.

He retreated, his back against the sullied wall, and began to snarl. As even decrepit *fauves* will, if forced beyond the point of endurance. No matter how desperate the odds or futile their struggle.

1955

The book was small but vitriolic. It contained his poetic testament: an angry settling of accounts with didactic professors and all the other inept surveyors of his works; an affirmation of his still-formidable stylistic powers. But not formulated in treatise fashion or high-flown language, for laughter must be mingled with terror even here (the same need must have spurred Villon on)—in a series of outrageous, imaginary interviews[12] which had the overtones of a soliloquy directed against an enemy who voiced all the doubts and failures he had internalized.

Through it, he would achieve vindication; catharsis through humor; power over the intellectual-ineffectuals by virtue of invectives. And victory by force of words: the irrepressible war-machine he had devised (the "underground of the emotions") to thrust the reader into a cage of style, render him helpless and willing—force, seduce, rape him if necessary—submissive to the virile thrusts of language.

He must have known that he was resorting to a familiar weapon. Whose form and intent were not unlike the pamphlets of the past, except that now he aimed to demolish— not political systems, racial formations, or medical iniquities —but all literature other than his own.

I write in order to make the others unreadable. . . .

he would one day admit.[13] But he had already passed his pitiless judgment upon them:

Gide is a notary . . . no poetic trance in him at all, except at the sight of a Bedouin's ass. . . .

Sartre is a maniac of the "self." . . . He renders us some service, by vulgarizing certain forms of audacity . . . that puppet with his hands full of parchments. . . .

Giono . . . a delirious nature bard with a huge dose of artifice. . . . He would have triumphed, if only he had been born an Englishman . . . in French, he makes one laugh—he's a pain . . . Rabindrathagorist [*sic*] of the leeks. . . .

That pretentious egomaniac Jules Romains is a joke
. . . Montherlant too—Sacha Guitry, of course—and
Aragon, the next Commissar of the People of Letters
. . . Mauriac the Jesuit—Malraux, the darling of De
Gaulle—all a bunch of paranoiacs fit for strait jackets
—but crammed full of prevailing notions, vast concepts,
remedies for the human condition. . . .

That poor Cendrars has been trying to write a novel for
thirty years. He'll never make it—nor will Miller.

Claudel, Cocteau, Mauriac, Colette, and a lot of others
were positively indulged by the Nazis. . . . They also
adored Giraudoux.

Proust explains too much for my taste—300 pages just
to inform us that Tutur fucks Tatave up the ass, that's
too long. . . .

The Talmud is constructed, conceived just like the novels of Proust, twisted, arabescoid [*sic*] . . . a disorderly
mosaic . . . without head or tail. From which end
should one grab it? . . . the work of a caterpillar
which crawls, returns, twists around, forgets nothing. . . .[14]

He railed against all those that had not "paid" like he had.
Who dared to write without having put a price on their own
heads or sounded the depths of despair:

The music of Time changes and is never the same from
one century to the next—it's death alone which can furnish this music—one must pay—it is hideous and sad.

As for all those jabberers of literature, they don't understand a thing about it—even the most committed—the
most rabid of them. . . . They resemble the people
who, long ago, used to taste the urine to determine
fever. The thermometer is what's needed—they don't
even suspect that—don't want to admit it—so they go
on guzzling urine—shit! [15]

He would prove his physician's skill by further blood-letting. And arise as the only true prophet amidst an assembly of false augurers.

It was time to launch into the final tirades that spelt out the elements of doom. And raise his hand to trace the dread words on the wall. Slowly. With great effort. At the risk of self-immolation.

> It takes me two years to get a book done, because I start each sentence ten, twenty times over. . . . And the poor cretins who think I improvise! . . . It's all measured down to the last millimeter, man! . . . The only thing is, it's killing me. . . .[16]

1955–1961

The last trilogy was taking form. Drawing its strength from his body; growing as he withered. Leechlike, it swelled as he was drained. He knew that it would kill him, as surely as a bullet in exaggeratedly slow motion, or the blade of an ax that takes five years to fall.

But with a rhythm of creation as relentless as the blows that fell giant oaks. Three books in half a decade. A cycle of endings that began with the gates of France clanging shut and led to the north, the land of prison and exile.[17] From one maw of hell to another. A dance of death, performed under death's eyes; filled with the drumbeat of annihilation— the trembling earth that opened in successive bursts under one's feet; the chaotic rhythm of the bombs falling, as if programmed in random sequence; the boiling innards of the world breaking through at irregular intervals.

The inner nightmare world he had long harbored, now proved to be real fiction. A prophecy of doom all too well fulfilled.

Dates and events were, quite naturally, subject to upheaval. Chronology, that simplistic traditional cope founded
on linear hopes of survival and the belief in an ordered motion of the spheres, had to be abandoned. Instead, a jumbled
no-man's-land in which pieces of puzzles flew about like limbs
severed in an explosion. Without identity, links, clues to their
origin. It was a mosaic of chaos, in which each fragment
mirrored a different species of horror; a splintered image
where every jagged morsel became a jab to the heart or
bowels:

Inquisitorial cretins, epileptic assassins, flagellants on
horseback, orgiastic death-cultists, mongoloid dwarfs, fake
surgeons and anachronistic heretics, weeping maidens that
trailed their silken hair in the outpour of urinals, parturient
nymphs, giant pallbearers and female executioners in red
boots, hellhounds and martyred mares, prisoners chained to
resemble blood sausages, princesses with pink parasols who
emerged from subterranean passageways, ministers with inflamed prostates, pyromaniacs and imitation Jesuses; prosthetic phalluses, cadavers in cesspools, funeral trains decked
out as for a Mardi gras, Charon's bark and the auguries of
crows, perverts and saintly cats, hunting horns and lyre-
birds; cartomancy and castration, cacophony among cattle
cars, nettles and cyanide.

A whole world that had taken so great a fall that nothing could put it together again.

In which even language had tumbled off the last remaining
traditional wall. And rhythms—savagely staccato, limping,
syncopated with silence—spoke of the fragmentation of the
universe, the maze of feeling, of thought, from which there
was no exit. Tones alternated ruthlessly—from vicious to
tender; hilarity gave way to tragedy, delirium to detailed

realism. The very words seemed to hasten toward annihilation. Slang, engendered by violence, carried within it the germ of its own destruction:

> Slang . . . consists of images born of hate, it's hate which creates it. . . .
>
> What's more, slang can't remain alive, because it's not a structure, it's like that house I knew in Berlin, where the walls had crevices thirty feet wide, but the doors could no longer be opened. . . .[18]

Neologisms too, and other forms of word inventions, flashed into life for an instant on the page, the better to let you contemplate their rapid demise. And imply their fragile hold on existence, their readiness to topple into the void. (Like that other house in Berlin whose odd appearance—the top story suspended like a hammock above the chasm below—was a constant reminder of its imminent fall.[19]

Yet, the constantly varying pace never allowed one to become numb or indifferent to this dying. It jarred one awake, like a pail of ice water thrown into the victim's face between torture sessions. Produced new awareness to inflict further pain. With the infernal skill of the master inquisitor.

From it all, a vast sense of panic arose. As though the entire world had become a trap. Where steps taken forward or back, leaps into the air and the halting limp of the maimed, rigadoon or frantic blindman's buff, lead nowhere; and retreats or advances in time are futile in this enclosure of an everlasting present.

Finally, one tires even of the apocalypse. For heaven and hell are obviously doors that can no longer be opened. Despite the crevices in the world-edifice that yawn on every side. Emptied of judgment, and without end, until it becomes nothing but a statement of diminishing returns. A vast abnegation. World without end, ending.

1960

Within this center of the holocaust, in the eye of the
tornado, he had carved out his world. And built his last fictional kingdom.

> Curiosity got me into it. Curiosity can be costly. I've be-
> come a chronicler, a tragic chronicler. Most writers look
> for tragedy but can't find it. The Greeks, you'll say. The
> Greek tragic poets were under the impression that they
> communed with the gods . . . so you see . . . hell,
> it's not every day that you get a chance to ring up the
> gods. . . .
>
> There's been a cataclysm. . . . I was in the middle of
> it . . . I got something out of it. . . .[20]

He had chosen the perfect culminating scene for his
talents. Where he could move among the actors—seer and
seen—record and partake of the hideous revelry. Only in
such a setting could tragedy reign (Racine had known it;
for him also, "tragedy is the dance before death"). The steps
followed a predetermined pattern—as ancient as the maze-
dance whose ritual demanded maiming, the sacrifice of victims, violent death before transfiguration.

He plunged ever more deeply into a labyrinth of castles,
tree-groves, ghost cities, cemeteries, and prisons. From which
only the thread of his art—stretched to impossible tautness,
wearing and ever ready to snap—could lead him into the
light.

And ventured into the deepest pits of a sulfurous inferno, compared to which, some said, "Sartre's hell was
nothing but a girls' finishing school." [21] Where every jest
became a shot of vitriol, each breath was wrenched from
lungs constrained by succubi, and every hope turned grotesque by bouts of mocking laughter.

To tell his story with clinical precision, as the moribund physician of doom. Himself as corrupt as those whose symptoms of putrefaction he notes. (His method in the past, some argued, had helped him to resist death: by inoculating life with the germs of decay, he had created a vaccine that immunized him against it; and cured his life by injecting it with small doses of evil—homeopathy of the most elementary kind).[22] Now, however, the vaccine had worn off and he had not renewed it. His own rotting carcass was offered up for all to see, in the midst of a decomposing world. No longer exempt from the general evil: avowed Azazel and Beelzebub, leading a horde of scapegoats and devils. Bearer and progenitor of guilty acts. Doomed among the doomed. In the dawn of an impossible judgment day.

As he moved toward his own death, he saw the world ending. As though his personal nightmare still demanded to be applied to life, like some dread decalcomania. And all must share his march to oblivion:

> Oh, yes, I tell myself, soon everything will be finished . . . ouf! . . . *we've seen enough* . . . at sixty and some odd years, what does one care about the worst super-bomb H? . . . Z? . . . Y?. . . .[23]

(He began to contemplate his exit scene. Sometimes with fury, sometimes in a more nostalgic vein, often with the defiance of a man who reserves the right of dying as he chooses—robbing his enemies of the satisfaction of murdering him, and those who feigned concern, of selecting a practical mode of suicide:

> . . . another spring . . . two . . . three . . . I won't be here anymore . . . it'll be too late. . . . I'll have died a natural death. . . .

(CAS, 13)

> . . . gas! . . . not so good! . . . they don't always
> make it . . . far from it! . . . they get revived . . .
> they don't die but they suffer plenty . . . on the way
> out and on the way back . . . a thousand deaths, a
> thousand recoveries! and the smell! . . . no, gas is a
> bad business . . . the safest method, take it from me,
> I've been consulted a hundred times, is a hunting rifle in
> your mouth! stuck in deep! . . . and bang! . . . you
> blow your brains out . . . one drawback: the mess!
> . . . the furniture, the ceiling! brains and blood clots.
> . . . Prison . . . that's another way of crossing out
> your existence! . . . Suicide little by little. . . .
>
> . . . as for me, I'll finish myself off in the garden . . .
> out there . . . plenty of room . . . or maybe the cel-
> lar would be better? . . . The police will investigate
> . . . cause of suicide? . . . neurasthenia. . . .
>
> (*CAS,* 32–33)

And thus he played the game of his own disappearance; explored the various endings of the drama.)

But he was not quite ready to make the exit. The play could
not end without his writing and directing the finale.

"I'll make your prison cells sing!" [24] he vowed.

—Sing a song of death wails, a pocketful of cyanide,
a swarm of ravens, trapped in fire. Of a king who was in his
Baltic hut, counting out his days; a queen in her leotard,
wearing out her shoes. When the gates were opened, the
ravens began to croak. Oh, wasn't it a lovely dish to set before the world.—

Nor would he allow his work to come to a conclusion. Even
when death stopped the moving hand, it would continue to
rankle the living. Open-ended as a stream of black water
(flaunting its sewer origins, its obvious products of pollu-

tion), it emptied forever into the sea. All of his books had insured such continuity, for none had ever ended. The last words of every one spelled only a momentary pause—an intermission during which strength was gathered—in order to plunge more deeply still into another facet of suffering; a deceptive curtain call, which implied that the show was permanent, and any respite simply a delay that prepared for a sharpened awareness of pain.

Even after his death, his shriek would continue to hang in the air, calling us fiendishly, each by our own, most shameful name.[25] As we continue having to recognize our abject images in the mirror of man.

1969

Even the fate of his last novel had this effect. For it left the final cry of damnation hanging midair for more than seven years. Silence seemed to have closed over Céline. The voice appeared to have been successfully stilled. Yet rumors circulated, crisscrossed, clashed, canceled each other out: "Rigodon" had burned; it had disappeared; it was lost or stolen; parts of it had been salvaged; it was intact but hidden for safekeeping. The manuscript taunted, tantalized, baited the waiting audience; making it writhe in a trap from which escape was impossible, and the *coup de grâce* was nowhere in sight.

A rigadoon as devastating as the one described throughout its pages.

When it finally appeared, it contained the disconcerting assurance that Céline's last word would not be spoken. For there was no ending, even posthumously. The concluding phrase only exposed a series of panoramas of limitless number; the fall of one screen revealed an infinity of other, unspoken perspectives of terror. And ever larger circles of hell.

True, the voice had sunk almost to a whisper. Broken, stumbling (and perhaps worked over by alien hands)[26] phrases, and halftones that betrayed its ailing nature, gave it the character of a deathbed confession. Or the subdued despair of a last testament.

But it bequeathed despair also to those who survived. Fulfilling his earliest oracles of doom. And giving substance to his dream of all-engulfing chaos.

1961

In the end, he had conquered his land. And established his kingdom in a shipwrecked world. Death could now exercise its dictatorial functions, reign free of every former constraint.

The catastrophic cycle was approaching culmination. The wheel of misfortune had come full turn, before it ground to a stop. Man's one-way street was established as an unequivocal cul-de-sac. The game of blood-poker had claimed almost all the players.

The fair grounds were emptying out. The tents were ready to fold. For all the attractions there had long been working at a deficit. The aerialist was no longer in demand; the bareback riders had fallen into disfavor; the ballerina was aging; even the fire-eaters and snake-charmers were outmoded now. Perhaps a hunger-artist might still draw a small crowd. Certainly, the freak show alone would thrive and multiply.

The barker's voice rose in a dread and jubilant cry:

"Time to return to the void!"

It was a call which resounded through the ruins (of his own life and the world at large). Celebrating the rebirth of nothingness. Mingling his own coming extinction with total annihilation. Ready to quench an old thirst for the dissolution of being, the dispersion of atoms, which had already plagued him three decades ago.

> That body of ours, that travesty of banal and agitated molecules, revolts constantly against this hideous farce of enduring. They want to get lost, as fast as they can, within the universe, those darling molecules of ours! They suffer from being only "us," cuckolded of infinity. If one had any courage, one would explode. . . . Our cherished atomic torture is locked up in our very skin, together with our pride.
>
> *(VOY, 333)*

The only relief in sight was the return to original chaos, into the dark of non-being.

But a final outcry must accompany the dissolution. The old sin of pride demanded that only he furnish the fitting accompaniment to this plunge into oblivion.

Before the silence became complete, one haunting scene would evoke the terror and beauty of this sinking world:

It was in the center of Copenhagen, in a public garden. His body felt emptied of all its substance, almost transparent. Only where his fingers and ankles crossed, did there remain a vestige of feeling. All the scenes were growing numb. Only the eye still perceived (not outer forms, but those that appear to the seer) a few shadowy semblances of life.

> There . . . in the grass, a bird . . . but not the usual kind . . . one would call him "rare" in any zoo . . . a bird about the size of a duck, but half pink, half black . . . and fluffy! its feathers all in an uproar . . . I look further in the distance . . . another one! that one I know! . . . I saw him first! an ibis . . . funny duck for this region . . . and a heron! . . . that one, surely not a native of Denmark! . . . now a peacock

. . . they're deliberately approaching . . . and a lyre-
bird . . . they have come to be fed . . . though the
place is certainly not inviting, ruins, thorns, pebbles . . .
still another! . . . this time, a toucan . . . they're ten
. . . twelve feet away . . . they'd become tame if one
had something to give them, but truly, truly, there's
nothing left to give . . . surrounded by birds, like this,
what if someone came . . . he'd wonder what we're
doing to them, if we weren't perhaps enchanters, bird
charmers. . . .

(*RIG*, 313)

Until the very last, he would proclaim the right to cast
spells; to penetrate into the underworld and return victorious
though empty-handed; to reveal secrets that would make the
world topple. To ordain himself herald of an apocalypse
that would not spare him its cataclysms.

Like any ancient sacred king, submitting to sacrifice
so that his voice might be heard—refined of being—when
he had been rent asunder. For only at this price could Orphic
melodies ring out, and Osiris, Hercules, Atys, Dionysus prevail. Or, for that matter, the poet whose face is covered by
a bloody stancher.

Finished, it's finished, nearly finished, it must be nearly finished.

S. BECKETT

11

ENDGAMES

What they call my life . . . is . . .
just my way of being dead,
nearly dead, already dead.[1]

1961

It was a day or so before the end. The visitor sat looking at him, outlined against the darkening trees.

His face was that of an old country doctor, worn out,
full of despair, human from having grimaced so much
. . . it evoked the startling beauty of a mask.[2]

One could sense that the play was coming to a close.
The moments stretched into an interminable pause before
the curtain fall: the interim in which one must divest oneself
of life, let all its antics fall away (grain upon grain), certain
in the knowledge that one can't be punished anymore. That
seeds would never sprout again; sight was failing; the world
was corpsed; that soon there would be no more speech.

In the diminishing light, the wait continued. Rendered
more tolerable only by painkillers (the 2 ccs. of morphine,
greatest of all lullabies, which he had come to put to ritual,
almost sacramental use).[3] And when these also failed, by the
telling of tales.

For dying is a very demanding task. A role that takes infinite skill to play; and must be paid for, more dearly than all the rest. —This was not news to him. He had known it as long as a quarter of a century ago:

> Kicking in isn't free of charge. A beautiful shroud embroidered with tales—that's what the Pale Lady wants. The last gasp is very exacting. It's the last Movie. . . . I'll hear my ticker give its last slobbery *pfutt* . . . and then plop! . . . It'll be all over. They'll open it up to check . . . on that sloping table. . . . They won't see my beautiful legend, nor my music either. The Pale Lady will have taken it all. . . . Here I am, Madame, I'll say to her, you're the greatest connoisseur of all. . . .
>
> (*DIP,* 41)

He now prepared to play his endgame before her discerning gaze. With every flourish he could muster; and the entire array of masks he had ever worn. Tragedian and ham; poet and buffoon; pauper and dying king. Unable to breathe his last with the utter simplicity of animals. Who did not have to win over the dread muse, nor pay a price for the cessation of being.

> The trouble with men's death agonies is the song and dance . . . a man is always on the stage . . . even the simplest. . . .
>
> (*CAS,* 140)

1951–1961

The road to death was full of roles to be played (offerings and divertissements; trifles intended to tide one over). He undertook them all. Sometimes brazenly, sometimes feigning indifference or shyness. Ambivalent in his mode of action. Protesting too much, for desire not to transpire in his words.

The prospect of being filmed, for example, alarmed and

intrigued him. After the first gruff refusal, he hastened to write:

January 23, 1960

Dear Sir,
    The trouble is that I'm not an actor at all. . . .
*I'm only a worker who relates to things—paper, pencil
—but not to men. That's another profession, entirely!
I'm a disaster on stage, it's no place for me! . . .*
    *But, if you want to talk to me, come any evening
towards 4 o'clock.*
    I'm always there.

*Very cordially,
L.-F. Destouches*[4]

But when they attempted to photograph him, he had another impulse of recoil:

Oh . . . that's a bad joke. I'm against iconography.
I'm a Mohammedan. No photos of me . . . I don't
like that business at all! [5]

(Perhaps he would have been less Mohammedan in his views if some vestige of vanity did not rebel at the way his appearance had deteriorated with age—despite his mocking self-portraits:

I don't often look in the mirror it's true, but the few
times I did, in the course of the years, I found that I was
getting uglier and uglier . . . that was also my father's
opinion . . . he found me hideous . . . advised me to
grow a beard. . . .

(*EPY*, 12)

Or if the descriptions usually given of him were less harsh.)
    Abundant word-portraits had appeared, similar in tone, and usually depicting him as a faintly repugnant, aging vagabond.

Some sounded like the descriptions issued in the "Wanted for . . ." posters of criminals:

> Sixty-seven years old, sorrowful face, hands swollen, deformed by illness, three sweaters, a battle-jacket plus a cape, sealskin slippers . . . surrounded by animals.[6]

Some betrayed revulsion mingled with pity:

> An old gardener who had been loading manure, approached, spewing forth dreadful curses at the dogs. . . . The supposed gardener is wrapped in a filthy cape out of which a lined face emerges, the face of a weary anchorite in which the sad mouth contrasts with the half-closed lids through which a hard flame sometimes shoots. It's Doctor Destouches, better known as Louis-Ferdinand Céline. . . .[7]

Others were frankly jubilant when describing him in his dilapidated state (while slyly hinting at depravity):

> He's pretty broken-down, one must admit. His own mother wouldn't recognize him. . . . He has the head of a dog, a growth of grayish stubble. Some sort of shirt hidden by a large dark blue scarf, a sheepskin vest, a pair of brown wool pants with a shapeless bottom. In the back, as he walks, the belt hangs down to the level of what one presumes to be his buttocks. . . . In the front, the trousers are held up by a rope; the fly is permanently open unto the long gray underwear. There are large stains which have trickled down almost to the knees, maybe in Denmark, maybe before.[8]

Not that he spent his time trying to contradict them. Instead, he often seemed to agree to play this role. It was as if he merged his own wrecked state with the abject nature of his best-known protagonist, and took on the mask of Ferdinand-Bardamu (that pilgrim of all disasters). Adding stories in illustration of this fact, as if he were attentively watching his own decomposition, noting its progress, and reporting the events which supported it by means of evidence:

> Last week, they threw me out of a café in Paris. Al-
> though I was a bit better turned out than now. As I ap-
> proached the bar, the owner said to me: "No, no, not
> here, let's go, let's go . . ." And he led me to the door.
> And yet, it was a most humble establishment, with very
> modest customers. . . .[9]

But the tyranny of his word still reigned unchallenged. As
soon as he began to speak, the paltry body was effaced by
the powerful flow of his monologue.

His improvisations were so apt, so full of mastery that
almost none could tell whether they were aimed to terrify,
amuse, charm, devastate. Or simply embroidered smoke
screens behind which his vulnerable being could cower.
Words, grimaces, gestures, never ceased to do his bidding.

He seemed to take malicious delight in leading intruders
(and who was not an intruder?) astray. Sometimes, by giving them an overpowering feeling of guilt. A game especially
piquant, when the circumstances did not warrant such sense
of culpability at all. As when a friendly critic had been lulled
into a state of confidence and sat, smilingly expectant in his
garden:

> We were speaking about a subject of the greatest inter-
> est, full of nuances, delicacy, in just the right tone; a
> subject which it had taken me a great deal of trouble to
> introduce. . . . Suddenly, thunder rumbles in the sky!
> Insistent, unrelenting thunder.
>
> The helicopter. . . .
>
> We find ourselves reduced to using the language of deaf-
> mutes: you can imagine how useful that is for metaphys-
> ical discussions. . . .
>
> —"It's Belgian," Céline says with disgust.
> You don't exactly understand what lesson should be
> drawn from this determination of nationality.

—"It's Belgian," he repeats. "That flying machine is Belgian!"

He looks at you with severity. And if, by some chance you were born in Belgium, which can happen to anybody, you start feeling responsible. . . . In less than half a day . . . you would be convinced that you were morally at fault. . . .

the critic reported later, apparently still abashed by the experience.[10]

Metaphysical discussions were hateful enough, but when questioners pried into his own life, he reared up in fury. The defense then consisted of inventing any plausible tale—or an implausible one, so well told and so seriously presented that it resembled the truth—that could be offered as bait. They snapped it up, swallowed it whole, got hooked and smugly made their getaway. Convinced that they had captured a trophy, one of his prize secrets. So confident that some spread it as gospel, a revelation to be reveled in, an inside story straight from Céline's innards. It was repeated, even put into print—where it gained further authenticity—, perpetuated and magnified.

(One suspects that such was the case of the myth of Céline's trepanation, until recently in use.)[11]

Sometimes, however, his patience wore thin and the game was not worth the effort it took to play. To be asked to provide details about his past life, was the final straw.

"Invent them!" he snapped. "Use my books!" [12]

For he saw through their motives. And was convinced that they had come, either to observe him as some curious wild beast, or to enjoy his grilling.

They wanted me to do an acrobatic act on the high wire, up there at a height of a hundred and fifty feet, all alone, exposed, in the glare of the projectors; to have me play the pig, rolling in its own muck. . . .

(a sight as thrilling as the tormented pig which had appeared, twenty-five years earlier, in *Voyage au bout de la nuit.*)

His reactions to such trials varied. Sometimes, he seemed indifferent to the outcome:

> I gave in to my habitual mania for sacrifice. I became the perfect sponge, nice and slimy. They're drooling with joy over that. It doesn't matter. . . . I don't give a damn about my image.[13]

Or proceeded to exaggerate the hideousness they had come to see. He took a pose straight out of a Kafkaesque nightmare; became the monster who was an incarnation of cowardice and hate. Enlarging upon their vision, as though he were himself a fictional construct.

But he also felt an unwarranted sense of triumph at times (in face of evidence to the contrary which stared him in the face):

> How they wanted to hear my usual outrages and obscenities! . . . But they didn't manage to sniff out or uncover a thing. . . . You know, when one's been tracked down by the world for so many years, inside the cage and out, one's vocabulary becomes measured down to the last millimeter. . . . How could those baboons hope to surprise me? I could teach them a thing or two! Those heavy-handed morons. . . .[14]

Or justified his actions by comparing them to the antics of a weary jester:

> When one doesn't have *the strength,* one is forced to play *the clown* . . . better sitting down than standing up![15]

It was a game which he clung to, knowing the power of laughter. (Had it not, in the past, saved his life?) It became almost a reflex in the face of their goading, or the siege they laid to his house with film cameras, microphones, and arc lights.

As in the instance when one of them decided to "televise" him. Before they seated him in a broken-down armchair near his worktable where the technicians had conspicuously placed the manuscript of his next novel, and trained the enormous eye of the camera on his face. And he was still able to clown:

> No, let's not speak of the Apocalypse . . . (he drawled) let's speak of light things (he imitated the flight of a butterfly with his hands).

But as the session continued, he was no longer able to sustain this tone. He grimaced, cursed, snapped back at those who baited him with such phrases as: "Louis-Ferdinand Céline, you're a peculiar character. You excite strong passions. Your works, your ideas, your way of life, have increased your chances of being despised. . . ." Then threw supplicating glances at his tormenters, as if asking them why he was being subjected to this slow fire. Little by little, however, he gave in and let himself be led to confess—a victim conscious of descending into the lowest depths of his being. And brought forth feelings that were startling in their rawness, purity, and truth.[16]

It was not unusual for him to protest before allowing himself to speak of those matters which were central to him. To grumble, for example:

> I'm being asked to speak of my masterpieces in the setting of an electric chair . . . !

before voicing his convictions on style, the atrophy of the French language, the lack of faith, warmth, and enthusiasm of his people which made them cling dully to the past.[17]

Somehow, he protested too much.

There was also some glee, a sly sense of triumph in being heard, consulted, solicited, even misunderstood. Undoubtedly, also, the exhilaration of playacting; the vanity which leads old actors to undertake even the most grotesque roles.

The effect he had upon others could not have become totally indifferent to him. It passed the time—just as pain and passion did. One could not neglect a single one of the figures in the dance before death.

Despite his rantings that these appearances were necessary publicity for his books, that he was being forced to "play the game," [18] the game remained a profoundly personal one. Nor had it changed (except in the interpretations he chose to give) in the past forty years. Voyeur, actor, and dying king were masks that illustrated, in varying guise, the triple nature of his face.

The literary games had not radically changed either. Except, perhaps, in that his fears and cautions had somewhat increased:

Whereas, in pre-exile days, he had worn the brief case containing his manuscripts chained to his wrist, he now lived in constant dread of losing them despite the most extravagant precautions. As letters such as the following show:

> *Dear Marie,*
> *With a lot of fear and trembling I sent you the first 56 pages of* Féerie *by "special delivery". . . . Would you be kind enough to inform me immediately when they have arrived. Thanks!*
> *I think that the original copy (the beautiful one) should be reserved for your own use; send me one carbon. Put another carbon in your vault—as for the fourth, think of someone who can be trusted to keep it in a safe place. . . .* [19]

He had not exercised such caution with either his gold or his own life. But then, more exacting care had always been given to his manuscripts than to those other matters. Thousands upon thousands of pages yielded the final versions of several hundreds that constituted a book. No effort, no ferocity was spared in perfecting the smallest phrase.

> One must correct, down to the last carat . . . savagely. . . .

he roared. If he decided to change a word, it never sufficed to merely replace it with another. He recomposed the entire sentence, and often the neighboring ones also, according to the demands of his "cadence." (Often, tapping his foot as though he were counting the beat.) Sometimes, the attack occurred hours later; a night, or several days, might pass. Then, he would telephone Marie, ask her to read the specific phrase, and proceed to effect the transformation. His inventions were prodigious; but never subject to any rule. When Marie, puzzled by his inconsistencies in the spelling of a word, objected that he had switched within the space of a few pages, he shouted:

> So what! . . . if one has several wives, why would one always want to sleep with the same one? [20]

In the end, his ear seemed to have become more sensitive than his eye. His "music" revealed itself most profoundly in this way. Just as it did in his rare readings of his work. Suddenly, it was no longer a jester who spoke, or a ham actor playing to those who writhe in the pit. A voice which few ever heard, now rose to give his phrases their true meaning:

> He read very slowly, spacing the words, putting more wisdom and greater kindness into them than one might imagine; full of real gravity with many solemn allusions and undertones. No longer the slightest trace of clowning. The king's fool, the village idiot mourns a death in the family. Or he is meditating on grave matters. . . .
> As though the unlucky poet, assured of the final ef-

fect of the curse which weighs upon him, has ceased to feign madness. Hamlet after the scene with the actors. . . .[21]

However, the moment of truth could not be allowed to continue. A mask of derision was almost instantly clapped on. As though he had been caught waxing lyrical and must counter with harshness. Deny the seriousness of his calling.

> "What a lousy profession . . . ," [he muttered]. Me and my three dots . . . my supposedly original style! . . . all the real writers will tell you what to think of it! . . . but what does the grocer think of it? . . . that's what counts! . . . that gives me food for meditation! Hamlet of the carrots. . . . I meditate up here in my garden . . . about carrots and taxes. . . .
>
> *(CAS,* 338)

Lower it to the level of breadwinning only. Which would cease instantly, if only the world were not so full of grocery bills.

> Good Lord, how nice it would be . . . never to say another word, never to write anything again, to be left completely alone . . . to go somewhere by the seashore to die . . . absolutely at peace, forgotten . . . but look here, Toto, how about the grub? . . . trumpets and bass drum! . . . get up on those ropes, you old clown! . . . keep moving! . . . higher! . . .
>
> *(CAS,* 228)

Obviously the circus was not ready to close. He was condemned to the ring, until the last.

And so, he continued to climb the paper ropes, knowing that each completed work was only a platform on which he was allowed to rest for an instant, before the next ascension began. (Even when death was imminent, he spoke of his next project—"the last one, irrevocably the last. It'll be called

'The Ambassadress' . . .")[22] And cursed those who forced
him to go on—the circus owner, the ringmaster, the other
performing clowns, the whole rotten freak show of life.

His publisher irritated him most, who kept him going
through his paces, with whip and chair, debts and deadlines,
monthly doles and promises of becoming entombed alive in
the Pléïade.[23]

His revenge was to insult Gallimard in the very pages
of the works he published. (The typesetters must have re-
galed themselves as heartily at his curses, as those who had
composed the pages of *Voyage au bout de la nuit*.) While
nostalgically recalling Denoël out of the past, to contrast him
with his present-day counterpart:

> Oh, he [Denoël] had his nasty ways . . . ! There's no
> denying it, he sold you down the river when necessary
> . . . he tied you hand and foot, he sold you out . . .
> but he had one saving grace . . . his passion for litera-
> ture . . . respect for writers. . . .

While

> Achille Brottin[24] is your sordid grocer, an implacable
> idiot . . . the only thing he can think about is his
> dough . . . all he reads is the financial page . . .
> his reading is done by the "Pin-Brain-Trust" . . . their
> idea of reading is to smoke, wash their feet, and play
> the trumpet! they decide heads or tails . . . who cares?
> one author more or less . . . they've got thousands in
> the cellar. . . .
>
> (*CAS*, 10)

But often, weariness crept even into his railing. All channels
into which pride could flow, had been blocked off. The field
of action was so diminished that there seemed no purpose
in moving. Writing and medicine were equally humiliating.

When out of sight of his audience, he shrank together.

Sat motionless for hours, in the center of the maze of bird-cages. Or took to his sofa, rolled himself in layers of wraps and covers, until he resembled a cocoon that has despaired of metamorphosis.

The overcoat, however, was the best shelter for ruminating his stories.

And somehow, there was never a dearth of overcoats.

> I bury myself . . . under the mountain of overcoats.
> . . . I don't remember how many overcoats! I'm poor in everything, but Christ, not in overcoats! That's what people who see our misery send us . . . they keep sending them . . . overcoats! they always have too many . . . oh, not overcoats you could wear, absolutely threadbare! You can't go out in them, but in bed with a fever you're very glad to have them!
>
> (*CAS*, 173)

They were the covers of despair, where one retired as to a shabby womb. To nurse one's nausea of the world, to gather a few dregs of solace. Or simply to wait for the impossible weariness to abate a little.

(Ferdinand had known this, thirty years ago, when he fled to his uncle's retreat, trembling with disgust at having seen life, knowing the score of negation already, at the end of his first youth.

> I was still shaking like a leaf. . . . He covered me all up, he buried me under a pile of overcoats. . . . I had all his bearskins on top of me. . . . There was a whole selection in the closet. . . . I kept on shivering just the same. . . .
>
> "If you get up, put on an overcoat. . . . Just reach into the pile, it doesn't matter which. . . . There's no shortage of coats. . . ."
>
> "No, Uncle."
>
> (*DIP*, 588)

The only difference now, was that the shape of his protector
had changed: from uncle Edouard to Lucette. And that a
more complex past fed his ruminations. Otherwise, the refusal of solace had remained the same:

> I never want anything. . . . I refuse everything. . . .
> I don't want a kiss . . . and I don't want a napkin.
> . . . I want to reminisce. . . . I want to be left alone
> . . . that's it . . . my memories . . . all the circum-
> stances . . . that's all I ask. . . .
>
> (*CAS,* 111)

As had the necessity to look. Even though from the bottom
of the heap, from the gray center of the cocoon.)

The eye opened—furtively alert at all times, though veiled
to the observer—and cast its penetrating gaze about, pierced
through appearances and seized upon truths despite their
masked nature and cosmetic embellishments.

> I look out the window. . . . I accuse other people of
> being voyeurs . . . but actually I'm hopeless . . . the
> complete peeper. . . . I can't stand being looked at
> . . . but I myself, I admit . . . I'm terrible . . .
> wherever I am . . . I look into the distance. . . .
>
> (*CAS,* 79)

A voyeur turned seer.

> Ah, those piercing eyes of mine!
>
> (*CAS,* 81)[25]

The third eye had become the organ of poetry. The
present scene diminished; gave way to larger panoramas,
more intense in imagery. The visions spread, unfolded out
of a simple incident, as infinity can be evoked by circles in
water which a mere pebble has set in motion.

He employed his otherwise diminished state to fabricate
a shroud that would inevitably be embroidered with tales.

Only when his lids finally closed (and coins pressed down on them assured his passage with the dread ferryman) would his seer's role be finished.

Now, the game was so absorbing that it negated all the rest: pride, solicitude, outer reality, life that raged somewhere beyond (or else had been reduced to ashes). He clung to it, all the more because the end was drawing near.

> Just a minute . . . I'm pretty far gone, I'm not through yet. . . . I wish the bed would cave in. . . . If I could only open a gash in it . . . a watercourse . . . and me and my bed would sink!
>
> (*CAS*, 111)

To drift to submarine depths or float upon it as on a vessel of hallucination. He would have been willing to go to any length to produce the necessary trance state.

His regime, for example, was carefully designed to such an end. He had reduced his food intake to the minimum (some farinaceous elements, tea, or water); prescribed nightly intestinal irrigations to rid his body of its poisons; allowed his migraines and insomnia to go almost unrelieved, so that the mind twisted and burned in its skull cage.

Until there was hardly anything left of his body. Nothing but a voice, that spoke of voyages untold; of phantoms and near-phantoms; of all the past suddenly become clear. In tales of a growing void, told in the void growing.

Endgames within a game of endings.

1963; 1964; 1969

As might be expected, the games were played posthumously also.

In 1963, Céline (who had been accused of sympathy

with the Germans and owed his original conviction and imprisonment to this fact) was convicted for libel by a Berlin
court. The book in question was *Nord*—with which he had
made his literary comeback in France—and the lawsuit had
been instituted by one of the characters who figured promi-
nently in the novel. One of the phantoms had reared its head:
Schertz and his family (whom Céline had long considered
extinct and buried behind the Iron Curtain) returned to
haunt the author beyond the grave. The case was won; a
heavy fine imposed on the author's estate; his publisher forced
to withdraw the book from circulation.[26] Henceforth, it had
to be published in changed form, somewhat mutilated to
avoid too-personal allusions, the names with their wonderfully macabre plays-on-words, toned down to anodyne versions of the originals.

A year later, the game was called "The Manuscript in the
Closet": one of Céline's best novels, written during the period
which many critics bemoaned as a gap in his writing career
(1937–1944), and considered either lost or nonexistent for
almost twenty years, suddenly turned up.

It was a strange story. In several versions: the first, that
Marie Canavaggia, Céline's secretary, had unearthed the
large manuscript one day, "while cleaning out an old
closet." [27] The second, provided by the lady herself, who
protested (and was still protesting five years after the event)[28]
that Céline had entrusted her with the manuscript before
leaving France in 1944; that she had hidden it; and, upon
the author's return from exile, offered to return the property
to him. "We'll see . . . we'll see . . ." he reputedly answered (while generally declaring that the manuscript had
been stolen). Mlle. Canavaggia also explained that she had
thought Céline indifferent to the work, since its first volume

(*Guignol's Band*) had not been too well received, and he did not seem eager to revert to the faraway past when many more pressing incidents were haunting him. She reiterated the fact that she had never forgotten about the existence of the manuscript. "It's true," she went on, "that I had hidden it too well and that it took me some time to find it again. But I have never lost anything that has been entrusted to me . . ." [29]

The story of the publication of the work (*Le Pont de Londres*) was as controversial as its discovery. After the manuscript had been put into the hands of Céline's widow and literary executor, she in turn, entrusted it to Robert Poulet (critic, writer and interviewer of the author). There were three packets of pages, which he studied assiduously, concluding that two were identical (although their pagination was at first confusing) and that the third was a more polished version which, however, stopped about two-thirds of the way in the story. —Perhaps one day the missing chapters would be found. —But now, he saw no other way than to tack the ending of the less polished (but complete) version onto the polished (but incomplete) one. It was a somewhat regrettable solution, he readily admitted.[30] Fortunately, no phantom of an angry Céline appeared, demanding "savage correction."

For a while, only fragments of his writing emerged here and there. In bookstores, other closets, trunks stored in various cellars. To be bought up by amateurs, speculators, and those concerned with bringing them to light through publication.

But no other novels "mysteriously" appeared.

The suspense about his last work continued. It was of course known that, on the day of his death, Céline had terminated "Rigodon." (There were even photos showing the handwritten final page.)[31] But the years passed, and still it did not appear. Almost eight years. While rumors around it multiplied, crossed, canceled each other out; grew wildly exorbitant at times. The fire at Meudon, in 1968, had added fuel to the more dismal conjectures.

When the book finally appeared in the spring of 1969, it seemed a minor miracle.

The manuscript's private life had been a complex and arduous one: upon recovering somewhat from Céline's death, his widow devoted long evenings (after her dance lessons) to photocopying the many bundles of pages. She removed the manuscript part by part from the enormous metal chest in which it was kept (so heavy, it took two people to move it), copied it with her unwieldy and primitive equipment; then replaced it into the improvised strongbox. Soon, rumors of thefts and the unexplained disappearance of objects around the house made her uneasy; she transferred the manuscript for safekeeping into the hands of Maître Naud (the lawyer who had once defended Céline in exile). It made the work slower and more difficult. And convinced her of the impossibility of tackling such a vast task alone.[32]

In 1965, she gave this account of its progress:

> It's four years now, since Louis' death, that we've been working on it. We pore over it, decipher it. . . . But it'll be ready very soon. To put the novel into its proper form hasn't been easy. We only have a first version. But a definitive one! Since he wrote with much difficulty, because of the pains in his arm, we've had a lot of trouble.
>
> *Qu.*:
> How did you proceed to work, exactly?
>
> *Ans.*:
> It's my lawyer who took care of it, who recopied it, by hand, with the help of his secretary, without changing anything, respecting everything. . . . Of course, there

are still some indecipherable words, but the essential thing is to get it finished.

Qu.:
What will you do about the indecipherable words?

Ans.:
I'll respect everything, that is to say that I won't replace them by others. Undoubtedly, they are words he had invented, and if we can't manage to uncover them, it's best to leave them blank. I'll have them photocopied and put them at the end of the book. . . .[33]

But more than three years passed, and still "Rigodon" had not appeared. And the story of its preparation and unveiling had changed. At its publication, it was the following:

Qu.:
How did it happen that *Rigodon* had to wait seven years before being published by Gallimard?

Ans.:
Céline didn't have time to recopy his manuscript; words that had been erased several times, and the handwriting which had often become difficult to read, caused by his ailing arm, made the re-transcription a delicate problem. This task was undertaken in two stages; I first gave the manuscript to a lawyer, Maître Damien, who did the hard job of clearing up the text, to which he devoted all his leisure hours; but a vast and delicate task remained. It was with Maître Gibault that the second phase of the labor was undertaken; there was still the problem of punctuation and of certain words that had remained incomprehensible. It was above all, a question of patience and honesty. We did not omit, add, or change anything. Céline had read me a large part of the book; thus we were able to find certain words, by the rhythm alone . . . we listened to find out if they sounded right. . . .

Qu.:
And those manuscript thefts of which Céline so often spoke? Can one expect to see entire novels suddenly reappear?

Ans.:

Yes. At least four or five sketches of manuscripts were
stolen. . . . But a large number of these documents
will only reappear after my death.[34]

(To date, Mme. Céline is alive and well and living in Meudon. And no other novels have come to light.)

The critics—as might be expected—had somewhat
sneering comments to make about the two lawyers who devoted all their leisure time ("between court sessions ad-
journed and judicial vacations") to this literary task. And
seemed to find it hard to decide whether to disparage the
work of the moribund author, or the version of his novel
submitted for publication.[35] The latter was admittedly a
difficult puzzle to decipher (as the second lawyer admits in
the Preface of *Rigodon*):

> Two successive versions of *Rigodon* show Céline's enor-
> mous labor, for there isn't a page or even a line that
> hasn't been erased or crossed out; one word replaces
> another, then the third is finally replaced by the first,
> then the whole phrase is revised, plastered over, re-
> written; it's a continual patching job. . . .[36]

It is not too difficult to imagine Céline's disdainful grimaces
at the antics that accompanied the posthumous appearance
of his work. The snarl with which he would have greeted
the titles under which some of its reviews appeared ("Pavane
of the Collaborator";[37] "Céline, the Madman").[38] Or the
shrug of his shoulders at hearing one of his fervent admirers
of former days ask:

> But how could he, in his old age and misery, rehash the
> same things over and over again: his 75% disability, the
> prison stay, the "three dots" which characterized his
> style? He who had once been so proud, so haughty, who

could not bear pity and had a horror of accepting help
—All this is very bizarre.[39]

Surely the shrug would have superseded snarls and grimace. For the game, all along, had never been to conserve but to lose.

Progressing from loss to loss, until the world itself was played out.

And life concluded on a scene of trancelike nothingness: the invasion of France by the Chinese who, in turn, would lose themselves in drunken revelries in the wine cellars of Cognac, Reims, and Epernay,

Those bubbly depths where nothing exists any longer. . . .

(*RIG*, last phrase)

The fade-out of existence. The final orgy which gives way to silence. The close of the play, complete with stage directions recalling those which had already ended his first drama:

Softly

curtain

on all that.

(*EG*, last phrase)

SUMMER 1961

—"That's it. This time I'll croak!" he announced.

His friend chuckled.

—"Go on, you old joker; you're a born comedian. You never mean a single word you say!" [40]

And the friend left, not giving Céline's words another thought.

He laid down his pen and turned to Lucette.

—"It's finished," he said. "We'll go away. To the
sea." [41]

She acquiesced with a smile, remembering the many times
he had made similar pronouncements before.

—"It's my high blood pressure that will get me in the
end!" he roared. "If I don't watch my diet, I'm finished;
if I eat the least little thing. . . ."

But his doctor knew that his high blood pressure was an
imagined state—self-diagnosed—and probably nothing more
than an anxiety symptom. The diet also (which Dr. Destouches had prescribed in order that Céline might attain a
ripe old age); and the nightly clysters administered to wash
away the toxins he swore had accumulated in his body.[42]

—"I only write to pay my debts to Gallimard—9 million francs' worth!" he assured one reporter who had
come to interview him.[43]

A year later, another reporter brought back another
story:

—"Circumstances force me to [write]. I owe 6 millions
to my editor. That's the whole story. It's simple; each
time a book of mine comes out, it costs me money.[44]

His performances were done with consummate skill. As
nimbly as those of a circus clown whose life depended on
pratfalls and subtle variations of mime. "Ferdinand, make
your funny faces!" [45] a chorus seemed always ready to shout.

And he complied, all of his life. Unable to stop, even at
the very end. For they had to recognize him as the great
"master of farce: a man without hope, neck-deep in quicksand and sinking fast, telling outrageous stories until the very
last gasp." [46]

Even those who saw his graver face, did not always de-
tect the macabre undertones of his pronouncements. The

young writer who visited Céline in his cellar kitchen one day, recalls:

> As evening fell, the room became a sort of odorous cave, in which Céline took on the appearance of an anchorite. He got up. . . . I heard an intonation of fatigue creep into his magnificent voice:
>
> —"Please consider yourself free to leave. . . ."
>
> Another sleepless night was beginning for Céline. The city did not know that this generous and blaspheming monk was orbiting around the sun for the last time. Nor did I. . . . I didn't know yet that the "freedom" which he had accorded me so casually, would be mine forever.[47]

So lightly did he trip the lines on his tongue—or in such exaggeratedly solemn tones—that almost no one knew when the game was about to come to an end.

As though, at an interminable auction, the call of: "Going . . . going . . . gone!" was never followed by the sound of the hammer falling.

Only when the nails were driven into the coffin, did the reality of his dying become manifest.

The game of paradoxes did not end there, however. It surrounded his death. A shroud of tales covered the event and what followed: the rumors of suicide;[48] the announcement of his death, made on July 4, 1961, by the Paris radio, when his funeral was coming to a close;[49] the ceremony, during which the game of *non sequiturs* was so skillfully played (Arletty to the gravedigger's son: "You know, that's a great poet they're burying." Boy: "Yes, thank you very much, Madam"),[50] the tomb, unblessed by any priest and adorned by a plant sacred in druidic rites, while requiem masses would be said for Céline each year to commemorate the day of his death[51] advertised in the local newspaper in Switzerland, between maudlin expressions of traditional grief in alphabetical order:

..........ile CAPPELLARO
1968 — 1er juillet — 1969
327565 X   *Pourquoi si tôt ?*

IN MEMORIAM
Célerine ROVEYAZ
1968 — 1er juillet — 1969
Maman chérie, une année déjà que tu nous a quittés, mais ton doux souvenir demeure au plus profond de nos cœurs.
                    Alice et Marcel.

IN MEMORIAM
Louis-Ferdinand CÉLINE
1961 — 1969
Puisse-tu avoir enfin trouvé la paix, après ce long voyage..
41341 Se   *Tes amis suisses.*

REMERCIEMENTS

La famille de
Monsieur Albert DROMAZ
très touchée de la sympathie qui lui a été témoignée, remercie sincèrement toutes les personnes qui ont pris part à son grand deuil.
                    327.831 X

It seems that Lucette had inherited his talent for dissembling. The gift of hiding grief beneath harsh, commanding tones. On the day of the funeral, she pinned a note to the garden gate, that read:

CLASSES AT THE USUAL HOURS, STARTING
MONDAY, JULY 10TH.[52]

She had learned the rules of the endgame well.

No matter how numerous, though, the masks of grief he wore
—they all spelled out a truth that he had lived with for more
than thirty years:

> For those who have no imagination, dying is a small
> matter; for those who do, it's too much. . . .
>
> (*VOY*, 22–23)

Nothing in a lifetime of poses, games and disguises, had
altered the severity of this law.

Few epitaphs would have been more fittingly carved upon his
grave.

Except perhaps, the one that Shakespeare wrote for mad
King Lear:

> Vex not his ghost: O, let him pass!
> he hates him much
> That would upon the rack of this
> tough world
> Stretch him out longer.
>
> (V, iii)

Daedalus in Cnossos once contrived

A dancing-floor for fair-haired Ariadne

HOMER

12

THE MINOTAUR

On the outskirts . . . life comes to you in the morning . . . during the small hours, along the Boulevard Minotaur. . . .[1]

From the very first, he sensed that life flows, rushes, staggers, ebbs away on this road. —Labyrinthine in its ways. —From dawn to nightfall; beneath waning and waxing moons; from ovule to obliteration. Along the vast, twisting boulevard whose very name indicates that it leads into the center of the maze, where man lies spread-eagled by his manifold destiny, and polar extremes unite to form an inexplicable knot of Gordian complexity. Where the incomprehensible monster dwells: nature's puzzle; loftiest and most base of earth's creatures. The sacred, hideous abode of the composite beast.

For he knew that he, also, bore its mark; shared its attributes; belonged to its disciples.

"Diversity is my law!" he cried.[2]

"Admirable monster that you are!" another answered.[3]

Genius and aberration. Bastard and saint. Madman and

analyst. Atheist-priest. Hermit-adventurer. Pacifist-soldier.
Generous miser. Biologist-poet. "Hell's Angel" in evening
attire.[4] Creator-destroyer. Charlatan and healer. Gargoyle
and demon. Dr. Destouches and Ferdinand Agonistes.[5] La-
borer and alchemist. Jew and anti-Semite; dybbuk and possessed.[6] Aristocrat of language and expert of gutter slang.
Anti-erotic eroticist.[7] Scatological perfectionist. Inquisitor
and heretic. Communist-Fascist-Anarchist-Nihilist. Catastro-
phist-opportunist. Chaste satyr. Seasick lover of ships. Terrified hero. Sightseer in handcuffs.[8] Convict and "prince of
free men." [9] Leper and physician. Gravedigger and *accoucheur*. Traitor and patriot. Actor and spectator. Voyeur-
Voyant.[10] Man, woman, child, animal. All, or none of these.

Juggler of parody and paroxysm; guffaws and growls;
obscenities and cemeteries; orgiastic joy and dread; weight
and weightlessness; movement and immobility; music and
cacophony; ecstasy and stasis. Of dancers and amputees;
alligators and the pipes of Pan; tripod and oracle; oak and
holly; solstice and equinox; air, water, earth, and fire.

Labyrinth. Daedalus. Ariadne. Theseus. And Minotaur.

> The best thing . . . is to imagine a tapestry, up, down,
> sideways, all the elements at the same time and all
> the colors . . . all the motifs! . . . everything upside
> down! . . . to pretend presenting them to you lying
> flat, standing up, or reclining, would be a lie . . . do
> your best to find your way! . . . in time! in space!
>
> (*NO*, 26)

Words written in the last years of his life, when almost nothing existed for him anymore. And all that remained was a
thin, almost invisible thread that linked him to life. (It is not
hard to divine that it was spun out of words.) [11] Taut, brittle,
weak, it threatened to break under the slightest strain. But, as

before, it led to the core of the labyrinth, where the Minotaur waited to be slain—but also contemplated face to face, as a reflection in a mirror. Thread that uncoiled the pattern of the dance from most ancient times, tracing the endless ritual of death and life; described the wheel that keeps ruthlessly, magnificently turning.

> In him, there is neither high nor low, neither entry nor exit. He does not suggest a single geometric shape. . . .[12]

except perhaps, that of the double spiral (signifying eternal return) or the maze pattern that had once adorned Ariadne's dancing floor.

How then, could fixity reign, even after his death?

No machine can program the course of his mind. He escapes homage, niche, shrine, sordid or solid sepulchres. All mortuary statues are smashed as fast as they are erected.[13] Nor could it be otherwise for this man who considered micturation into a flowing stream a gesture of eternity, the phallic emblem of the raised pen sufficient monument; and curses an inverted prayer.[14]

Even his death mask does not evoke quietude.

Nor would he accept being enshrined in stone to become one of the pillars of our time, content to be assigned the guardianship of one point upon which the axis of this world turns:

> He is one of the poles of our epoch. Chaplin is the other. Mr. Einstein will make them both sizzle in the same frying pan.[15]

For his fluctuating powers encompass Chaplin's creatures (those derelicts, kicked universally in the seat of their shapeless trousers) and the worst holocausts that haunted Einstein's atomic brain. As he portrays nobodies in a no-more-world, enacting clown-shows on doomsday launching pads—their sad animal eyes melting in the heat of gamma rays, their gauche feet tripping on spaghetti, into the void. And conjures up both wandering Jews and cremators; *Luftmenschen* and their mound of earth or universe-sized funeral pyre; Infra- and Super-Man; juggler and atom-splitter; comedy and nuclear fission; a Hiroshima-circus where charred corpses dance on high wires in the sky and sparrows drop violets from their shattered beaks.

His is a vast peep-show rigged by a seer. Where pornography suddenly turns into prophecy, and lascivious atoms dissolve, no longer cuckolded of infinity.[16] A panorama of global dimensions, in which opposite poles spin past with such speed that they can no longer be distinguished or isolated. A gigantic mobile, whose elements achieve unity through constant fluctuation.

From largest spheres to minute matters, the sign he moved under was diversity.

("Astroflash" would probably attribute it all to his being born a true Gemini.)[17]

The face alone was startling in its duality. Monolithic at first glance, it soon showed contradictions that merged, as though it were an image produced by double exposure:

> The left eye, with its lowered lid, was dull; full of nobility and suffering and as calm as that of a martyr who musters his last reserves of strength. The right eye was wide open, hard, fiery, and piercing. . . . The left is that of an honest man, laboring under a painful surprise . . . the right continues to emit glances of irresistible power . . . the nose is asymmetrical also; higher on the left than on the right. . . .[18]

("It's probably a vestige of his trepanation," the observer mused,[19] under the spell of the legend that had so long been propagated.)

The mouth also was enigmatic. Laughter and derision lay on the same curved line; smiles easily gave way to snarls. The lips ready to break into alternating utterances. Only a hair's breadth divided humor and fury. It was simply a question of a slight twist in the mask. Yet the whole world seemed to shift countenance about him:

> How can I explain my amazement when seeing Céline guffaw for the first time, suddenly rejuvenated, his eyes moist, as gentle as a sheepdog offering its paw.

> He spoke with lowered lids, clenched his teeth, muttered imprecations that grew more and more unintelligible.

> He was close to delirium; he trembled, the face darkened and grimaced; he cast a look into the void . . . that was so incendiary that one expected to see cities and plains go up in smoke . . . transformed into a sorcerer drunk with rage . . . about to annihilate the whole world.[20]

Even the hands were inexplicably different: The right (which did all the writing), clawlike, reminiscent of the parrot and various lower animals; inhuman. The left, simply an old man's hand, veined and marked by purely human toil.

But his twin nature underwent such protean shifts of form that the results were always disconcerting: reflections that went suddenly askew; sets (imperfectly matched) that gave a momentary illusion of kinship yet provoked uneasy feelings of subtle discrepancies. As though a mirror image had slipped ever so slightly; or a breeze had disturbed the reflection in the water on a windless day. Resulting in a fabulous beast that was cause for wonder, irritation, puzzlement.

*   *   *

Even his most prized possessions were subject to playful jug-
gling.

Akin to Humpty Dumpty—whose sovereign disdain for
language made him say, "When I use a word, it means what I
want it to mean, nothing more, nothing less," [21]—he indulged
in what frequently seemed mere arbitrariness or haughty
child's play. Only a few saw the creative concern it implied,
the invention of words as new as the objects that recent
painting had devised, "where words are no longer used for
their strict meaning . . . but *with art,* the way jugglers use
hats, eggs, and handkerchiefs—with an entirely different aim
than to wear them, eat them, or blow their noses." [22] Or the
conviction that language must contain the seeds of its own
annihilation (a "self-destruct" mechanism built into its very
vitals, that would prevent its falling into the enemy hands of
classicism) : a dose of argot which dies more swiftly than more
traditional forms of speech.

> It dies quickly, this language of mine. Therefore it has
> lived, it *lives,* as long as I use it. . . . A language is like
> all the rest, it's continually dying. . . . The traditional
> novel's language is dead, its syntax dead, everything
> about it dead. My works will also die, probably very
> soon; but they'll have this small advantage over so many
> others—for a year, a month, a day, they will have
> *lived.* The quest for an absolute language, an eternal
> form in writing, is stupid and unbearably preten-
> tious. . . .[23]

He preferred to be a stylist who carried explosives that would
blow style sky-high; to perfect phrases with a lapidary's skill,
while insisting that the polished reflection must soon crack,
shatter, return to fragments indistinguishable from rock. If,
from the hidden matrix, new gems were one day to glow.

For he had always known that:

> One never has one's fill of the unknown. . . .
>
> A book is already a sort of death, and often a mucky death. . . .[24]
>
> Nothing ruins and condemns like routine. The Spirit flees, seeing itself always identical. . . .[25]

Not only style then, but also one's life-style must be subject to flux. One role could not suffice him, no absolute self, nor fixed identity. Even a single name implied stagnation. Louis-Ferdinand Destouches (or even Des Touches) had to give way to other incarnations: Dr. Destouches, Céline, and their literary doubles—Robinson, Bardamu, Ferdinand, Ferdine.

How irritated he was when others were made uneasy by this diversity and had to be reassured:

> I am indeed L.-F. Céline and also Destouches. No mystery! It's all quite benign, I assure you. . . .[26]
>
> My Lord, why such alarm! Because I'm a doctor and Destouches besides! One has to have some small alibi, some technique for earning one's bread.[27]

As if his twin calling were some guilty secret! Or he were living the life of a double agent. (The memories of London days were, of course, delightful and he sometimes thought that espionage would have suited him well.) It had to be admitted that varied identities amused him; fed his appetite for contradiction, for proliferation and vitality of being.

The first real split, however, did not occur until he plunged into the literary adventure. Some thought of it as a seesaw motion, by which "a writer would emerge and a man go under." [28] But in reality, it was a process of multiple selves growing—the nighttime double that wrote, grew side by side

with the physician of the daylight hours. Together with a third
(the narrator) who would disparage them both:

> I haven't always practiced medicine . . . that shitty
> trade. . . .[29]

> My trouble is insomnia. If I had always slept properly,
> I'd never have written a line.[30]

Soon, the diverse lives intertwined, crossed over, threatened to merge. Creating misgivings on his part (probably
mixed with joyful apprehension) and exclamations of fear
(that made life more palatable by the spice of danger).

> As for Dr. Destouches, let nobody except Denoël iden-
> tify him with that hideous cacographer-pornographer
> who wrote *Voyage,* or suspect one of the other. . . .
> Literature is looked at askance in the medical world.
> . . . A doctor-novelist like me has to hide his game
> well. Dr. Jekyll and Mr. Hyde. . . .[31]

Some would call the game schizophrenia. Others might call it
realism—for complexity is often subject to suspicion, and
creatures that outgrow their pigeonholes seldom escape attack.

He might have countered with the retort that life was
one long *non sequitur.*

So great was his drive for contradiction, that even the simplest formulas had to be reversed (greetings, forms of address,
consistency of signature). What joy there was in calling a
friend, not "Old boy," but "J.J." ("Young One");[32] or in addressing a much older companion always as "Son";[33] most of
all, perhaps, in never signing one's name the same when writing to the same correspondent—to affix at least ten different
signatures to the letters sent to one friend over the space of a
decade or so.[34]

Mere dichotomy seems elementary by comparison. Puzzling only to those who seek a single line of explanation, and, plagued by the least sign of enigma, complain:

> Céline presents a Hamlet-like problem to the critic. Is he a madman or an artist assuming the symptoms of a madman? [35]

While poets have a tranquil answer to the dilemma:

> Céline is . . . a sane man handling hallucinations . . . a nut, a freak, an exccentric [sic] . . . like all our geniuses verily. . . .[36]

Because they know that opposites are the stuff that art is made of; that individual mutiny must reign; and extravagant incompatability marks the man who creates it.

(Which has been true for other sacred monstrosities —sphinx, chimera, basilisk, Garuda, Melusine, hippogriff, Ganesha, sea monk, naga, harpy, Anubis, Sekmet, Isis, Thoth, Hathor, gryphon, werewolf, Minotaur, and the seven-headed, ten-horned red dragon of the Apocalypse.)

The mark which cannot be effaced by simplification. And escapes all reductive logic. Tantalizing as a riddle. Anathema to those who would square every circle. Heresy for manufacturers of gummed labels. Source of continuing delight to addicts of versatility who identify life with movement, the flux of all things. And smilingly affirm the most paradoxical combinations.

Céline's image is made of words—his, those of others—of a chorus of voices that chant in contrapuntal manner, discordant, pursuing separate or opposing themes, pitched in a dozen different keys, varied in tone and rhythm, mindless of melodic confluence, resolution, or harmony. But swelling into a statement of inexplicable power:

"He kept his dough stashed
away under his mattress. . . ."

"He detested money, dis-
dained it. . . ." [37]

"My voice is only good for
yelling, 'Fire!' . . . not fit
to be heard."

"Those who knew him, com-
pared [his voice] to that
of Louis Jouvet." [38]

"In real life, Céline's
speech was that of a mighty
lord. . . ."

"[He was] timid, had a
stentorian voice and spoke . . .
with a Parisian street-
accent. . . ."

"He spoke like a true aristocrat. . . ."

"He cursed like a
sailor. . . ." [39]

"He wore a cowboy hat and
danced naked in his house. . . ."

"He looked like an inspired
clochard. . . ."

"When they expected him
to look disreputable, he
appeared in immaculate
evening attire, feigning
indifference at their surprise. . . ." [40]

"He had a passion for his-
torical studies. . . ."

"He read everything. He
adored encyclopedias and consulted them constantly."

"He never really read anything. He merely glanced
at a book and put it
down." [41]

"He had lost all taste for
living in the end. He let
himself die. . . ."

"He wanted to live to be
very old. That was the
aim of the odd diet he
prescribed for himself." [42]

"He suffered from sea-
sickness. . . ."

"His love of ships was lifelong. He was happiest when
he was at or near the sea." [43]

"Having an innate fear of
horses. . . ."

He chose the cavalry over
all other branches of military service when he en-
listed.[44]

"Toto, my parrot. . . ."

"Toto is more precisely
Tototte."

"Céline's parrot, Coco." [45]

"The main thing is to choose
the party which will suc-
ceed."

"Independence is my sole
boon. The world is full of
domestics."

"Céline had perfected the art of always putting himself in the wrong." [46]

"In the end, he loved only
his animals. . . ."

"Hoodlums . . . toads! A bunch
of half-breeds, bastards as ugly
and rotten as humans. . . ." [47]

"He had a deep feeling for
friendships and always
showed a rare fidelity in
his affections."

"He was impossible with his
friends. Even the most
patient of them were finally
driven away. . . ." [48]

"[He knew that] he was the
greatest French writer of
his time. . . ."

"Great writers! . . . I don't
give a fuck about adjectives.
First you have to croak, and
then you're classified."

"I'm the greatest writer
in the world! . . . Aside from
me, nothing exists! except
charlatans. . . ."

"I'm nothing but the in-
ventor of a little trick. . . ." [49]

"Not one first-rate female
in a thousand. . . ."

"This vice of perfect
forms. . . ."

"I love the physical perfections of
women to the point of madness. . . ."

"I'm neither a voluptuary nor a
sensualist. . . ." [50]

"I'm the complete voy-
eur. . . ."

"Lucid Super-Voyant that I
am. . . ." [51]

"Nihilist that you are. . . ."

"His greatest rages were
aroused by anything that
abased man, or by self-
defeatism. . . ." [52]

"He consulted a psychiatrist;
he was probably in analy-
sis. . . ."

"I wanted to become a psychiatrist . . . the work involved would have suited
me. . . ." [53]

"[In Baryton's asylum] a
kind of vertigo seized me. . . .
I wondered . . . if I hadn't,
by some chance, been locked
up once and for all with
their insanity. . . ."

"The human personality is
broken as cruelly as the
body when madness turns
the torture wheel."

"Madness has been hot on my trail . . .
no exaggeration . . . for twenty-two years." [54]

"[The Jews] are a bunch of
vampires! phenomenally
filthy bastards that must be
sent back to Hitler! to
Palestine!"

"Céline's granddaughter
spent some months in Israel,
digging potatoes on a
Kibbutz. . . ."

"Céline's fate resembles
that of the contemporary
Jew. . . ." [55]

"In a hundred years, the whites
of New York will be living in a
ghetto: the Blacks will go to
New-Harlem to watch the 'pale-
faces' dance the polka."

"The white race is condemned
to death . . . it's nothing more
than cream-makeup!"

"Race . . . or what you call
race, is nothing else but
that heap of ragpickers
to which I belong, flea-
bitten, pursued by hunger,
pestilence, tumors, and
cold . . . it's all the van-
quished come from the four
corners of the earth."

"The Chinese are coming . . . the yellow peril!"

"We must create a new form of racism on biological foundations—All the elements are there—."

"The blood of colored races is 'dominant' . . . whites' blood is 'dominated' . . . always! children . . . will never be white again!" [56]

"I write . . . when the right wind blows . . . but without a fixed date . . . ! I travel by sail. I have no timetable. . . ."

"Another two thousand pages, at least! How hard it is to get down to work! . . . I promised, I must!

"I'm nothing more than a work tool and I treat myself as such. Existence is too heavy and monotonous without continual artifice." [57]

"He enjoyed the game of making [those who questioned and wished to observe him] lose their way in a labyrinth of . . . contradictory opinions . . . taking pleasure in presenting a shocking paradox. . . ." [58]

"All this might seem a bit contradictory to you, but only contradictions have any life. . . ." [59]

(Even when they applied to his own death: when the entire French press centered its attention on Hemingway—who, by some odd quirk of fate, had died the same day as he. The irony was first-rate. They dedicated headlines and cover photos to the American whom some considered "a far greater hunter than writer";[60] while his own death was dismissed as an event of secondary importance, easily covered by short, sometimes spiteful announcements.)

A more apt necrological notice could not have been devised by Céline himself.

Except, if one considers that he had written his own

obituary almost forty years ago (disguised as a summary of
his earliest Doppelgänger's life):

> His methods . . . are and will continue to be brand-
> new. His work is eternal. Although, in his day, he was
> totally misunderstood. . . . The reasons why he was
> the victim of such extraordinary hostility . . . cannot
> be explained by facts, ideas, or words. There is so much
> one doesn't know and will never know.
>
> (*SEM,* 131–132)

And that Céline's comments on the departure of Semmelweiss, might have borne repetition at his own demise:

> Really, it was time for him to go.

> But he clung to this world as long as anyone can with
> an impossible brain attached to a body in shreds. . . .
> At the core of this man, there was no indulgence at all
> for the common fate. . . .
>
> (*SEM,* 130)

So uncommon, so incongruous was this creature that there
was no finality even in dying.

A semblance of life remained, so strong that even the
being closest to him was led astray:

> I didn't understand right away that he was dead . . .
> I gave him mouth-to-mouth resuscitation for three
> hours. . . .[61]

The face continued to retain its enigma. Long after death.
For though cast in plaster, the mask is not immobile: One
side appears carved in classical marble—lofty, massive, impassible; the other, as if molded in wax—flaccid, shapeless,
partially decomposed.[62]

(Janus-face that incarnates the grandeur and baseness
of man; his mortal and immortal destiny; his high and low

estate—earthworm and giant; blind beggar and super-seer; king of the universe and swarm of dispersed atoms.)

The mask of a Minotaur. Symbol of all that lurks in the heart of the labyrinth; of being and non-being:

Creation that destroys and in turn awaits destruction. Annihilation that alone assures rebirth. Dread jubilation. Ultimate union of the monstrous and the magnificent. The equal sacredness of victim and sacrificial priest. Tender brutality. Loving hate. Lucid hallucination. Mythic biology. Elemental puniness. Mad sanity. Deadly life and living death. Coitus of finite and infinite, male goddesses and female gods.

Circle in which the aged child rejoins infantile octogenarians; embryo and maggot merge; where blood of birth, hymen, and death are one. And human and inhuman meet.

Heart of the labyrinth to which every journey to the ends of night must lead. And where all rigadoons patterned on the maze-dance inscribed upon antique floors, are fated to terminate.

Epilogue

13

*I wish the storm would make
even more of a clatter, I wish
the roof would cave in, that
spring would never come again,
that the house would blow down.*

(DJP, 15)

MAY 1968

Fire had swept over everything; singed the grass and trees, meadow, gates, and the house on the hill. Its core stood outlined against the sky, worked by flame into a fretted stone citadel. Rafters and beams jutted through the shell, like quills of a gigantic porcupine or fractured bone fragments that protrude from flesh. Through empty windows . . . doorways, sudden gusts of wind raised an odor of smoke. The nonexistent lawns were littered with bedsteads that had been hacked apart, molten silver knives in amoebic shapes, pages of manuscripts, contorted birdcages, books with back broken. All sodden under a film of soot and water.

A flagstone trail led upwards—among burned rosebushes—into the ruin of the house.

There, a spiral staircase turned charcoal remained inexplicably standing; pointed to the torn roof. Windows gaped; revealed, unframed, the splendor of the Seine valley below.

Floorboards rose and fell at the approach of a step, as if to mimic the motion of ships in rough waters. Bent stovepipes had merged with splintered timber. In a recess, a monumental toilet stood intact. Mute excremental witness.

While teapots, twisted by fire into legendary dragon shapes, rattled across the stone tiles; and vast mirrors—where grace of dancers had long dwelt—now stood like cracked sentinels against exposed iron doorframes, their web of black fissures reflecting the desolate garden that stretched beyond the house.

The cry of a bird.

A gray parrot shrieking in the silence. Silence even greater than the stillness of July heat.

Seven years ago. The day he had died.

Silence in his workroom, now destroyed. Outside, the river flowed on. From far away, a boat horn blew.

> Its call passed the bridge, an archway, still another, the locks, another bridge, far, still farther. . . . It called all the barges on the river towards it, all, and the whole city, and the sky and the countryside, and us, it took everything with it, the Seine also, everything, so that all would be said and done.
>
> (*VOY,* 493)

The room had been put to the torch. Fumigated by fire. Rendered aseptic, nonvirulent. No trace of struggle, illness, or creation remained. Not an imprint on the charred walls. Neither blurred yellow outlines in the places where pictures of a Baltic hut and maps of seafarers' journeys had hung; nor smudges made by his feverish head when he turned on the sofa during long insomniac nights. No trail of pages, fastened with clothespins, on which scrawled phrases were hammered into successive shapes. Not even a mark where his dead body had lain, wound in a shepherd's cape.

Nor sound. . . . Yes. . . . The bark of dogs approaching in the distance. His dogs. Two only—all the others having died: Totom after the fire, Balou shortly after his master's death (the shepherd with the wolf's face, the Great Dane who had accompanied him on his walks along the Baltic Sea). Those that remain, run sniffing up the hill. Follow the scent of smoke, crash through the gates that had once secured the house from the streets below, where they stood guard to keep intruders at bay.

The plaque that had hung there to shield his writer's activities from view, had vanished in the flames with all the rest.

DR. L.-F. DESTOUCHES
DE LA FACULTÉ DE MÉDECINE DE PARIS

A plaque gray with age, that had accompanied its owner on all his journeys. Terse sign which pointed to the other domain of his double life: Back bent over bedside, deathbed, dissecting table. Eyes diagnosing advance of labor, progress of agony, death throes and thrust of placenta. Hands deftly probing—*accoucheur's* hands, fingers of healer, palms to close glazed eyes and elicit first breath. Hands that are the familiars of pain, wield syringe of morphine and acid pen with equal skill. Hands twisted by labor and shrapnel wounds; resembling simian paws or the tenacious claws of a parrot. Stilled now. Unmoving. Consumed by earth and fire.

*   *   *

A woman slowly approaches, across the burnt grass. The remnants of a dancer's grace in her halting gait. The dogs recede and follow; zigzag, confused by smells of flame; retreat in terror; plunge quivering noses into the wet debris. She calls them off with a weary cry.

Her face resembles a torn Flemish painting below the turbaned hair.

One hand fumbles to close her robe over a singed leotard. With startled gaze pausing here and there in the wreckage, she stoops to right a fallen clothes rack (the parrot's perch), absently strokes the wounded cat that follows. He lurches forward, his black fur matted, a wooden splint grotesquely hindering his moves. The cat who sparked the fire.

> You see, it wasn't the fault of the May "wildcats." It all happened because of a wounded kitten she had picked up on the road. She rushed it to a veterinarian. When she returned, there were firemen everywhere; the house had been reduced to an eggshell with blackened walls. This Noah's ark was fated to perish, the victim of one of its boarders.[1]

Unaware of his betrayal he wanders about. Sniffs at the ruins without suspicion of the role he has played, or how he became the instrument of the house's final, fitting fall.

She moves toward the garden shed with its canvas roof strangely intact. Reminiscent of nomadic tents or anchored sailings ships. Boat lanterns sway in the high wind, knock against a row of empty cages. From which a hundred many-colored birds have vanished.

In the fire. . . . No. . . . It was another time. . . .

When their cries, resounding through the house during the long winter, had suddenly became a nightmare sound. Rage and exhaustion had made her throw the windows wide.

The screens fell. In a wild frenzy of color, they escaped. First covered the trees with sound-filled bloom; then were gone. Dead or dispersed to die in the dark wood that bordered the end of the garden—Yveline Forest of ancient witchcraft fame.

The shed where his last days were spent; where he sat, wrapped in layers of fur and old coats, his canes leaning against the chair, the large feet swathed in cloth or paper. Now snarled a response when questioned, now brooded silently as do caged beasts.

Mostly, he held dialogue with a gray bird.

The parrot who mirrored his thoughts and could best echo the shrill halting voice. Companion of the last refuge. Into which the woman would now retreat. Under the singed trees. In the silence of the dead garden.

Spring had gone. The roof had caved in. Charred mirrors froze the vast desolation; enlarged and projected its image in an unending chain. She stared at the blind wall of the house.

There's nothing like odors and flames, for forcing memories into the open. . . .

(*VOY,* 175)

A broken bed stood waiting there. Offering—in mockery—death, sex, or sleep.

Grotesque stillness after flames. The waves of fire had receded. Only the empty shell of the house lay before her. Gaping and dry as a sea creature tossed, irretrievably, up to shore. Without the sound of waters roaring in its intricate spiral husk. Sear and hollow. A soiled ossature, unpurified by burning. (Although his mother had often affirmed, when throwing old bandages into the flames, "Fire purifies everything," [2] and his father maintained the cleanest of records during his long years of service in the Phoenix Insurance firm.) [3]

Sullied and further defiled by shadowy forms that gathered about the house at nightfall: human jackals who probed the wreckage for pages of manuscripts, scraps of a life, offal to turn into lucre. So like the dim figures beyond the windowpane, whom she had seen lurking about and dragging heavy sacks across the ground. The day after the funeral.

It was ended for her now. Twice robbed—both of the man and all vestiges of his life—she sat, mechanically stroking dogs and one maimed cat.

Until all anguish froze when the parrot shrieked his name. The harsh syllables rent the air. Split the silence. As on the day he had died.

"Louis . . . Louis . . . !" [4]

Exit Louis-Ferdinand Céline.

JULY 4, 1961

The coffin stood in the cellar kitchen. All the windows were closed. Musty walls and decay in July heat. Odors of rotting oranges, dog urine and fetid air from the plumbing below. His cloak still hung on a peg near the door. Flies slowly wandered over the lead casket with its lurid crucifix (last irony, due to a supply shortage among the village coffin makers). It had been placed on wooden vegetable crates. The dogs sniffed about, the oldest one howling in low tones. The others solemnly paused to urinate on the coffin sheets.[5]

*   *   *

Two women descend the stairs. —Not the nuns, who had refused to anoint the body or sit at the wake. —One slender figure, moving as if blind: Lucette. The other, larger in stature and younger than the first, her blue eyes glancing wildly about (eyes that resemble the dead man's): Colette, his child. She stands terrified, struck by each ludicrous detail —food and death smells mingled; crucifix, urine, and rigor mortis combined. The mind stops. Grief and nausea producing only a frozen stare.

"No . . . no . . ." she croons, holding her sides; as if rocked in an invisible cradle of pain. And cut off by this final rupture. Broken, the fragile bond that had united them; despite the intermittent love, the long intervals of silence.

"Papa . . . papa . . ." the child in her moaned.

As long ago when, feverish with typhoid, she had lain in her grandmother's narrow bed that smelled of lavender and stale skin.

Until he had appeared—as if by enchantment—at her side. From the other side of life. To diagnose, and chide those about. Thundering for milk and alcohol rubs. To stand at her bedside, tears streaming down his face, over her eyes, wetting the sheets, cooling the feverish room. Bathed in his tears she had lain and grown well. While he slept for ten nights, like a dog, at the foot of her cot.[6]

Guardian and sorcerer, father.

The other woman bent low. All dancer's grace gone now. Panting as if in labor; her dry womb heaving to no avail. Childless child-wife of his late years. Silent companion of all the final journeys; whose presence was meant to keep the cold of age at bay. —Lost now. Lost as the dogs who wandered mute through the house, or the gray parrot disconsolately screaming his name.

The harsh desolate cry rose. Echoed through the rooms. Voicing their anguish. Daring to call up the dead.

"Louis . . . Louis . . . Louis . . . !"

Name she had often uttered. So intimate that only she and his mother called him thus (all the others resorting to the more staccato Ferdinand). Name of her birthplace also —rue St. Louis-en-l'Ile, Ile St. Louis;[7] doubly destined to mark the course of her life. Name mouthed in passion and whispered through barriers of prison walls; light as lacework in joyous days, sudden as a laugh; dark monosyllable at the edge of the mute Baltic Sea, no more than a gasp during the final hours.

Name to be spoken no more. Silenced now. Entombed.

JULY 1, 1961—6 P.M.[8]

Night in the room. Dusk filtered darkly through the curtains he had shut earlier that day when pain jabbed through his head at every touch of light. (First sign of death —noted and diagnosed.) To Lucette, he had said lightly: "It's finished. We'll go away. To the sea. Some place far. . . ." And then had written a note to his publisher, stating that the last manuscript was completed.[9]

The throbbing in his head was stronger than usual. He staggered to the cellar to make tea; left it untouched; dragged himself back to the workroom again. Impelled to touch the white page, not yet to abandon all words. The clawlike hand moved across the expanse of paper, and wrote:

". . . so that nothing more may exist . . ."

The last phrase. Which trailed off into nothingness.
"Finished . . ." he snarled.

*   *   *

The music upstairs grew shriller. Each note a sharp jab to his head. Were they castanets, those drumming relentless sounds? Or his pulse racing in final, exacerbated leaps? The pain in his temples increased. Blotted out lifelong, familiar throb of migraine and injured nerve cells. The usual buzzing in his ears (a sound of trains rushing to and fro, as in some infernal station) was drowned out now by an internal tidal wave of blood. He grimaced, almost producing a smile. That "small music of death" he had so often written about, was now about to swell into a fully orchestrated tune.

He pulled himself across the room. Sprawled on the sofa against the wall. Drew his limbs together in foetal closeness, and wrapped the shepherd's cape tightly about him. Armor or winding sheet. To fight off, or succumb to, the great Pale-face (as he had mockingly called her in his books). Hedge-hog or mummy. Ready for final attack or burial ground.

Agony in his temple. Veins burst in the brain. Flooded one side of the head in massive hemorrhage. A rictus twisted the lips into a grin. Paralyzed the workings of his huge voice.[10]

A wave of pain lifted the body, threw it obliquely across the bed. The invalid right hand was seized by a final convulsion. It rose menacingly for an instant; then fell back inert. All movement stopped.

> The truth is Death! . . . I've fought against it as long as I could . . . danced with it, festooned it, waltzed it around, dressed it up and all that! . . . decked it out in ribbons, titillated it with wild farandoles. . . . Alas! I know only too well that everything breaks, gives way, falls apart, at a given moment . . . I know that one day the hand falls, limp at the side of the body . . . I've seen the gesture thousands and thousands of

times . . . and the shadow . . . the weight of the
dead! . . .

(PL, 34)

Death no longer on the installment plan, but paid in
full. Decay held no longer in abeyance. Man's bag of maggots ready to be opened. The final dissolution about to begin.

J U L Y 5, 1961—8:30 A. M. [11]

Ten minutes ago, the Paris radio had announced his
death.

The mourners filed in slowly. Gathered for secret burial,
in an effort to give a modicum of dignity to his dying. To
shield his tryst with death from vulgar words, the corpse from
further defilement by microphone and acetylene glare.
Though unwilling to carry out his express wish to be buried
in a common grave.[12] Considering it sufficient that the cadaver, unanointed by nuns, unblessed by the village priest,
was to be carried, unknown, to an old cemetery nearby.

> There will no nobody at my funeral: everybody will be
> quite content, and I most of all.[13]

> There were thirty people at Musset's burial; Mozart had
> only his dog to accompany him to the cemetery.
> Modesty.[14]

There were about thirty mourners. The dogs were not allowed
to enter the cemetery. (Rules of modesty had obviously
changed since Mozart's day.)

A thin funeral cortege on the long hot walk. Along the
winding road to *Bas-Meudon* where the burial ground had
been prepared. The widow's face ready to give way; her
black-turbaned head outlined against wreaths of blood-red
flowers.

The cemetery was small, with rusted gates. Among the

half-forgotten tombs, near a stone dolmen, the earth yawned. The gravediggers stood ready. Implacable as executioners, spades held like axes ready to strike. In the dark earth, a profusion of white roots—or maggots already preparing for the funeral feast.

> All those worms . . . the big ones . . . the fat ones with feet . . . gnawing, swarming about in there. . . . All that decay . . . millions of them, in all that swollen pus, the stinking wind. . . .
>
> (*DIP*, 111)

The coffin sank down. Around the open grave, a cat stalked. A small boy cycled unconcerned, tracing large circles on the ground (perhaps the gravedigger's son, bred among tombs). A woman detached herself from among the mourners —Arletty, the famed actress now almost blind. She murmured something to the boy. The child stared with indifferent eyes; shrugged, and went on to circle tombstones and graves.

A holly bush had been planted to mark the spot.[15] (Its seeds would be eaten by birds so that, from their excrement, others of its species could grow. Until the roots, in insidious proliferation, would reach the oak coffin beneath the crucifix. Coffin of Celt.[16] Whose ancestors may have practiced druidic rites in the holly-month of wrath, at midsummer when heat and violence reach their height and the tanist dies to make way for the oak king.)

Rain had begun to fall. The clumps of earth hit the lead cover, buried the lurid Christ in earth. Lucette threw—instead of holy water—a blood-red carnation on the falling sods. Gravediggers swiftly covered the hole over, their spades moving in mechanical rhythm. As in a Punch-and-Judy show.

The mourners turned and went up the hill. The whole ceremony had taken 21 minutes from start to finish.[17]

The rain increased. Bathing the earth, enveloping tombstones in mist and water. Like so many sails . . . adrift. . . .

Then I was really alone! Then I saw the thousands and
thousands of little skiffs. . . . Each one had a shriveled
little corpse under its sail . . . with his story. . . .
                                                        (*DIP*, 47)

One day, a tombstone would rise above the grave, to tell his
story: A sailing ship carved on a stark slab of Breton granite;
and the terse summary of a double life.

LOUIS-FERDINAND CÉLINE
LE DOCTEUR DESTOUCHES
1894–1961

Now, only rain and silence. The holly bush stood forlorn in
the wind. No oak grew there, no sacred oak of Celtic days
(forbidden tree whose defilement brought on dread chastise-
ment). Only some oak boards beneath lead covers. A poet
whose body rots, defiled by death; no longer there to probe
our entrails with his words, nor chastise trespassers with
terrible and sacred craft.

The rain stopped as soon as the funeral party had left
the cemetery. A fierce summer soon was blazing.

MAY 1969

Out of fire, new life. The burnt shell remained standing
on the hill. A ruin his widow had thought of preserving in
varied ways: to cover its whole vast expanse with mirrors so
that it would sparkle and reflect the sun (a giant fun-house
edifice); or erect bamboo supports and let it be grown over
(until it evoked Inca palaces swallowed up by jungle
growth). Dreams of a dancer, as nebulous as the gauze stage
sets among which she had long moved. Mitigating life's harshness with fantasy of forms.

Even when architects intervened, and insurance agents
attempted—with cash arguments—to crash through the web

of artifice, she had escaped intact. Persistent in the dream.

The gates were now painted bright blue. The dance studios had been rebuilt among the high trees of the back garden that bordered the Yveline Forest. (Recalling geishas' pleasure pavilions such as are found on painted scrolls of silk.)

Suspended below the roof of the burned-out house, she had fabricated a bird's airy retreat: Her apartment hung among the rafters, an impossible perch bounded by glass. There, the Seine and the forest appeared to meet; a medieval fireplace seemed to be suspended in space, yet burned brightly. The bath's splendor floated incongruously above the emptiness below. Beds covered in fur rose to the level of the windows, making the dreamer merge with the landscape's flow.

The old peasant woman who served her, smiled. Confidante of the mirage, enmeshed in the lacy fantasy about, she moved with the ease of familiars in fairy tales. Unquestioning, wordless, she carried wrapped teapots from garden to these swaying heights. Never challenged the existence of the void below. Nodded, approved.

The garden had been terraced and was shielded from view. Large earthen pots held rosebushes from Dieppe, grown by the sea. A small pool reflected the light on naked dancers' limbs. Portuguese gardeners planted the lawn, their soft lisping voices in council over the placement of shrubs.

A brazen hen wandered among the dogs. Two Flemish rabbits hopped about; described a large circle around the stealthy form of the cat—as, sleek and healed of his wounds, he stalks among renewed rosebushes and freshly sown grass.

Up on the hill, musical instruments mingle with the rasping crickets' sound. (Summer is once again beginning.) And dancers glide from within the oriental walls, melt into the landscape about. Their forms merge with the trees, return and gather in new groupings. Modeling their moves on the gestures of a central form.

On a raised platform in their midst, Lucette sways in elaborate grace, freshly enthroned.[18]

Strains of Stravinsky animate the dance.

From far below a parrot calls.

Voice undiminished though changed. Fire and birdcalls jointly renewed. In endless variation. Metamorphosis by flame in a continuous present.

LIST OF
ABBREVIATED REFERENCES

I. *Works by Céline*

AB: *A l'Agité du bocal.* Paris: P. Lanouve de Tartas, 1948.

BAM: *Bagatelles pour un massacre.* Paris: Denoël, 1941.

BD: *Les Beaux Draps,* 79th ed. Paris: Nouvelles Editions Françaises, 1941.

CAS: *Castle to Castle,* tr. Ralph Manheim. New York: Delacorte Press, 1968.

CP: *Casse-pipe,* 4th ed. Paris: Gallimard, 1952.

DIP: *Death on the Installment Plan,* tr. Ralph Manheim. New York: New Directions, 1966.

EC: *L'Ecole des cadavres.* Paris: Denoël, 1938.

EG: *L'Eglise, comédie en cinq actes,* 4th ed. Paris: Gallimard, 1952.

EPY: *Entretiens avec le Professeur Y.* Paris: Gallimard, 1955.

FEE: *Féerie pour une autre fois,* I. 12th ed. Paris: Gallimard, 1952.

GB: *Guignol's Band, I.* Paris: Gallimard, 1952.

MC: *Mea Culpa,* in *Mea Culpa suivi de La Vie et l'oeuvre de Semmelweiss.* Paris: Denoël & Steele, 1936.

NO: *Nord.* Paris: Gallimard, 1960.

NOR: *Féerie pour une autre fois, II. Normance.* Paris: Gallimard, 1954.

OC: *Oeuvres de Louis-Ferdinand Céline,* ed. J. A. Ducour-
     neau. Paris: André Balland, 1966–1969, Vols. I–V.

PL: *Le Pont de Londres (Guignol's Band, II).* Paris: Galli-
     mard, 1964.

RIG: *Rigodon.* Paris: Gallimard, 1969.

SEM: *Semmelweiss,* 10th ed. Paris: Gallimard, 1952.

VOY: *Voyage au bout de la nuit suivi de Mort à crédit.* Bibli-
     othèque de la Pléïade. Paris: Gallimard, 1962.

II. *Works on Céline*

LH: *Cahiers de l'Herne,* ed. Dominique de Roux. Paris, No.
     III, 1963; No. V, 1965, both devoted to Céline.

NOTES

Chapter 1

1. Cited by Albert Paraz, in *Le Gala des vaches* (Paris: Ed. de l'Elan, 1948), p. 137.

2. In Céline's Preface to Albert Serouille's *Bezons à travers les âges* (Paris: Denoël, 1944).

3. Information obtained by the author during a conversation with Mme. Céline. Also mentioned in a letter from Céline to Milton Hindus (May 29, 1947), *LH*, V, p. 77.

4. Letter to M. Hindus, *loc. cit.*

5. *NO*, pp. 242–243.

6. Letter to M. Hindus, *loc. cit.*

7. Nicole Debrie, "La Méthode Almanzor." Unpublished treatise on Lucette Almanzor's dance theories and techniques: "As a sort of bet, Lucette Almanzor had taken this case, condemned by doctors to a fate of permanent immobility. . . . Eight years of constant and devoted work have reduced the pronounced edema, equalized the legs which had suffered from an asymmetry of several centimeters, awakened this mind, at least to the art of the dance. . . ."

Chapter 2

1. Letter from Céline to M. Hindus (June 22, n.y.), *LH*, V, p. 83.

2. "Chronologie," *OC*, I, p. xxi.

3. Marcel Brochard, "Céline à Rennes," *LH*, III, p. 14.

4. Story recounted by M. Brochard, during an interview with the author, Nantes, June 1969).

5. "Chronologie," *OC*, I, pp. xxii–xxiii.

6. Kléber Haedens, "L.-F. Céline," *Candide* (July 29, 1964).

7. Georges Geoffroy, "Céline en Angleterre," *LH*, III, p. 11.

8. *Ibid.*, p. 12.

9. Recounted by M. Brochard, during an interview with the author (Paris, May 1969). Also suggested by Dominique de Roux, in a conversation with the author (Paris, July 1968).

10. "Carnet du Cuirassier Destouches" (also known as the "Black Notebook"), *LH*, V, 10. Céline's first known writings, dating from his cavalry days in 1914.

11. Robert Poulet, *Entretiens familiers avec L.-F. Céline* (Paris: Plon, 1958), p. 105.

12. In André Maurois' *Histoire de la France*, II (Paris: Albin Michel, 1947), p. 295.

13. "Carnet du Cuirassier . . . ," *op. cit.*, p. 10.

14. "Chronologie," *OC*, I, p. xxii.

15. Letter from Céline to M. Hindus (May 29, 1947), *LH*, V, p. 76.

16. For the complete version of this work, see *LH*, V, pp. 9–11.

17. Interview with Céline (1960), in *CAS*, p. viii.

18. M. Brochard, "Céline à Rennes," *op. cit.*, p. 15; Jean A. Ducourneau, "La Fin d'une légende," *OC*, I, pp. xxv–xxix. See also Robinson's statements concerning his trepanation, in *VOY*, p. 466.

19. Letter from Céline to M. Hindus (July 19, 1947), *LH*, V, pp. 86–87; see also R. Poulet's *Entretiens . . . , op. cit.*, pp. 77–78, for Céline's descriptions of this exploit.

20. Claude Bonnefoy, "Dernier Adieu à sa jeunesse," *Arts* (August 5–12, 1961).

21. Dr. Guy Morin, "Destouches médecin," *LH*, III, p. 18.

22. Stated by M. Brochard, during an interview with the author (Nantes, June 1969).

23. *VOY*, pp. 344–345.

24. R. Poulet, *Entretiens . . . , op. cit.*, p. 75.

25. Recounted by Mme. Edith Lebon (nee Follet), Céline's first wife, during an interview with the author (March 1969).

26. *VOY*, p. 238.

27. C. Bonnefoy, *op. cit.*, quoting Céline.

28. *VOY,* pp. 123–180.

29. Recounted by Mme. Lebon, interview cited.

30. *Ibid.*

31. *SEM,* p. 82.

32. *CAS,* p. 192.

33. *Ibid.,* p. 240.

34. Original in the private collection of M. Brochard, Nantes. Copy kindly presented to the author by M. Brochard.

35. M. Brochard, *op. cit.,* p. 14.

36. André Lwoff, "Quand Céline était 'chercheur' à l'Institut Pasteur," *Le Figaro Littéraire* (April 7–13, 1969).

37. Unpublished manuscript of an early tale written by Céline in 1917. At present, in the possession of the Librairie Nicaise, Boulevard St. Germain, Paris.

38. Jean Guénot, "Voyage au bout de la parole" (Interview), *LH*, V, p. 252.

39. Unpublished Preface to *Semmelweiss, LH*, III, p. 163.

40. *Ibid.,* p. 164.

41. Quoted by Dr. Villemain, during an interview with the author.

42. M. Brochard, *op. cit.,* p. 16.

43. Letter from Céline to A. Paraz (June 19, 1957), *LH*, III, p. 157.

44. Alastair Hamilton, "Céline's Paris," *London Magazine* (February 1968), p. 42.

45. Interview with Céline, *CAS,* p. x.

46. R. Poulet, *Entretiens* . . . , *op. cit.,* pp. 78–79.

47. See *VOY,* p. 208, for example.

48. "Hommage à Zola" (1933), *LH*, III, p. 169.

49. In 1928, Céline (then Destouches) submitted a communiqué to the Paris Medical Society, entitled "L'Organisation sanitaire des usines Ford," and subsequently published an article "Les Assurances sociales et une politique économique de la santé publique" in *La Presse Médicale* (reprinted in *OC*, I, pp. 721–730). What one may assume to be a synthesis of these two works, entitled "La Médecine chez Ford," first appeared in *Lecture 40,* August 1941

(reprinted in *OC,* I, pp. 711–720). It is in the latter that much of the material concerning the hiring of the disabled, used in my text, is to be found.

The work is a mock-serious study which (provided it is not read in naïvely straightforward fashion) emerges as a minor masterpiece in irony. The tone is close to that of the "pamphlets" which Céline was writing at the time of its publication, and might well be included among them, although it was conceived at a much earlier date (ca. 1928).

The literary transposition of Céline's experiences in the Ford factories appears in *VOY,* pp. 222–231.

50. Céline makes numerous references to the fact that he considered *L'Eglise* a "flop." See, for example: *BAM,* p. 78; his letter to Eveline Pollet (October 1933), *LH,* III, p. 102.

51. Céline defines *L'Eglise* as "a comedy." The title is ironic, as the following quote from the play indicates: "Life isn't a religion . . . it's a prison! you mustn't try to make its walls resemble those of a church . . . there are chains everywhere."

The play satirizes various power groups: colonialists, bankers, theatrical magnates, the police, the dignitaries of the League of Nations (especially the central power elite, consisting of Jews, whom Céline already attacks at this date but to whom he will address the most violent diatribes of his "pamphlets"), and ends in the faubourgs of Paris where life, love, and even death stagnate. The hilarious—though hideous—circumnavigation of the globe closes on a note of macabre fantasy: a dance performed around a dancer named Elizabeth Gaige (a thin disguise for Elisabeth Craig, an American dancer who had become Céline's mistress at this date).

The central message of the play resembles that of *Semmelweiss* (although it has now been satirically treated): "The truth of this world . . . is death! Life is a moment of intoxication, a lie!" (p. 102).

52. *VOY,* p. 237.

53. In *VOY,* Clichy becomes Garenne-Rancy. Céline's predilection for plays-on-names is evident: Rancy evokes the verb *rancir* ("to grow rancid").

54. Céline's Preface to *Bezons à travers les âges, op. cit.*

Chapter 3

1. Jeanne C[arayon], "Le Docteur écrit un roman," *LH*, III, p. 23.

2. Recounted by Eliane Bonabel, in an interview with the author (June 1969).

3. Utterance of Louis XVI which Céline had inscribed on his wall; recounted by Jean Loiret during an interview with the author (June 1969).

4. Henri Mahé, *La Brinquebale avec Céline* (Paris: La Table Ronde, 1969), p. 27.

5. Paul Chambrillon, "En 'brinquebalant' avec Céline," *Valeurs actuelles* (April 21, 1969), p. 42.

6. R. Poulet, *Entretiens* . . . , *op. cit.*, p. 43.

7. J. Guénot, "Voyage . . . ," *op. cit.*, p. 252.

8. Statement made by Gen Paul on the French TV program "Dans Céline, l'autre," Part II (May 18, 1969).

9. Letter from Céline to M. Hindus (September 2, 1947), *LH*, V, p. 94.

10. Letter from Céline to M. Hindus (September 10, 1947), *LH*, V, p. 96.

11. Recounted by H. Mahé, *op. cit.*, p. 61.

12. M. Brochard, *op. cit.*, p. 17.

13. Jeanne C., *op. cit.*, p. 21.

14. Recorded in the intimate journal of Colette Turpin (unpublished), which Mme. Turpin (nee Destouches, daughter of Céline by his first wife) kindly allowed the author to consult during her visit.

15. R. Poulet, *Entretiens* . . . , *op. cit.*, p. 23.

16. Recounted by Mme. Juliette Delannoy, during an interview with the author (September 1962).

17. *Ibid.*

18. Lucien Rebatet, "D'un Céline l'autre," *LH*, III, p. 43.

19. Letter to E. Pollet (September 14, 1933), *LH*, III, p. 101.

20. Jeanne C., *op. cit.*, p. 23.

21. Recounted by Jeanne Carayon, during an interview with the author (Chartres, September 1962).

22. See notes in *OC,* I, p. 743.

23. *Ibid.*

24. Letter from Céline to Lucien Descaves (1932; right after the publication of *Voyage au bout de la nuit*), *OC,* I, p. 745.

25. *Ibid.*

26. "L'Homme au bout de la nuit" (Interview with Céline by Albert Zbinden, broadcast by Radio Lausanne, July 25, 1957).

27. Jeanne C., *op. cit.,* p. 24.

28. Letter to L. Descaves, *OC,* I, p. 755.

29. Originally published in *Candide,* March 16, 1933. Reprinted in *OC,* I, p. 734.

30. *OC,* I, p. 735.

31. Letter from Céline to Léon Daudet (December 30, 1932), *LH,* III, p. 92.

32. Letter to Elie Faure (n.d., probably August 1934), *LH,* V, p. 56.

33. A character named Gologolo already appears in *L'Eglise.* The use of the same name for a human and an animal character is again noted in *Voyage* and the later novels: Bébert is both the name of a small boy whom Bardamu attempts to save, and that of the cat who accompanied Céline during exile and plays a prominent role in the writer's final trilogy.

34. C. Turpin's journal, *op. cit.*

35. Letter to M. Brochard (1930), *LH,* III, p. 16. The play-on-words is suggested by the name Brochard: Céline's nickname for M. Brochard was "La Broche" (*broche* in French means "rod," or "prick").

36. Other evidence can be found in *VOY,* p. 227, where Bardamu contrasts the football team's sexual prowess with his own "somewhat impotent" efforts. Opinions concerning signs of impotence in Céline were voiced by M. Brochard and Pierre de Boisdeffre in a radio broadcast by Jacques Legris, Paris, May 15, 1967 (text in the personal collection of the author).

37. Henri Mahé dixit.

38. "Secrets dans l'île," in *Neuf et une* (Paris: Gallimard, 1936), pp. 71–79. Lesbianism, encouraged by Céline, is also alluded to by H. Mahé, *op. cit.*, pp. 27–28.

39. H. Mahé, *op. cit.*, p. 101.

40. *Ibid.*, p. 103.

41. *Ibid.*, p. 102.

42. Postcard from Céline to L. Descaves (August 2, 1934). Unpublished. Quoted by special permission from Mme. Céline.

43. Letter from Céline to E. Pollet (August 30, 1934), *LH*, III, p. 102. Also quoted in E. Pollet's novel *Escaliers* (Brussels: La Renaissance du Livre, 1956), p. 61 (a book in which her liaison with Céline is fictionalized, according to Mme. Pollet's own statement during an interview with the author—Brussels, April 1969).

44. Letter from Céline to M. Hindus (September 10, 1947), *LH*, V, p. 96.

45. The ballet is published in *Bagatelles pour un massacre* (1937) and reappears in the collection *Ballets sans musique, sans personne, sans rien* (1959).

46. Céline asks Mme. Pollet permission to change her first name from Eveline to Evelyne, in a letter of February 1933, *LH*, III, p. 96.

47. "Secrets dans l'île," *op. cit.*

48. E. Pollet, *op. cit.*, p. 107.

49. *Ibid.*, p. 119.

50. *Ibid.*, p. 117.

51. *NOR*, p. 50.

52. Letter to Erika Landry (October 30, 1933), *LH*, V, pp. 43–44.

53. *Ibid.*, p. 44.

54. E. Pollet, *op. cit.*, pp. 121, 175.

55. Letter to Eugène Dabit (ca. 1936), *LH*, III, p. 88.

56. Letter to E. Pollet (January 31, 1937), *LH*, III, p. 103.

57. Irrgang which, in German, means "to go astray," or "to go mad"; changed to Landry by her marriage.

58. Letter from Céline to E. Landry (April, 1936), *LH*, V, p. 46.

59. Information obtained during a lengthy correspondence between Mme. Landry (now living in Costaraneira, Italy) and the author. Letters in the personal collection of the author.

60. Recounted by Mme. Lucienne Delforge during an interview with the author (May 1969).

61. Letter from Céline to L. Delforge (n.d.). Unpublished. Cited by special permission from Mme. Céline.

62. *Ibid.*

63. *Ibid.*

64. Louis Aragon and Elsa Triolet translated *Voyage au bout de la nuit* into Russian, in 1936. Preface by Anissimov (reprinted in *LH*, V, pp. 165–172).

65. *Mea Culpa, OC,* III, p. 341.

66. Letter from Céline to M. Hindus (May 29, 1947), *LH*, V, p. 77.

67. See reprints of the major critical articles of the time, in *OC,* II, pp. 733–760.

68. Recounted by Mme. Céline in a conversation with the author (Summer 1967).

69. *Paris Soir,* May 15, 1937. Originals of Céline's letters to the French Consul of the Isle of Jersey in the private collection of the author. Also published in *LH*, III, pp. 93–95.

70. Letter from Céline to the French Consul of the Isle of Jersey (n.d.), *LH*, III, p. 94.

71. Recounted by Mme. Bonabel during an interview with the author (June 1969).

72. Letter from Céline to M. Hindus (May 17, 1949), *LH*, V, p. 109.

73. Letter from Céline to M. Hindus (February 28, 1948), *LH*, V, p. 104. Note also the accounts by H. Mahé, *op. cit.,* pp. 118–119, which suggest that Céline encouraged lesbian encounters at a much earlier period of his life and was aware of the fascination and pleasure which they provided him.

74. Recounted by C. Turpin during her interview 'with the author; corroborated by various friends of Céline.

75. Incident recounted by H. Mahé during an interview with the author (April 1969).

76. Letter from Céline to Perrot (July 1, n.y.), *LH*, V, p. 127.

77. Letter from Céline to Denise Thomassen (December 31, n.y.), *LH*, V, p. 113.

78. Letter from Céline to M. Hindus (July 7, n.y.), *LH*, V, p. 84.

79. Letter from Céline to Ernst Bendz (n.d.), *LH*, V, p. 125.

80. Recounted by Mme. Céline in a conversation with the author (July 1968).

81. Letter from Céline to Raoul Nordling (March 28, 1949), *LH*, III, p. 137.

82. See Céline's letters to E. Pollet (August 1947), *LH*, III, p. 111; (February 1948), *LH*, III, p. 112.

83. Contrast with Céline's letter to A. Paraz (March 4, 1951), *LH*, V, p. 121.

84. *VOY*, p. 463.

85. Letter from Céline to M. Hindus (Augst 23, 1947), *LH*, V, p. 92.

86. Letter from Céline to A. Paraz (July 15, 1951), *LH*, III, p. 150.

87. Letter from Céline to E. Bendz (n.d.), *LH*, III, p. 129.

88. Letter to L. Descaves. In the collection of the Descaves family. Cited by special permission from Mme. Céline.

89. Recounted by M. Brochard during an interview with the author (May 1969).

Chapter 4

1. R. Poulet, *Entretiens* . . . , *op. cit.*, p. 38.

2. M[arie] C[anavaggia], "Mlle. Marie, ma secrétaire," *LH*, III, p. 31. Similar incidents also described by Mlle. Canavaggia during interviews with the author (1962, 1964).

3. Letter from Céline to M. Hindus (July 7, n.y.), *LH*, V, p. 84. See also Céline's letters to E. Pollet, which express similar feelings: (August 16, 1933), *LH*, III, p. 100; (May 31, 1938), *LH*, III, p. 105. See also Epigraph, *FEE:* "L'horreur des réalités!"

4. In: *FEE,* and *NOR*.

5. M. Brochard, *op. cit., LH*, III, p. 14.

6. Letter from Céline to E. Faure (1932), *LH*, V, p. 48.

7. Letter from Céline to M. Hindus (August 10, 1947), *LH*, V, pp. 89–90.

8. Letter from Céline to M. Hindus (July 19, 1947), *LH*, V, pp. 86–87. It must be noted that this letter was written during exile—resulting, in part, from anti-Semitic feelings expressed in Céline's writings. In writing thus to Hindus (of Jewish extraction) Céline may have been resorting to calculated flattery (via his portrait of Rajchman). This seems confirmed by a letter from Céline to Dr. C[amus] (July 17, 1948), *Ecrits de Paris* (October 1961), p. 107, in which he states: "I've only one admirer left in the world, and he's a rabbi!" (obviously referring to Hindus).

9. Letter from Céline to M. Hindus (August 10, 1947), *LH*, V, pp. 89–90.

10. Observations made by Alexandre Garbell during an interview with the author. M. Garbell had ample opportunity to observe Céline and his entourage during the Montmartre days, since they both frequented the same restaurant (Chez Birnbaum) for many years.

11. Letter from Céline to Perrot (n.d.), *LH*, V, p. 127.

12. Letter from Céline to A. Paraz, in Paraz' *Le Gala des vaches, op. cit.*, p. 146.

13. Statement made by Arletty during an interview with the author (September 1962).

14. Paris: Gallimard, 1959.

15. *Le Monde* (February 15, 1969), p. v; *Paris Match* (September 1960); *CAS*, pp. 88–89.

16. Letter from Céline to M. Hindus (July 18, 1947), *LH*, V, p. 85.

17. Visit to the home of Jacques Deval; interview with the author (May 1969).

18. Unpublished essay by C. Bonabel, "D'un Logis l'autre: itinéraires céliniens précédé de Du Côté de Destouches" (kindly put at the author's disposal by M. Bonabel). Supplemented by an interview with M. Bonabel by the author (1969).

19. Stated by Marcel Aymé during a conversation with the author at M. Aymé's summer home (September 1964).

20. Le Vigan, as portrayed in *NO*, pp. 116–118.

21. For these contrasting images, see two letters from Céline to M. Hindus: (May 15, 1947), *LH*, V, p. 75; (n.d., ca. 1949), *LH*, V, p. 111.

22. Letter from Céline to M. Hindus (June 22, n.y.), *LH*, V, p. 83.

23. *DIP*, pp. 325–529, deals with Courtial des Pereires. Contrast this example of literary transposition with descriptions of the actual inventor who served as Céline's model: Letter from Céline to M. Hindus (July 7, n.y.), *LH*, V, p. 84; Pierre Andreu's article, "Un Modèle de Céline," *La Quinzaine Littéraire* (July 15, 1966), pp. 11–12.

24. Gen Paul illustrated an edition of *Voyage au bout de la nuit* (Paris: Denoël, 1942), which is now a collector's item.

25. *Hommage à Zola.* Speech delivered by Céline in October 1933 upon the request of L. Descaves. Text in *LH*, III, pp. 169–172; also, *OC*, II, pp. 501–508.

26. Quoted by Pierre Monnier, in "Résidence surveillée," *LH*, III, p. 78.

27. René Héron de Villefosse, "Prophéties et litanies de Céline," *LH*, III, p. 34.

28. This and other details concerning the ambiance at the studio of Gen Paul, established during an interview with André Pulicani by the author (May 1969).

29. *NOR*, pp. 29–267.

30. *Ibid.*, pp. 318–321.

31. *CAS*, pp. 89–104.

32. In: *DIP, VOY, EG; CAS, NO, RIG*, respectively.

33. *NOR*, p. 24.

Chapter 5

1. See: *OC*, III, p. 336.

2. *Ibid.*, p. 342.

3. *idem.*

4. See letters written by Céline after the publication of *Mort à crédit*, *OC*, II, pp. 711, 717, 719–721.

5. They had already done so, after the publication of *Voyage au bout de la nuit:* see, for example, Louis Aragon, "A Louis-Ferdinand Céline, loin des foules," *Commune* (November 1933), pp. 179–181; Trotsky's comments about Céline at the Moscow

Writers' Congress of 1934, cited by A. Hamilton, *op. cit.*, p. 45; Paul Nizan, "Voyage au bout de la nuit," *L'Humanité* (September 12, 1932).

6. Letter from Céline to C. Bonabel (1937), in C. Bonabel's unpublished essay, *op. cit.* Quoted by special permission from Mme. Céline.

7. *BAM*, pp. 11–24; 24–33.

8. Remark made by Céline and reported by a number of his friends (H. Mahé, M. Brochard, *et al.*).

9. *BAM*, p. 33.

10. *Hommage à Zola, LH*, III, pp. 169–171.

11. The doctor's name was revealed much later by Céline in a conversation with R. Poulet: Dr. Idouc. See R. Poulet's *Entretiens . . . , op. cit.*, p. 51.

12. Letter from Céline to A. Paraz (May 18, 1951), *LH*, III, pp. 168–169.

13. Letter from Céline to M. Hindus (March 19, 1947), *LH*, V, p. 70.

14. Céline seems to expect any peak in life to be followed by a downward plunge. His apprehensions of the future are perhaps best expressed in a letter to E. Pollet, written at the height of his success with *Voyage au bout de la nuit* (September 28, 1933): "I have always had a horrible dread of the future, of future humiliations." *LH*, III, p. 101.

15. Letter from the painter Vlaminck (friend of Céline) to L. Descaves, a month after the publication of *Bagatelles pour un massacre* (January 19, 1938). In the private collection of the Descaves family. Photocopy kindly presented to the author by Mme. Descaves.

16. Letter from Céline to E. Pollet (June 2, 1939), *LH*, III, p. 108.

17. Letter from Céline to Lucien Combelle (1940), *LH*, V, pp. 64–65.

18. Letter from Céline to E. Pollet (June 21, 1941), *LH*, III, p. 109.

19. Céline, "Rabelais, il a raté son coup," *LH*, V, p. 21.

20. Admonition to Jean-Paul Sartre, in Céline's *A l'Agité du bocal* (Paris: P. Lanouve de Tartas, 1948).

21. Rabi, "Un Ennemi de l'homme," *LH*, III, p. 265.

22. Robert Chamfleury, 'Céline ne nous a pas trahi," *LH*, III, pp. 60–66.

23. Rabi, "Un Ennemi . . . ," *op. cit.,* p. 265.

24. This opinion is also expressed by Alain Penel, in "Si Céline n'avait pas existé," *Tribune de Genève* (May 16–17, 1964); and in "Céline, chroniqueur des grands guignols," *Tribune de Genève* (February 6, 1969).

25. Letter from Céline to Dr. Camus (Gibraltar, January 9, 1940), *LH,* III, p. 114.

26. In *BAM*.

27. In *EC*.

28. Georges Altmann had noticed this tendency as early as 1932 (in *Voyage au bout de la nuit*). See his comments in *LH,* V, p. 136.

29. L. Rebatet, *op. cit.,* p. 47.

30. Emmanuel Mounier, "Bagatelles pour un massacre," *Esprit,* No. 66 (March 1938).

31. Unpublished doctoral thesis, "Les Idées politiques de L.-F. Céline," by Jacqueline Morand.

32. *BAM,* p. 132.

33. Simone Mittre, "Témoignage," *LH,* V, p. 283.

34. Céline refutes his article in *La Gerbe* (February 18, 1941), reproduced in Michèle Cotta's *La Collaboration. 1940–1944* (Paris: Armand Colin, 1964), p. 136. He writes to L. Combelle: "the letter published in *La Gerbe* has been absolutely mutilated . . . truncated, falsified . . . I don't recognize myself at all . . . *it has nothing to do with me.*" Unpublished letter. Copy kindly presented to the author by M. Combelle. Quoted by special permission from Mme. Céline.

35. Robert Aron, *Histoire de Vichy,* II (Paris: Anthème Fayard, 1954), pp. 178–179.

36. Rabi, "Antisémite?" *Magazine Littéraire* (February 1969), p. 11.

37. John Webster, *The Duchess of Malfi*.

38. L. Rebatet, *op. cit.,* pp. 46–47.

39. Paul de Swaef, "Toujours entre le trône et la potence," *Le Peuple* (June 11, 1964).

40. M. Brochard, *op. cit.,* p. 16.

41. Rabi, "Un Ennemi . . . ," *op. cit.,* p. 265.

42. L. Rebatet, *op. cit.,* p. 47.

43. Robert Poulet, "Le Pont de Londres," *Rivarol* (April 30, 1964).

44. Letters to E. Faure (1932, 1933), *LH*, V, pp. 48, 55.

45. Six million francs, according to Kléber Haedens in "Le Dernier Rigodon de Céline," *Journal du Dimanche* (March 2, 1969), p. 2.

46. "Révélations sur Céline" (unsigned), *Candide* (January 10–17, 1963).

47. L. Rebatet, *op. cit.*, p. 54.

48. "Chronologie," *OC*, I, p. xxviii.

49. *CAS*, pp. 36–37.

50. *FEE*, p. 14.

51. R. Aron, *op. cit.*, II, pp. 439–440.

52. K. Haedens, "Le Dernier Rigodon . . . ," *op. cit.*, p. 2.

53. R. Aron, *op. cit*, II, p. 446.

54. L. Rebatet, *op. cit.*, p. 50.

55. *NO* (especially p. 41).

56. Karl Epting, "Il ne nous aimait pas," *LH*, III, p. 59.

57. Renamed by Céline in an ironic play on words: "Siegmaringen" (*Sieg* in German means "victory").

58. L. Rebatet, *op. cit.*, p. 51.

59. R. Aron, *op. cit.*, II, pp. 446, 448.

60. *Ibid.*, p. 456.

61. *Ibid.*, pp. 451–453.

62. *Ibid.*, p. 459.

63. S. Mittre, *op. cit.*, p. 284.

64. L. Rebatet, *op. cit.*, pp. 52–53.

65. *Ibid.*, p. 51.

66. R. Aron, *op. cit.*, II, 463.

67. L. Rebatet, *op. cit.*, p. 54.

68. R. Aron, *op. cit.*, II, 463.

69. L. Rebatet, *op. cit.*, p. 54.

70. Mme. Céline states that this occurred ten days after the start of their twenty-one-day-long journey. Interview published in *Magazine Littéraire* (February 1969), p. 18.

71. The actual itinerary of the Céline couple has been established by K. Haedens, "Le Dernier Rigodon . . . ," *op. cit.*, as: Berlin, Rostock, Warnemünde; Berlin, Ulm, Sigmaringen, Hanover, Flensburg, Copenhagen.

72. *RIG,* p. 276.

Chapter 6

1. *FEE* (1952).

2. *RIG* (1969). Note the progression from the first to the second of these epigraphs.

3. P. Monnier, *op. cit.*, p. 74.

4. *NO,* pp. 46–47.

5. Letter from Céline to Dr. C[amus] (June 30, 1947), *Ecrits de Paris* (October 1961), p. 104.

6. Story recounted by Mme. Céline during a conversation with the author (Summer 1964).

7. Name of a large department store in Paris.

8. *NO,* p. 296.

9. *Ibid.*, pp. 132, 174, 308–309.

10. *Ibid.*, pp. 356–357.

11. Ole Vinding, "Vu par son ami danois," *LH*, III, p. 69.

12. Recounted by Mme. Céline during a conversation with the author (Summer 1967).

13. R. Poulet, *Entretiens* . . . , *op. cit.*, p. 12.

14. Jean Pommery, "Bestiaire de Céline," *LH*, V, p. 302.

15. R. Poulet, *Entretiens* . . . , *op. cit.*, p. 5.

16. J. Pommery, *op. cit.*, pp. 301–302.

17. *Ibid.*, p. 306.

Chapter 7

1. Letter from prison (Céline to his wife), March 15, 1946; transmitted by his lawyer. *LH,* V, p. 310.

2. English word *finish* appears in original.

3. According to the French penal code, Article 75 applies to those who have "had intelligence with the enemy." See J. Morand, *op. cit.*, p. 360, for its application to Céline's case.

4. *FEE*, pp. 169–178.

5. *Ibid.*, pp. 157–159.

6. *Ibid.*, p. 224.

7. Maurice Nadeau, "La Fin du voyage," *La Quinzaine Littéraire* (March 15, 1969), pp. 3–4. One informant claims that Céline and his wife were betrayed by the friend who "preferred their gold to their necks." See Dominique de Roux's "Céline: toujours dans les beaux draps," *L'Esprit Public* (March 1963, p. 59).

8. Letter from Céline to M. Hindus (April 31, n.y.), *LH*, V, p. 74.

9. The letter in question read:

> *Copenhagen,*
> *December 18, 1945*
>
> *Monsieur le Ministre,*
>
> *I have been informed that M. Destouches, Ferdinand, a French subject accused of treason and subject to a warrant of arrest issued April 19, 1945 by the Seine Court, has sought refuge in Denmark and, according to the latest reports, is residing on the top floor of 20 Ved Stranden, in the apartment of Mme. Karen Jensen.*
>
> *In the name of my government, and according to our reciprocal agreement policy, I have the honor of asking you to order the arrest and extradition of the person concerned.*
>
> *Attached please find a copy of the order for arrest, as well as the texts (Articles 75 and 76 of the penal code) upon which the guilt of M. Céline is based.*
>
> *With my profound respect,*
>
> *G. de Girard de Charbonnière*

10. In December 1945, Jean-Paul Sartre published his "Portrait de l'antisémite," in *Les Temps Modernes* (I, No. 3), pp. 442–470. Céline's retort to this work (most likely conceived in prison), "A l'Agité du bocal," was first published in A. Paraz' *Le Gala des vaches, op. cit.*, where it passed unnoticed; it was later brought out in an edition of 200 copies by P. Lanouve de Tartas, Paris. Text reprinted in *LH*, V, pp. 22–24; *OC*, III, pp. 415–417.

11. Cited by P. Monnier, *op. cit.*, p. 74.

12. Michaël Donley, "L'Identification cosmique," *LH*, V, p. 193.

13. Stated by Lucette Céline in "Céline. Le Testament d'un maudit" (interview with Mme. Céline), *Les Nouvelles Littéraires* (February 6, 1969), p. 7.

14. "Madame Céline raconte son mari," *Télémagazine*, No. 702 (April 5–11, 1969), p. 74.

15. Recounted by Mme. Céline during a conversation with the author (July 1968).

16. The document can be found, in its entirety, in *LH*, V, pp. 319–325.

    The major points made by Céline are: a total denial of all crimes he has been accused of; proof of his innocence; a reminder of the fact that he had volunteered during both world wars to fight on the side of France; that his trip to Germany was made only with the aim of reaching a peaceful retreat; that, rather than a "collaborator," he should be considered an "abstentionist"; that he is a victim of mass hysteria and the envy of his literary rivals.

    The document is signed by Céline, and dated November 6, 1946.

    It should be noted that Maurice Vanino's *L'Ecole du cadavre, L'Affaire Céline* (Paris: Editions Créator, 1952) refutes Céline's defense and cites examples which inculpate him.

    The controversial nature of accusations and denials leaves the *legal* guilt of Céline open to question. J. Morand, *op. cit.*, for example, does not find proof of any substantial character; M. Cotta, *op. cit.*, cites only two instances in which Céline published articles during the occupation, and of these two, only the first could be described as "collaborationist" (a call to arms against the Jews, urging the Vichy government to take a position against them; published in *La Gerbe*, February 18, 1941), p. 136; the second consists of an attack against Charles Péguy, admired by the collaborationists as the creator of French national-socialism (published in *L'Appel*, April 12, 1941), pp. 233–234.

    The question of *human* guilt, however, is a much broader and more profound one, and cannot be minimized.

17. Letter from Céline to A. Paraz (June 1, 1947), in *Le Gala des vaches, op. cit.*, p. 86.

18. J.-P. Sartre, *op. cit.*, p. 462.

19. *AB*.

20. Letter from Céline to A. Paraz (June 22, 1957), *LH*, III, p. 159.

21. J.-P. Sartre, *op. cit.*, pp. 469–470.

22. *AB,* in *OC,* III, p. 417.

23. Letter from Céline to E. Bendz (1948), *LH,* III, p. 120.

24. In a letter to Bendz, Céline describes the work as: "a bit of non-sense, an old scenario for a cartoon, which I'm having published in order to try to pay my typist in France! (secretly)!"—*LH,* III, p. 126; or as: "a little diversion, whose only merit is that it was written during my 18 months' imprisonment at the *Vestre Faenjsel* (known the world over!)"—*LH,* III, p. 118.

25. Recounted by Mme. Céline during a conversation with the author; substantiated by E. Bonabel.

26. Letter from Céline to E. Pollet (August 1947), *LH,* III, p. 111.

27. Story recounted by Céline; quoted by P. Monnier, *op. cit.,* p. 77.

28. Letter from Céline to M. Hindus (June 22, 1947), *LH,* V, p. 83.

29. Letter from Céline to M. Hindus (March 30, 1947), *LH,* V, p. 70.

30. Letters to E. Bendz (1948), *LH,* III, pp. 117–118.

31. Unpublished letter from Céline (March 13, 1947). In the Descaves estate. Quoted by permission from Mme. Céline.

32. Letter from Céline to M. Hindus (August 1947), *LH,* V, p. 92.

33. Letter from Céline to G. Altmann (October 27, n.y.), *LH,* V, p. 135.

34. Céline, "Vive l'Amnistie, Monsieur," *LH,* V, p. 28.

35. Letter from Céline to M. Hindus (June 14, n.y.), *LH,* V, p. 81.

36. Letter from Céline to M. Hindus (May 29, 1947), *LH,* V, p. 77.

37. Letter from Céline to M. Hindus (June 11, 1947), *LH,* V, p. 79.

38. Letter from Céline to L. Descaves (n.d.), *LH,* III, p. 118.

39. Letter from Céline to M. Hindus (n.d.), *LH,* V, p. 80.

40. Interview with Céline. *L'Express* (June 14, 1957).

Chapter 8

1. Letter from Céline to E. Faure (1934), *LH,* V, p. 56.

2. "Letters from Exile" (to Dr. C[amus], November 15, 1948). In *Ecrits de Paris* (October 1961), p. 108.

3. *Ibid.* (May 17, 1948), p. 105.

4. *Idem.*

5. *Ibid.* (October 15, 1948), p. 108.

6. *Ibid.* (July 14, 1948), pp. 106–107.

7. *Ibid.* (June 15, 1948), p. 106.

8. Letter from Céline to M. Hindus (June 30, 1949), *LH*, V, p. 111.

9. "Letters from Exile" (June 7, 1948), pp. 105–106.

10. Quoted by P. Monnier, *op. cit.*, p. 77.

11. Céline had originally entitled this work "La Bataille du Styx," and liked to refer to it as his "prayer-wheel." See *OC*, III, p. 599.

12. A few years after the assassination of Denoël, his publishing house was acquitted of having published works in favor of the enemy or containing racist or totalitarian doctrines. See *LH*, V, p. 311, for the text of the document which (by extension) seems to acquit not only the publisher but also the authors he published (such as Céline).

13. Letter from Céline to M. Hindus (n.d.), *LH*, V, p. 102.

14. Letter from Céline to M. Hindus (September 12, 1948), *LH*, V, p. 111.

15. For example, a job for Lucette as dance instructor or a physician's post for Céline in Alaska (*LH*, V, pp. 84–85); as well as publications in the U.S. or nylons to be used in barter for food (*LH*, V, pp. 69, 71, 76, 77, 82, 91–93).

16. Information concerning the work of Hindus, based on his visit to Denmark, as well as the developments that followed, can be found in *LH*, V, pp. 67–68.

17. Letter from Céline to M. Hindus (January 20, 1949), *LH*, V, pp. 111–112.

18. In France, where Céline claimed he had been "excommunicated" (see his letter to M. Hindus, *LH*, V, p. 107), Monnier *did* succeed in having some of Céline's work published once again: the Editions Paul Chambriand, Paris, brought out *Casse-pipe* in 1949, and the ballet "Scandale aux abysses" in 1950 (before Céline's exoneration and return from exile).

19. Letter from Céline to Perrot (n.d.), *LH*, V, p. 129.

20. Letter from Céline to E. Pollet (February 21, 1948), *LH*, III, p. 112.

21. See Céline's correspondence with R. Nordling, A. Paraz, Pastor Löchen, E. Bendz, for examples (*LH*, III, pp. 117–150).

22. Letter from Céline to L. Descaves (December 1947), *LH*, III, p. 116.

23. Letter from Céline to E. Bendz (August 9, 1948), *LH*, III, p. 117.

24. Letter from Céline to Perrot (n.d.), *LH*, V, p. 131.

25. *SEM*, pp. 103, 105.

26. Reported by R. Héron de Villefosse, *op. cit.*, p. 34.

27. Letter from Céline to P. Monnier (n.d.), *LH*, III, p. 79.

28. Judgment pronounced upon Céline (by default) on February 21, 1950, by the court of the 3rd departmental subsection of the Seine. For details, see "Céline est condamné à un an de prison," *Le Monde* (February 23, 1950), p. 3; also *OC*, I, p. xxxi.

29. The Association Israélite pour la Réconciliation des Français. For details, see Michel Legris' "L'Antisémite," *Le Monde* (July 6, 1961); also *Le Monde* (February 23, 1950), p. 3.

30. "Céline s'en tire avec une tirade de rires inédite," *Paris Match* (March 4, 1950), p. 29. Se also P. Monnier, *op. cit.*, p. 80; A. Paraz, *op. cit.*, p. 291.

31. Letter from Céline to E. Bendz (n.d.), *LH*, III, p. 124.

32. Surgery for a fibroma, performed May 1950.

33. Letter from Céline to Perrot (n.d.), *LH*, V, p. 127.

34. Letter from Céline to L. Descaves (n.d.), *LH*, III, p. 116.

35. See Céline's letter to E. Pollet (February 21, 1948), *LH*, III, p. 111.

36. See numerous letters by A. Paraz, *LH*, V, pp. 285–298, on this subject.

37. Letter from Céline to P. Löchen (December 26, 1947), *LH*, III, p. 132.

38. Reported by P. Monnier, *op. cit.*, p. 75.

39. A. Hamilton, *op. cit.*, p. 41.

40. Letter from Céline to D. Thomassen (n.d.), *LH*, V, p. 114.

41. *Féerie pour une autre fois, II. Normance.* To be published by Gallimard in 1954.

42. Letter from Céline to Perrot (n.d.), *LH*, V, p. 125.

43. P. Monnier, *op. cit.*, p. 76.

44. Letter from Céline to M. Hindus, *LH*, V, p. 85.

45. Letter from Céline to M. Hindus, *LH*, V, p. 69.

46. In a conversation with the author (Spring 1969), H. Mahé suggested the link between *"argot"* and *"art gothique,"* stating that *argot* originated as the secret language of cathedral builders, in order to allow them to convey the formulas for constructing these edifices without running the risk of their being understood by outsiders or the uninitiated.

47. Two articles in *Le Monde* relate to the struggle for the application of the amnesty rule to Céline: the first, "Louis-Ferdinand Céline ne peut être amnistié," *Le Monde* (December 15, 1951), p. 7; the second, "Monsieur L.-F. Céline est amnistié," *Le Monde* (April 27, 1951), p. 7, also states that Céline's case was handled by MM. Tixier-Vignancour and Naud (the latter having also been Laval's defense lawyer).

48. *OC*, I, p. xxxi.

49. Letter from Céline to E. Bendz (n.d.) *LH*, III, p. 130.

50. Letter from Céline to R. Nordling (March 24, 1951), *LH*, III, p. 139.

51. Letter to A. Paraz (May 27, 1951—Céline's 57th birthday), *LH*, III, p. 149. The same pronouncement was made on numerous other occasions by Céline (in interviews, letters to various friends, etc.). It might be considered his "famous last words" (since, ironically, the paralysis of his vocal cords at the time of death did not allow him to utter any final pronouncement).

52. See Céline's letters to A. Paraz written during this period, in which the key words and phrases cited appear: *LH*, III, pp. 143, 150, 151.

53. Letter from Céline to A. Paraz (July 19, 1951—just before the novelist's return from exile), *LH*, III, p. 151.

Chapter 9

1. Letter from Céline to A. Paraz (Menton, July 10, 1951), *LH*, III, p. 150.

2. Letter from Céline to A. Paraz (July 15, 1951), *LH*, III, p. 150.

3. On August 18, 1951, Céline signed a contract with Gallimard, who, from this time on, became the publisher of all his works.

The house in question is the one located at 25 ter, Route des Gardes, Meudon, where Céline spent the remaining years of his life and which is still inhabited by his widow. The purchase of the house was made with the aid of the Marteaus and the family of Lucette Almanzor.

4. Tape interviews with Céline by J. Guénot and J. Darribehaude, reproduced in *LH*, III, p. 190.

5. Letter from Céline to A. Paraz (June 26, 1953), *LH*, III, p. 153.

6. Letter from Céline to A. Paraz (January 14, 1953), *LH*, III, p. 152.

7. Letter from Céline to M. Hindus (August 29, n.y.), *LH*, V, p. 93.

8. Letter from Céline to A. Paraz (November 1, 1953), *LH*, III, p. 154.

9. *CAS*, p. 11.

10. Letter from Céline to M. Hindus (March 30, 1947), *LH*, V, p. 72.

11. Letter from Céline to A. Paraz (June 26, 1953), *LH*, III, p. 153.

12. One critic had already remarked this in Céline's *Pont de Londres* (written ca. 1944; published 1964): see Renaud Matignon's article in *Mercure de France* (July 1964), pp. 545–546.

13. Jean Guénot, "De la Parole à l'écriture," *Le Monde* (February 15, 1969), p. 12.

14. Letter from Céline to A. Paraz (February 24, 1951), *LH*, V, p. 120.

15. See Dominique Rolin's remarks on this subject in "Ni avant, ni après, ni ailleurs," *LH*, III, pp. 290–291.

16. Letter from Céline to A. Paraz (August 14, 1957), *LH*, III, p. 160.

17. Reported by Mme. Céline during a conversation with the author (Meudon, September 1962).

18. Claude Sarraute, "Ecrire, c'est un truc qui vous tue le bonhomme," *Le Monde* (July 5, 1961).

Chapter 10

1. *Hommage à Zola, LH*, III, p. 172.

2. R. Poulet, *Entretiens* . . . , *op. cit.*, p. 99.

3. "Je sens les Parques me gratter le fil . . ." *RIG*, p. 290.

4. *Normance.* Volume II of *Féerie pour une autre fois.* Published by Gallimard in 1954.

5. *NOR*, pp. 93–95.

6. *Ibid.*, pp. 102–103.

7. *Ibid.*, pp. 104–105.

8. *Ibid.*, p. 114.

9. *Ibid.*, p. 119.

10. Letter from Céline to M. Hindus (July 28, 1947), *LH*, V, pp. 87–88.

11. Letter from Céline to A. Paraz (July 20, 1954—one month after the publication of *Normance*), *LH*, III, p. 156.

12. *Entretiens avec le Professeur Y.* Note that there might be a pun intended (Y = Why?) in the title.
    During a round-table discussion on Céline (New York University, January 1967), Prof. Hindus stated that he thought that this work of Céline contained his portrait. Was it Céline's answer to Hindus' *Crippled Giant,* by means of which Céline wished to establish that, despite his crippled state, he was still an adversary to be reckoned with?

13. Pierre Audinet, "Dernières Rencontres avec Céline," *Les Nouvelles Littéraires* (July 6, 1961), p. 1.

14. Selections from Cèline's letters to E. Bendz, M. Hindus, L. Combelle (contained in *LH*, III & V), reprinted in *Magazine Littéraire* (February 1969), pp. 20–21. Letter from Céline to Combelle, *LH*, V, pp. 65–66.

15. Letter from Céline to A. Paraz (August 4, 1952), *LH*, III, p. 152.

16. R. Poulet, *Entretiens* . . . , *op. cit.*, p. 5.

17. *D'un Château l'autre* (1957); *Nord* (1960); *Rigodon* (1969).

18. Céline, "L'Argot est né de la haine. Il n'existe plus," *Arts* (February 6, 1957); reprinted in *LH,* V, p. 31.

19. *NO,* p. 63.

20. Interview with Céline. *CAS,* p. v.

21. Walter Lenning, "Fragwürdige Abrechnung," *Hamburger Sonntagsblatt* (April 9, 1961).

22. Philippe Sénart, "Gide et Céline," *Combat* (February 14, 1963).

23. Preface to the original edition of *Nord* (Gallimard, 1960). (Edition withdrawn from circulation as the result of a libel suit; replaced by the revised edition now in common use.)

24. The original French reads: "Je les ferai chanter, vos cellules" (somewhat loosely translated in *CAS* as: "I'd make those cells talk"—p. 339). *Chanter* has a double meaning in French: (1) "to sing," (2) "to squeal" (betray guilty secrets or crimes).

25. Frederic Morton, "The First to 'Mine' Delirium," *The Nation* (March 17, 1969).

26. Céline's widow, with the help of two lawyer friends, edited and put *Rigodon* into its published form. Many French critics felt that some doubt might be cast upon the authenticity of the final product. Critical opinion concerning *Rigodon* is exemplified by: Annie Copperman, "Rigodon," *Les Echos* (February 21, 1969); Hubert Juin, "La poussière et les débris," *Combat* (February 6, 1969); François Nourissier, *"Rigodon,* roman de Louis-Ferdinand Céline." *Les Nouvelles Littéraires* (February 13, 1969).

Chapter 11

1. Quoted by R. Poulet, *Entretiens* . . . , *op. cit.,* p. 99.

2. Christian Dédet, "La Condition médicale de L.-F. Céline," *LH,* III, p. 314.

3. *Ibid.,* p. 313.

4. Quoted by J. Guénot, "Voyage . . . ," *op. cit.,* p. 249.

5. *Ibid.,* p. 250.

6. Léon Darcyl, "Céline le pestiféré," *Paris Match* (September 24, 1960), p. 89.

7. R. Poulet, *Entretiens* . . . , *op. cit.,* p. 2.

8. J. Guénot, "Voyage . . . ," *op. cit.*, p. 250.

9. P. Audinet, *op. cit.*, p. 4.

10. R. Poulet, *Entretiens* . . . , *op. cit.*, pp. 49–50.

11. See for example: Roger Nimier, *NRF Bulletin* (August 1961); J. Ducourneau's "Chronologie," in the Pléiade edition of Céline (Gallimard, 1962), p. xviii. Ducourneau refutes this myth a few years later in "La Fin d'une légende: Céline n'a jamais été trépané," *Le Figaro Littéraire* (October 27, 1966). It reappears, however, in Anatole Broyard's "Castle to Castle," *The New York Times Book Review* (January 5, 1969), p. 3.

12. A. Hamilton, *op. cit.*, p. 41; M. Brochard, *op. cit.*, p. 13.

13. André Brissaud, "Voyage au bout de la tendresse," *LH*, III, pp. 226–227. This article also includes information concerning the interview (*L'Express*, June 14, 1957) in which Céline was represented in a most unfavorable light.

14. Note that this letter to A. Paraz (*LH*, III, p. 157) was dated only four days after the above-mentioned interview had appeared.

15. Letter from Céline to A. Paraz, on the same subject (June 19, 1957), *LH*, III, p. 159.

16. Film made by Louis Pauwels which was not allowed to be shown. Parts of it appeared ten years later in a two-part television program "Dans Céline, l'autre," May 8, 18, 1969.

    Portions of the filmed interview have been quoted by A. Brissaud, *op. cit.*, p. 229.

17. "Louis-Ferdinand Céline vous parle." Recorded speech. Disques Festival, FDL-149M.

18. *EPY*, pp. 11–15.

19. Quoted by M. Canavaggia, *op. cit.*, p. 31.

20. *Ibid.*

21. R. Poulet, *Entretiens* . . . , *op. cit.*, pp. 15–16.

22. Quoted by P. Audinet, *op. cit.*, p. 4. Note that this book was never written, since Céline died shortly after having made the pronouncement. The title is nevertheless of great interest: "L'Ambassadrice" suggests a link with "L'Impératrice" (the "Empress")— the dancer Elisabeth Craig, to whom Céline had dedicated his first book, *Voyage au bout de la nuit*.

    Céline's widow also stated that her late husband had planned to write a book on the dance which would be his "last work." See "Céline cinq ans après," *Pariscope* (January 26, 1966), p. 20.

23. The Pléiade edition of Céline appeared posthumously (1962) but had been begun during the author's lifetime. He was thus one of three living writers to be included among the classics for whom the Pléiade is traditionally reserved—the other two being Montherlant and Malraux (whom Céline would parody as *Buste-à-pattes* ("Bust-with-paws") and *Dur-de-mèche* ("Tough-Prick"), respectively, in his posthumously published novel *Rigodon*). It is interesting to note that Céline was most eager to be included in the Pléiade and did not hesitate employing coercive measures in order to obtain his ends. (Evidence to this fact gathered by the author in the Gallimard archives.)

24. The reference here is very likely to Gaston Gallimard, whose offices are located at 5, rue Sébastien Bottin (the street name probably suggesting the play on words used by Céline). There are, however, many other names under which the publisher and various editors appear in the late novels of Céline. Moreover, disparagement of publishers is habitual with Céline, as his references to Denoël have shown.

25. The original term is "l'extra-voyant lucide."

26. See "Un Voile trop transparent," *Paris-Normandie* (March 8, 1963); "Nord," *Aux Ecoutes* (March 8, 1963).

27. Robert Poulet, "Une Oeuvre retrouvée de Céline," *Rivarol* (February 6, 1964).

28. "A Propos de Céline," *Le Monde* (March 8, 1969).

29. "Le Manuscrit dans le placard," *Aux Ecoutes* (April 17, 1964). The fact that Céline had lost interest in the work is substantiated in his letter to A. Paraz (April 18, 1951), *LH,* III, p. 144.

30. R. Poulet, "Une Oeuvre . . . ," *op. cit.*

31. See *Paris Match* (July 15, 1961), p. 31.

32. Recounted by Céline's widow during conversations with the author. Observations made by the author, as well as examinations of the manuscript version of "Rigodon," during the years following Céline's death.

33. Process described by Mme. Céline in her interview for *Pariscope, op. cit.,* p. 19.

34. "Comment fut écrit *Rigodon*" (Interview with Mme. Céline), *Magazine Littéraire* (February 1969), p. 18.

35. For example, Jean Freustié, "La Pavane du collabo," *Le Nouvel Observateur* (February 17, 1969).

36. Preface to *Rigodon* (Paris: Gallimard, 1969) by François Gibault, p. iii.

37. F. Nourissier, *op. cit.*, p. 2.

38. Title of an entire issue of *Magazine Littéraire* ("Céline l'enragé"), No. 26 (February 1969).

39. Letter from Mme. Pollet to the author (Brussels, April 30, 1969). In the author's personal collection.

40. M. Brochard, *op. cit.*, pp. 13, 16.

41. Stated by Mme. Céline during a conversation with the author (September 1962).

42. Stated by Dr. Villemain, Céline's attending physician, during an interview with the author (June 1969).

43. L. Darcyl, *op. cit.*, p. 91.

44. A. Parinaud, *op. cit.*, p. 3.

45. Philippe Sénart, "Céline: Le Pont de Londres," *La Table Ronde* (June 1964).

46. Kingsley Shorter, "Expressionist Mosaic," *The New Leader* (March 31, 1969).

47. Marc Hanrez, "Le Prince des hommes libres," *LH*, III, pp. 242–243.

48. Probably due to Céline's utterances in novels and interviews (such as his statement, "I hope to die of a heart attack . . . or maybe I'll finish myself off . . . that would be even simpler," quoted by A. Parinaud, *op. cit.*, p. 3); possibly also as a result of the clandestine nature of his death and burial.

49. P. Audinet, *op. cit.*, p. 1.

50. Statement made by Dr. Villemain, who had been present at Céline's funeral, during a conversation with the author.

51. A society named "Amis de Céline en Suisse" was founded by Gérard Nanzer in Bienne and Geneva, Switzerland, on July 1, 1964 (on the third anniversary of the writer's death). At present there are about eighty members. The organization sponsors read-

ings, lectures, forums and TV programs. It also sponsors an annual requiem mass for Céline (advertised in the notice shown which appears in *La Suisse,* Neuchâtel, on the anniversary of his death).

52. *Paris Match* (July 15, 1961), p. 32.

Chapter 12

1. *VOY,* pp. 237–238. Note that this passage occurs almost exactly in the center of *Voyage au bout de la nuit,* and might be said to divide the novel into two parts: "The Other World"; "Return from the Other World."

2. *CAS,* p. 135.

3. Letter from E. Faure to Céline (July 7, 1935), *LH,* V, p. 59.

4. Description given by Arno Breker (sculptor and friend of Céline) during an interview with the author (June 1969).

5. Very apt term coined by Michel Beaujour, "La Quête du délire," *LH,* III, p. 285.

6. An intriguing viewpoint developed by Arnold Mandel, "D'un Céline juif," *LH,* III, pp. 252–255; "L'Ame irresponsable ou Céline et le Dibbouk," *LH,* V, pp. 207–209.

7. Leon Trotsky, "Céline et Poincaré," *LH,* V, p. 147.

8. *CAS,* p. 22.

9. Title of study by M. Hanrez, *op. cit.,* pp. 240–243.

10. *CAS,* pp. 79, 81. Note that the second term, however, is mistranslated: "Moi, l'extra-voyant" is rendered as "Oh, those piercing eyes of mine!"

11. J.-M.-G. le Clézio, "Comment peut-on écrire autrement," *Le Monde* (February 15, 1969), p. 4.

12. *Ibid.*

13. Interesting coincidence related by A. Breker, *op. cit.:* a completed bust of Céline was inadvertently dropped by one of the sculptor's assistants and had to be begun once more; it has not been completed to date.

14. H. Miller, *The Intimate Henry Miller* (New York: Signet Books), p. 152.

15. René Barjavel, *Journal d'un homme simple* (Paris: Frederic Chambriand, 1951), p. 181.

16. See *VOY*, p. 333, for Céline's treatment of this notion.

17. For those interested in zodiac interpretations, Céline's Astroflash horoscope indicates the following:

> BIRTH SIGN: Gemini, with Scorpio rising. Gemini (suppleness, flexibility, adaptability, fluidity) opposed by Scorpio (intransigence, imperiousness, pride, stubbornness, aggressiveness, individualism). Instability of mixed signs.

> MOON IN PISCES: An unconscious with extreme "psychological plasticity"; an inner self enriched by sensations and emotions which in successive waves fill it and at times even submerge it. Possible result: a loss of inner unity, even inner chaos when these contradictory currents, this perpetual flux and reflux, enmesh the being like a piece of flotsam.

> VENUS "IN EXILE" IN ARIES: Desire overrides feeling and passion dominates tenderness. The peak of passion frequently foreshadows its inevitable end. In marriage: boredom, monotony and silence are the mortal enemies.

> MERCURY IN GEMINI: Unusual mental ability. Curiosity. Wit. Humor. A bent to embroider on reality.

18. R. Poulet, *Entretiens* . . . , *op. cit.*, pp. 70–71.

19. *Ibid.*

20. R. Poulet, *Entretiens* . . . , *op. cit.*, pp. 33, 7, 16.

21. Alain Hardy, "Rigodon," *LH*, V, p. 270.

22. Jean Dubuffet, "Céline pilote," *LH*, V, pp. 225–226.

23. Céline quoted by R. Denoël, in "Apologie de *Mort à crédit*," *LH*, V, p. 242.

24. Letter from Céline to E. Pollet (March 1933), *LH*, III, p. 97.

25. *Ibid.* (April 15, 1941), *LH*, III, p. 109.

26. *Ibid.* (April 1933), *LH*, III, p. 97.

27. *Ibid.* (May 15, 1933), *LH*, III, p. 97.

28. Jacqueline Piatier, "Louis-Ferdinand Céline," *Le Monde* (July 6, 1961).

29. On the very first page of *Death on the Installment Plan*. (The original reads "la médecine . . . cette merde" and has been softened in translation, to "medicine . . . crummy trade.")

30. *DIP*, p. 19.

31. R. Poulet, *Entretiens* . . . , *op. cit.*, p. 43.

32. See letters to A. Paraz (*LH*, III, pp. 144–160) in which Céline addresses his friend as "J.J." (abbr. for Jeune Jeune") or uses variations of this form of address, such as "Mon vieux J.J.," "Mon archi J.J.," "Mon jiji."

33. Described by Dr. Camus, *LH*, III, p. 114.

34. The following signatures appear in the letters of Céline to L. Combelle (dating from ca. 1941 to ca. 1957; unpublished; photocopies in the private collection of the author, kindly provided by M. Combelle) :

    LF Céline
    LFerdinand
    Destouches
    LF Destouches
    L Destouches
    LF
    LFC
    LFerd
    Des Céline (the second signature is superimposed on the first, as though the writer had changed his mind in the middle of signing his name. The original "Des"—first three letters of Destouches—has been covered over by the initials "LF" of "LF Céline.")

    Destouches ("Destouches" has been crossed out and replaced by LFCéline "LF Céline.")

35. Robert Kirsch, "Céline's 'Castle,' a Fascinating Freak-out," *Los Angeles Times* (April 2, 1969).

36. Letter from Allen Ginsberg to the author (September 24, 1964). Quoted with permission from Mr. Ginsberg.

37. Gen Paul; Lucette Destouches. "Dans Céline, l'autre," *op. cit.*, Part I (May 8, 1969).

38. *EPY*, p. 13; A. Hamilton, *op. cit.*, p. 47.

39. Dr. Villemain dixit; Max Dorian, "Céline, rue Amélie," *LH*, III, p. 26; J. Loiret dixit; H. Mahé dixit.

40. A. Hamilton, *op. cit.*, p. 43; A. Breker dixit; P. Audinet, *op. cit.*, p. 4.

41. Dr. Camus, *LH*, III, 113; Mme. Céline dixit; Dr. Villemain dixit.

42. Mme. Nadine Nimier dixit; Dr. Villemain dixit.

43. H. Mahé dixit; Mme. Céline dixit.

44. "Carnet du Cuirassier . . . ," *op. cit.,* p. 10; biographical detail, confirmed by various friends of Céline.

45. In his late novels, Céline refers to his parrot by this name; *Paris Match* and several other magazines (such as *Arts,* etc.) report the parrot's name as "Coco"; Mme. Céline dixit.

46. Letter from Céline to E. Landry (n.d.), *LH,* V, p. 39; letter from Céline to E. Pollet (May 29, 1939), *LH,* III, p. 108; Pascal Pia, "L'Art de se mettre dans son tort," *Magazine Littéraire,* No. 26 (February 1969), p. 9.

47. Mme. Céline dixit (statement repeated frequently); R. Poulet, *Entretiens* . . . , *op. cit.,* p. 6.

48. Marcel Aymé, "Non, Céline n'était pas un homme au coeur dur," *Combat* (October 1, 1966); A. Pulicani dixit.

49. M. Aymé, "Non, Céline . . . ," *op. cit.; RIG,* p. 32; A. Parinaud, *op. cit.,* p. 3; letter from Céline to M. Hindus, *Texas Quarterly,* V, 4 (1962), p. 26.

50. *CAS,* p. 190; *VOY,* p. 462; letter from Céline to E. Pollet (February 1933), *LH,* III, p. 96; letter from Céline to M. Hindus (n.d.), *LH,* V, p. 107.

51. *CAS,* pp. 79, 81.

52. Letter from E. Faure to Céline (1935), *LH,* V, p. 59; M. Aymé, "Non, Céline . . . ," *op. cit.*

53. Similar statements concerning this matter were made by Mmes. Pollet and Delforge (both of whom knew Céline intimately during the 1930s); quoted by C. Bonnefoy, *op. cit.,* p. 5.

54. *VOY,* p. 417; *SEM,* p. 121; *DIP,* p. 39.

55. *BAM,* p. 50; Mme. Colette Turpin dixit; A. Mandel, *op. cit.,* p. 252.

56. *BD,* p. 33; *RIG,* pp. 8–9; *RIG,* p. 318; letter from Céline to M. Hindus (n.d.), *LH,* V, p. 90; *VOY,* pp. 12–13 *RIG,* p. 8.

57. Unpublished letter from Céline to L. Combelle (n.d., ca. 1941). Photocopy in the private collection of the author; *RIG,* pp. 40, 44; letter from Céline to E. Pollet (August 16, 1933), *LH,* III, p. 100.

58. M. Aymé, "Non, Céline . . . ," *op. cit.*

59. Letter from Céline to E. Landry (n.d.), *LH,* V, p. 42.

60. M. Aymé, "Non, Céline . . . ," *op. cit.*

61. "Céline. Testament d'un maudit," *op. cit.*, p. 7.

62. Only the first side is usually shown in photos of Céline's death mask. One has to have examined the actual mask (as the author has done), in order to become aware of the startling discrepancy between its two halves.

Chapter 13

1. "Céline sort du tombeau avec un nouveau livre explosif" (unsigned), *Paris Match* (January 25, 1969).

2. *VOY*, p. 175.

3. Louis Montourcy, "Monsieur Destouches," *LH*, III, p. 9.

4. Information provided by Mme. Marcel Aymé during an interview with the author (Paris, June 1969).

5. Information furnished by Mme. Colette Turpin, during an interview with the author (Neuilly, June 1969).

6. Mme. Turpin's journal, *op. cit.*

7. Letter from Céline to R. Nordling (March 28, 1949), *LH*, III, p. 137.

8. "Madame Céline raconte son mari," *Télémagazine* (April 5–11, 1969), p. 70.

9. Attested to by Mme. Céline. Published in almost all accounts of Céline's death. Reappears in F. Gibault's Preface to *Rigodon, op. cit.*, p. iii.

10. Information obtained from Dr. Villemain, Céline's physician, during an interview with the author (Paris, June 1969).

11. Pierre Audinet, *op. cit.*, p. 1.

12. "Céline. Testament d'un maudit," *op. cit.*, p. 7.

13. P. Audinet, *op. cit.*, p. 1.

14. Letter from Céline to A. Paraz (February 24, 1951), *LH*, V, p. 119.

15. Attested to by Mme. Céline; Arletty.

16. Céline quite frequently spoke of his Celtic origins. See, for example, his letters to M. Hindus: (May 29, 1947), *LH*, V, p. 79; (September 2, n.y.), *LH*, V, p. 94.

17. "Céline était mort depuis samedi" (unsigned), *Paris-Presse* (July 5, 1961).

18. All descriptions of Céline's house (as seen in its various stages after his death), its occupants, its atmosphere, are based on the personal observations of the author made during her many visits to Meudon over a period of eight years (1961–1969).

BIBLIOGRAPHY

I. Works of Louis-Ferdinand Céline

IN FRENCH

A l'Agité du bocal. Pamphlet. Paris: P. Lanouve de Tartas, 1948.

Bagatelles pour un massacre. New edition with 20 photographs. Paris: Denoël, 1943.

Ballets sans musique, sans personne, sans rien. 2nd ed. Illustrated by Eliane Bonabel. Paris: Gallimard, 1959.

"Carnet du Cuirassier Destouches." *LH,* V, pp. 9–11.

Casse-pipe. 4th ed. Paris: Gallimard, 1952.

"Casse-pipe" (fragment). In *Entretiens familiers avec L.-F. Céline* by Robert Poulet. Paris: Plon, 1958.

"Casse-pipe" (fragment). Manuscript in the private collection of the author. Also published in *LH,* III, 167–169.

D'un Château l'autre. 20th ed. Paris: Gallimard, 1957.

Entretiens avec le Professeur Y. Paris: Gallimard, 1955.

Féerie pour une autre fois, I. 12th ed. Paris: Gallimard, 1952.

Féerie pour une autre fois, II. Normance. Paris: Gallimard, 1954.

Guignol's Band, I. Paris: Gallimard, 1952.

"Hommage à Emile Zola." In *Apologie de Mort à Crédit suivi de "Hommage à Emile Zola" par Louis-Ferdinand Céline* by Robert Denoël. Paris: Denoël & Steele, 1936. (Reprinted in *LH,* III, pp. 169–172; *OC,* II, pp. 501–508).

"L'Argot est né de la haine. Il n'existe plus." *Arts,* February 6, 1957 (Reprinted in *LH,* V, p. 31).

L'Ecole des cadavres. Paris: Denoël, 1938.

L'Eglise, comédie en cinq actes. 4th ed. Paris: Gallimard, 1952.

Les Beaux Draps. 79th ed. Paris: Nouvelles Editions Françaises, 1941.

Le Pont de Londres (Guignol's Band, II). Paris: Gallimard, 1964.

Mea Culpa suivi de La Vie et l'oeuvre de Semmelweiss. Paris: Denoël & Steele, 1936. (Reprinted in *OC,* III, pp. 334–348).

Nord. Paris: Gallimard, 1960.

Nord. Revised edition. Paris: Gallimard, 1964.

Oeuvres de Louis-Ferdinand Céline (the complete works of Céline, with the exception of the pamphlets *Bagatelles pour un massacre, L'Ecole des cadavres, Les Beaux Draps*). Edited and with notes by Jean A. Ducourneau. Preface by Marcel Aymé. Illustrations by Claude Bogratchew. Paris: André Balland, 1966–1969. Vols. I–V.

Rigodon. Paris: Gallimard, 1969.

"Secrets dans l'île" (Synopsis for a film). In *Neuf et une.* Paris: Gallimard, 1936.

Semmelweiss, 10th ed. Paris: Gallimard, 1952.

Voyage au bout de la nuit. Paris: Denoël & Steele, 1932.

Voyage au bout de la nuit suivi de Mort à crédit. Bibliothèque de la Pléïade. Paris: Gallimard, 1962.

IN ENGLISH TRANSLATION

Castle to Castle. Tr. Ralph Manheim. New York: Delacorte Press, 1968.

Death on the Installment Plan. Tr. Ralph Manheim. New York: New Directions, 1966.

Note: The author considers Mr. Manheim's translations of Céline far superior to any other existing ones. Passages in the text, drawn from the works above, are in Mr. Manheim's translation. All other translations are the author's own.

II. *Correspondence of Louis-Ferdinand Céline*

PUBLISHED

"Correspondance de Céline" (Letters from Céline to: Eugène Dabit, Mme. Eugène Dabit, Léon Daudet, the French Consul of the Isle of Jersey, Eveline Pollet, Dr. Camus, Lucien Descaves, Ernst Bendz, Pastor Löchen, Raoul Nordling, Georges Geoffroy, Albert Paraz). *LH,* III, pp. 85–160.

"Correspondance de Céline" (Letters from Céline to: Erika Landry, Elie Faure, Lucien Combelle, Milton Hindus, Denise Thomassen, Perrot, Galtier-Boissière, Georges Altmann). *LH,* V, pp. 35–137.

Letters from Céline to Albert Paraz. In *Le Gala des vaches* by Albert Paraz. Paris: Editions de l'Elan, 1948.

Letters from Céline to Paraz. In *Le Menuet du haricot* by Albert Paraz. Geneva: Editions Connaître, 1958.

Letters from Céline to Marie Canavaggia. In *Oeuvres de Louis-Ferdinand Céline,* Paris: André Balland, 1966–1969, Vol. II, pp. 709–710, 719–720; Vol. IV, pp. 489–492.

Letters from Céline to Lucien Descaves. In *Oeuvres de Louis-Ferdinand Céline.* Vol. I, pp. 745, 755; Vol. III, p. 570.

Letter from Céline to Eveline Pollet. In *Oeuvres de Louis-Ferdinand Céline,* Vol. II, p. 710.

"Lettre de prison." *LH,* V, p. 310.

"Lettres de l'exil" (Letters from Céline to Dr. C[amus]). Introduction by Robert Poulet. *Ecrits de Paris,* XCIII (October 1961), pp. 103–110.

"Louis-Ferdinand Céline: Excerpts from His Letters to Milton Hindus." Translated by Milton Hindus and Mitchell Smith. Introduced and expurgated by Milton Hindus. *Texas Quarterly,* V, No. 4 (1962), pp. 22–38.

UNPUBLISHED

Letters from Céline to Lucien Combelle (from ca. 1940 to ca. 1957; mostly undated). 34 letters. Kindly put at the disposal of the author by M. Combelle. Photocopies in the personal collection of the author.

Letters from Céline to Lucienne Delforge (1934–1936). Ten letters. Kindly put at the disposal of the author by Mme. Delforge. Typed copies in the personal collection of the author. Quotes from these letters with the permission of Mme. Céline.

Letters from Céline to Lucien Descaves and Mme. Descaves (from 1932 to 1951; some dated). Kindly put at the disposal of the author by Mme. L. Descaves and M. J.-C. Descaves, executors of

the Descaves estate. Quotes from these letters with the permission
of Mme. Céline.

Letters from Céline to C. Bonabel. In the latter's unpublished essay:
"D'un Logis l'autre: itinéraires céliniens précédé de Du Côté de
Destouches." Kindly put at the disposal of the author by M. Bon-
abel. Quotes from these letters with the permission of Mme.
Céline.

Printed announcement sent by Céline (then Destouches) to Marcel
Brochard at the birth of his daughter Colette. Drawing in the
hand of Céline. In the private collection of Marcel Brochard.
Copy, kindly provided by M. Brochard, in the collection of the
author.

III. Interviews with Louis-Ferdinand Céline

FILMED OR RECORDED

"L'Homme au bout de la nuit." Recording of an interview with Céline
by Albert Zbinden, originally broadcast by Radio Lausanne (July
25, 1957). Record out of print. Kindly put at the author's disposal by M. Pierre Monnier of Paris. Tape copy in the personal
collection of the author.

"Louis-Ferdinand Céline vous parle." Disques Festival. Collection
"Leur Oeuvre et Leur Voix." FLD–149M. Record out of print. In
the personal collection of the author.

"Dans Céline, l'autre." Television program (Télévision Française. 2e
Chaîne. Série "Bibliothèque de Poche"), directed by Michel
Polac and Michel Vianey. May 8 and 18, 1969, Parts I & II, re-
spectively. Program containing portions of a filmed interview with
Céline by Louis Pauwels; statements by friends and critics of
Céline; reminiscences of Mme. Céline. Tapes of both portions of
the program in the personal collection of the author.

PUBLISHED IN TRANSCRIBED FORM

"Céline au magnétophone." Interview by Marc Hanrez. *Candide*
(November 23, 1961), p. 14.

"Des Pays où personne ne va jamais. . . ." Interview by Jean Guénot
and Jacques Darribehaude. *LH,* III, pp. 185–190.

"L.-F. Céline." Interview by André Parinaud. *Arts* (August 12–18,
1961), p. 3.

"Le 'Voyage' au cinema." Conversation with Jacques Darribehaude. *LH*, III, pp. 191–194.

"Voyage au bout de Céline." Excerpts from the television program "Dans Céline, l'autre." *Le Figaro Littéraire* (June 2–8, 1969), p. 44.

"Rabelais, il a raté son coup," *LH*, V, pp. 19–21.

"Voyage au bout de la parole" by Jean Guénot. Contains an interview with Céline by Messrs. Guénot and Darribehaude. *LH*, V, pp. 250, 252–253, 254–260.

IV. Interviews with Mme. Céline

"Céline cinq ans après." Interview by Philippe Caloni and Gerard Guegan. *Pariscope* (January 26, 1966), pp. 19–23.

"Céline. Le testament d'un maudit." Interview by G. Rolin. *Les Nouvelles Littéraires* (February 6, 1969), pp. 1, 7.

"Comment fut écrit *Rigodon*." Interview by P. Djian. *Magazine Littéraire*, No. 26 (February 1969), pp. 18–19.

"Madame Céline raconte son mari." Interview by C. Leiber. *Télémagazine* (April 5–11, 1969), pp. 72–74.

Interviews with Mme. Céline by Erika Ostrovsky (unpublished to date). (Summer 1967). Tapes in the private collection of the author.

V. Interviews with Persons Related to the Life and Work of Louis-Ferdinand Céline

Almanzor-Destouches-Céline, Mme. Lucette. Widow of L.-F. Céline and executor of his literary estate. (September 1962–July 1969). Supplemented by voluminous correspondence with the author.

Arletty. Actress and friend of Céline. (September 1962).

Aymé, Marcel. Writer and lifelong friend of Céline. (September 1964).

Aymé, Mme. Marcel. Widow of the writer and friend of Céline and his wife. (September 1964; June 1969).

Bonabel, C. Friend of Céline since 1929 and author of "D'un Logis l'autre . . . ," *op. cit.* (May 1969).

Bonabel, Mme. Eliane. Artist and friend of Céline who had visited him in his Danish prison; illustrator of Céline's *Ballets sans musique* . . . (June 1969).

Bory, Jean-Louis. Novelist and critic who had attempted to visit Céline in exile. (April 1969).

Breker, Arno. Sculptor of the Third Reich and friend of Céline (Paris–Düsseldorf, June 1969).

Brochard, Marcel. Old friend of Céline, from his medical days in Rennes to his death. (Paris, Nantes; May, June, 1969). Correspondence with the author (January 1969–present).

Canavaggia, Mlle. Marie. Céline's secretary since 1935. (September 1962; July 1964).

Carayon, Mme. Jeanne. Céline's first proofreader and secretary during the period of *Voyage au bout de la nuit*. (Chartres, September 1962).

Combelle, Lucien. Journalist and friend of Céline. (May–June 1969).

Daragnès, Mme. Widow of the painter and friend of Céline during the latter's Montmartre days. (July 1968).

Dauphin, Jean-Pierre. Critic and author of a critical edition of Céline's *Entretiens avec le Professeur Y* (unpublished); owner of many first editions of Céline. (July 1966; July 1968; May 1969).

Delannoy, Mme. Juliette (formerly, Mme. Robert Beckers). Associate of Robert Denoël at the time of the publication of *Voyage*. (September 1962; May 1969).

Delforge, Mme. Lucienne. Pianist and companion of Céline from 1934–1936. (May 1969).

Descaves, Mme. Lucien. Widow of the author and member of the Académie Goncourt who had sponsored Céline; friend of Céline. (September 1963; July 1966).

Deval, Jacques. Playwright and old friend of Céline. (May 1969).

Ducourneau, Jean A. Critic, described in Céline's last work, *Rigodon;* editor of *Oeuvres de Louis-Ferdinand Céline;* author of "La Fin d'une légende," proving Céline's non-trepanation. (June 1969).

Garbell, Alexandre. Painter and habitué of the same restaurant in Montmartre as Céline. (May 1969).

Landry, Mme. Erika (nee Irrgang). Companion of Céline, ca. 1932–1933. Interviews by correspondence, since Mme. Landry presently resides in Costaraneira, Italy. (May 1969–present). Letters from Mme. Landry in the personal collection of the author.

Lebon, Mme. Edith (nee Follet). First wife of Céline. Mother of his daughter Colette. (March, May 1969). Followed by correspondence with the author.

Loiret, Jean. Painter. Alias Bonvilliers, actor. Friend of Céline. (June 1969).

Mahé, Henri. Painter; friend of Céline, especially during the 1930's; author of *La Brinquebale avec Céline* (Paris: La Table Ronde, 1969). (April–June 1969). Followed by correspondence with the author.

Manheim, Ralph. Translator of Céline. (August 1964; July 1966; May 1969).

Marteau, Mme. Paul. Widow of Paul Marteau who had received Céline at his home after return from exile: owner of an early draft of *Féerie* . . . , written in the Danish prison; owner of Céline's death mask. (Nice, July 1968).

Monnier, Pierre. Publisher and friend of Céline who had visited the writer in exile. Owner of out-of-print items on Céline. (September 1964; April 1969).

Morand, Mlle. Jacqueline. Member of the Faculté de Droit in Paris and author of a doctoral thesis "Les Idées politiques de L.-F. Céline." (April, May, 1969).

Nimier, Roger. Novelist; Céline's editor at Gallimard. Owner of a large unpublished correspondence with Céline. (September 1962).

Nimier, Mme. Roger. Widow of Roger Nimier; friend of Céline and his wife. (July 1966; April 1969).

Perrot, Jean. Friend of Céline from Montmartre days. (June 1969).

Pollet, Mme. Eveline. Novelist; companion of Céline during the 1930's. (Brussels, April 1969). Followed by correspondence with the author.

Pommery, Jean. Veterinarian and friend of Céline. (May 1969).

Poulet, Robert. Critic and friend of Céline. Author of various articles on Céline, of *Entretiens familiers avec L.-F. Céline* (Paris: Plon, 1958); editor of Céline's posthumously discovered work *Le Pont de Londres*. (September 1962).

Pulicani, André. Friend of Céline and Le Vigan, from Montmartre days. (May 1969).

Roux, Dominique de. Publisher and editor of the *Cahiers de l'Herne* which devoted two of its issues (III & V) to Céline; author of *La Mort de L.-F. Céline*. Paris: Christian, Bourgois, 1966. (September 1962, July 1966, July 1968).

Turpin, Mme. Colette (nee Destouches). Only daughter of Céline. (June 1969).

Turpin, J.-C. Grandson of Céline. (March 1969).

Dr. Villemain. Céline's physician during the last years of his life; longstanding friend. (June 1969).

All interviews by Erika Ostrovsky. Transcribed copies in the collection of the author. Unless otherwise indicated, the interviews took place in Paris or its suburbs, on the dates stated in parentheses.

VI. *Biographical, Critical and Historical Sources*

Accamé, Giono, "Céline, prophète de la décadence occidentale," *LH*, III, pp. 218–222.

Altmann, Georges, "Louis-Ferdinand Céline ou le 'Râleur grandiose.' " *Lumière*, No. 505 (January 9, 1937).

Andreu, Pierre, "Un Modèle de Céline." *La Quinzaine Littéraire* (July 15, 1966), pp. 11–12.

Anissimov, "Préface a la traduction russe de 'Voyage au bout de la nuit.' " *LH*, V, pp. 165–172.

Aragon, Louis, "A Louis-Ferdinand Céline, loin des foules." *Commune* (November 1933), pp. 179–181.

Arletty, "Interférence." *LH*, III, p. 197.

Aron, Robert, *Histoire de Vichy*. Paris: Anthème Fayard, 1954, Vol. II.

Audinet, Pierre, "Dernières Rencontres avec Céline." *Les Nouvelles Littéraires* (July 6, 1961).

Aymé, Marcel, "Non, Céline n'était pas un homme au coeur dur." *Combat* (October 1966).

Aymé, Marcel, "Sur une Légende," *LH*, III, pp. 213–217.

Balavas, Bugy, "Semmelweiss." *Communicationes ex Bibliotheca Medicae Hungarica*, Vol. 26 (1963), p. 192.

Barjavel, René, *Journal d'un homme simple*. Paris: Frédéric Chambriand, 1951.

Beaujour, Michel, "La Quête du délire." *LH*, III, pp. 279–288.

Benn, Gottfried, "Interférence" (Letter, dated December 11, 1938). *LH*, V, p. 141.

Bergère, Christian, "Un certain Docteur Destouches." *L'Etudiant Médecin Rondibilis* (June 1967), pp. 33–39.

Bernanos, Georges, "Monsieur Céline scandalise, c'est que Dieu l'a fait pour ça." *Candide* (July 6–13, 1961), p. 16.

———, *Le Crépuscule des dieux*. Paris: Gallimard, 1956. Especially, pp. 341–346.

Bernard, Richard, "Céline cinq ans après sa mort." *Gazette de Lausanne* (July 17, 1966).

Bertherat, Yves, "L.-F. Céline: *Le Pont de Londres*." *Esprit* (July 1964), pp. 176–178.

Boisdeffre, Pierre de, "Sur la posterité de Céline." *LH*, V, pp. 213–222.

Bonabel, C., "D'un Logis l'autre: itinéraires céliniens précédé de Du Côté de Destouches." (Unpublished.) Kindly put at the disposal of the author by M. Bonabel.

Bonnard, Abel, "A Sigmaringen." *LH*, III, pp. 67–68.

Bonnefoy, C., "Dernier Adieu à sa jeunesse." *Arts* (August 5–12, 1961).

Bonnier, Henri, "Céline." *La Dépêche* (February 23, 1969).

Bory, Jean-Louis, "Du Braoum dans la littérature." *LH*, III, pp. 223–225.

———, "Un Raz-de-marée dans les lettres françaises." *Magazine Littéraire* (February 1969), pp. 15–17.

Brenner, Jacques, "Le Dernier Rigodon de L.-F. Céline." *Paris-Normandie* (February 29, 1969).

Brissaud, André, "Voyage au bout de la tendresse." *LH*, III, pp. 226–231.

Brochard, Marcel, "Céline à Rennes." *LH*, III, pp. 13–17.

———, "Louis-Ferdinand Céline, tel que je l'ai connu." Lecture given by M. Brochard to the Rotary Club Ouest de Paris (March 28, 1963). (Unpublished.) Copy kindly presented to the author by M. Brochard.

———, Letter from M. Brochard to Mlle. Jacqueline Piatier of *Le Monde* (correcting certain biographical errors in Mlle. Piatier's article on Céline). In the private collection of M. Brochard. Copy kindly presented to the author.

Broyard, Anatole, "Castle to Castle." *New York Times Book Review* (January 5, 1969), p. 3.

Canavaggia, Marie, "Mademoiselle Marie, ma secrétaire." *LH*, III, pp. 30–32.

Carayon, Jeanne, "Le Docteur écrit un roman." *LH*, III, pp. 20–25.

"Céline" (unsigned). *Candide* (January 10–17, 1963).

"Céline" (unsigned). Notice of the novelist's death. *Paris Match* (July 15, 1961), pp. 29–30.

"Céline est condamné à un an de prison" (unsigned). *Le Monde* (February 23, 1950), p. 3.

"Céline était mort depuis samedi" (unsigned). *Paris-Presse* (July 5, 1961).

"Céline régicide" (unsigned). *Paris-Soir* (May 15, 1937).

"Céline s'en tire avec une tirade de rires inédite" (unsigned). *Paris Match* (March 4, 1950), p. 29.

"Céline sort du tombeau avec un nouveau livre explosif" (unsigned). *Paris Match* (January 25, 1969).

"Du Céline jamais lu, ni vu, ni entendu" (unsigned). *Le Figaro Littéraire* (January 12, 1963), p. 5.

"L.-F. Céline" (unsigned). Article containing facts concerning the novelist's London sojourn in 1915. *Minute* (March 20, 1964).

"Louis-Ferdinand Céline ne peut être amnistié" (unsigned). *Le Monde* (December 15, 1951), p. 7.

"Monsieur L.-F. Céline est amnistié" (unsigned). *Le Monde* (April 27, 1951), p. 7.

Chambrillon, Paul, "En 'brinquebalant' avec Céline." *Valeurs actuelles* (April 21, 1969), pp. 42–43.

Chamfleury, R., "Céline ne nous a pas trahi." *LH,* III, pp. 60–66.

————, Letter to the author, March 1969. Unpublished.

Copperman, Annie, "Rigodon." *Les Echos* (February 21, 1969).

Cotta, Michèle, *La Collaboration. 1940–1944.* Paris: Armand Colin, 1964.

Darcyl, Léon, "Céline le pestiféré." *Paris Match* (September 24, 1960), p. 89.

Darnar, P. L., "Un Céline retrouvé." *Le Dauphiné Libéré* (April 7, 1964).

David, Michel, "Céline et la critique italienne." *Le Monde* (February 15, 1969), p. v.

Debrie, Nicole, "La Méthode Almanzor." Unpublished treatise on the dance theories and practices of Lucette Almanzor (Mme. Céline). Copy kindly presented to the author by Mlle. Debrie.

Dédet, Christian, "La Condition médicale de L.-F. Céline." *LH,* III, pp. 312–316.

Delteil, Joseph, "Céline l'oral." *LH,* III, pp. 42–55.

Déon, Michel, "Les Beaux Draps." *LH,* III, pp. 238–239.

Donley, Michaël, "L'Identification cosmique." *LH,* V, pp. 189–200.

Dorian, Max, "Céline, rue Amélie." *LH,* III, pp. 25–27.

Dubuffet, Jean, "Céline pilote." *LH,* V, pp. 223–227.

Ducourneau, Jean A., "Chronologie." In *Oeuvres de Louis-Ferdinand Céline,* Vol. I, pp. xxi-xxxiii. (See listing on p. 376.)

————, "La Fin d'une légende: Céline n'a jamais été trépané." *Le Figaro Littéraire* (October 27, 1966).

"Enfer et gloire de Louis-Ferdinand Céline" (unsigned). *Le Monde* (February 15, 1969), p. iv.

Epting, Karl, "Il ne nous aimait pas." *LH,* III, pp. 56–59.

Faure, Elie, "D'un Voyage au bout de la nuit." *LH,* V, pp. 228–233.

Faurisson, Robert, "La Leçon de Bardamu." *LH,* III, pp. 306–311.

Fisher, Gerd, "Der Atem des Infernos." *Neue Ruhr-Zeitung,* Essen (October 12, 1960).

Ford, Henry, *The International Jew* (pamphlets). London: M.C.P., 1938. Originally published in the *Dearborn Independent* (the Ford international weekly).

Freustié, Jean, "La Pavane du collabo." *Le Nouvel Observateur* (February 17, 1969).

Friedman, Bruce Jay, " 'Céline, Céline!' " *The New York Times Book Review* (February 5, 1967), pp. 1, 52.

Geoffroy, Georges, "Céline en Angleterre." *LH*, III, pp. 11–12.

Gide, André, "Les Juifs, Céline et Maritain." *NRF*, No. 295 (April 1938), pp. 630–634.

Grover, F. J., "Céline et Drieu La Rochelle." *LH*, III, pp. 302–305.

Guénot, Jean, "De la Parole à l'ecriture." *Le Monde* (February 15, 1969), p. 12.

————, "Voyage au bout de la parole." *LH*, V, pp. 246–267.

Guilbert, Paul, "Louis-Ferdinand Céline dans sa nuit retrouvée." *Forces Nouvelles* (March 21, 1963), pp. 11–12.

Guinand, Jean, "Céline pas mort." *Dernières Nouvelles* (April 5–6, 1964).

Haedens, Kléber, "Celui que le monde repoussait." *Paris-Presse* (July 7, 1961), pp. 1, 4.

————, "Le Dernier Rigodon de Céline." *Journal du Dimanche* (March 2, 1969), p. 2.

————, "L.-F. Céline," *Candide* (July 29, 1964).

Hamilton, Alastair, "Céline's Paris." *London Magazine* (February 1968), pp. 41–52.

Hanrez, Marc, *Céline*. Paris: Gallimard, 1961.

————, "Enfin Céline vint . . ." *Le Français dans le Monde* (January–February 1966), pp. 8–9.

————, "Le Prince des hommes libres." *LH*, III, pp. 240–243.

H.h.h., "Ein gefärliches Genie." *Arbeiter-Zeitung*, Wien (March 24, 1961).

Hindus, Milton, *The Crippled Giant*. New York: Boar's Head Books, 1950.

Ikor, Roger, "Au Feu de l'enfer." *LH*, III, pp. 249–251.

Janières, Henri, "Ressuscité par 'La Vigue.' " *Le Monde* (February 15, 1969), p. v.

Jellinek, Roger, "An Ectoplasmic Gossip." *New York Times* (January 6, 1969).

Joannes, Alain, "Un Fantôme convoité: celui de L.-F. Céline." *Le Républicain Lorrain* (January 3, 1969).

Johansson, Eric, "Céline: l'Adolescent maudit." *Démocratie* (May 2, 1963).

Jouhandeau, Marcel, "Interférence." *LH*, III, p. 203.

———, "Magnificat." *Journaliers*, XIII (1969), p. 88.

Juin, Hubert, "La Poussière et les débris." *Combat* (February 6, 1969).

Kaminski, H. E., *Céline en chemise brune ou le mal du présent*. Paris: Les Nouvelles Editions Excelsior, 1938.

Kirsch, Robert, "Céline's 'Castle,' a Fascinating Freakout." *Los Angeles Times* (April 2, 1969).

"La Belle Américaine qui rendit Céline antisémite" (unsigned). *Minute* (April 17–23, 1969), p. 30.

Laurent, Jacques, "Il faisait la guerre au mal sans croire au bien." *Candide* (July 6–13, 1961), p. 16.

Le Breton, Jacques, "Un bien étrange confrère." *La Manche Médicale* (August–September 1962).

le Clézio, J. -M. -G., "Comment peut-on écrire autrement." *Le Monde* (February 15, 1969), p. 4.

Legris, Michel, "L'Antisémite." *Le Monde* (July 6, 1961).

"Le Manuscrit dans le placard" (unsigned). *Aux Ecoutes* (April 17, 1964).

Lenning, Walter, "Fragwürdige Abrechnung." *Hamburger Sonntagsblatt* (April 9, 1961).

Le Vigan, "Interférence." *LH*, III, p. 200.

Lioret, André, "Une doctrine biologique?" *LH*, V, pp. 210–212.

Lwoff, André, "Quand Céline était 'chercheur' à l'Institut Pasteur." *Le Figaro Littéraire* (April 7–13, 1969).

Maddocks, Melvin, "Fanatic of Disaster." *Atlantic Monthly* (January 1969).

Mahé, Henri, *La Brinquebale avec Céline*. Paris: La Table Ronde, 1969.

Mandel, Arnold, "D'un Céline juif." *LH*, III, pp. 252–255.

———, "L'Ame irresponsable ou Céline et le Dibbouk." *LH*, V, pp. 207–209.

Matignon, Renaud, "Céline." *Mercure de France* (July 1964), pp. 545–546.

Maurois, André, *Histoire de la France.* Paris: Albin Michel, 1947, Vol. II.

Mazars, Pierre, "Louis-Ferdinand Céline est mort." *Le Figaro Littéraire* (July 5, 1961).

Mazeline, Guy, "Cher Bardamu mon concurrent." *LH,* III, pp. 28–29.

Mittre, Simone, "Témoignage." *LH,* V, pp. 282–284.

Mondor, Henri, "Céline." *L'Express* (July 6, 1961), p. 30.

———, "Céline: Avant-Propos," in *Voyage au bout de la nuit suivi de Mort à crédit.* (Paris: Bibliothèque de la Pléïade, 1962), pp. vii–xvi.

Monneray, P. *La Persecution des juifs en France et dans les autres pays de l'Ouest.* Paris: Editions du Centre, 1947.

Monnier, Pierre, "Résidence surveillée." *LH,* III, pp. 72–80.

Montourcy, Louis, "Monsieur Destouches." *LH,* III, pp. 9–10.

Morand, Jacqueline, "Les Idées politiques de L.-F. Céline." Unpublished doctoral thesis, Faculté de Droit, et des Sciences Economiques, Université de Paris, 1968. Copy in the personal collection of the author, kindly provided by Mlle. Morand.

Morand, Paul, "Céline et Bernanos." *LH,* III, pp. 257–258.

Morelle, Paul, "Vie et mort de L.-F. Céline." *Le Monde* (February 15, 1969).

Morin, Dr. Guy, "Destouches médecin." *LH,* III, pp. 10–19.

Mort à Crédit. Major critical articles at the time of its publication. In *Oeuvres de Louis-Ferdinand Céline* (Paris: A. Balland, 1966–1969), Vol. II, pp. 733–759.

Morton, Frederic, "The First to 'Mine' Delirium." *The Nation,* March 17, 1969.

Mounier, Emmanuel, "Bagatelles pour un massacre." *Esprit,* No. 66 (March 1938).

Nadeau, Maurice, "Céline." *L'Express* (July 6, 1961), pp. 31–32.

———, "Contre-expertise." *L'Express* (April 23, 1964), p. 37.

———, "La Fin du voyage." *La Quinzaine Littéraire* (March 15, 1969), pp. 3–4.

———, *Littérature présente.* Paris: Corréa, 1952.

Nizan, Paul, "Voyage au bout de la nuit." *L'Humanité* (September 12, 1932).

"Nord" (unsigned). Report on the prohibition of sales of the novel in Germany, as the result of a suit for defamation. *Aux Ecoutes* (March 8, 1963). See also *OC,* V, pp. 503–506, for more information concerning this lawsuit.

Nourissier, François, *"Rigodon,* roman de Louis-Ferdinand Céline." *Les Nouvelles Littéraires* (February 13, 1969).

NRF Bulletin, "Céline et Hemingway." July–August 1961.

Ostrovsky, Erika, "Buffoons of the Apocalypse." *Saturday Review* (February 1, 1969), pp. 31, 63.

———, *Céline and His Vision.* New York: New York University Press; London: London University Press, 1967.

———, "Céline et le thème du Roi Krogold." *IH,* V, pp. 201–206.

———, "The Anatomy of Cruelty: Antonin Artaud; Louis-Ferdinand Céline." *Arts and Sciences* (Spring 1967), pp. 9–13.

Paget, Jean, "Hermantier retrouve une pièce de Céline." *Arts* (December 16–22, 1964).

Paillard, Auguste, "Le Pont de Londres." *Nouveaux Jours* (January 29, 1964).

Paraz, Albert, *Le Gala des vaches.* Paris: Editions de l'Elan, 1948.

———, *Le Menuet du haricot.* Geneva: Editions Connaître, 1958.

———, *Valsez, Saucisses.* Paris: Amiot-Jumont, 1950.

Penel, Alain, "Céline, chroniqueur des grands guignols." *Tribune de Genève* (February 6, 1969).

———, "Si Céline n'avait pas existé." *Tribune de Genève* (May 16–17, 1964).

Pia, Pascal, "L'Art de se mettre dans son tort." *Magazine Littéraire,* No. 26 (February 1969), pp. 7–9.

———, "Céline au bout de la nuit." *Carrefour* (February 13, 1963).

———, "Un Céline retrouvé." *Carrefour* (April 1, 1964).

———, "Rigodon." *Carrefour* (February 19, 1969).

Piatier, Jacqueline, "Louis-Ferdinand Céline." *Le Monde* (July 6, 1961), p. 16.

Picard, Gaston, "Le Renaudot: Comment je n'ai pas interviewé Louis-Ferdinand Céline." *Le Monde* (December 8, 1932).

Plumyene et Lasierra, *Les Fascismes Français. 1923–1963*. Paris: Editions du Seuil, 1963.

Poliakof, Léon, "Le Cas L.-F. Céline et le cas X. Vallat." *Le Monde Juif* (February 1950).

Pollet, Eveline, *Escaliers*. Brussels: La Renaissance du Livre, 1956.

Pommery, Jean, "Bestiaire de Céline." *LH*, V, pp. 300–306.

Poulet, Robert, *Entretiens familiers avec L.-F. Céline*. Paris: Plon, 1958.

———, "Le Pont de Londres." *Rivarol* (April 30, 1964).

———, "Où l'on retrouve Bardamu." *La Meuse* (September 28, 1933).

———, "Publications posthumes." *Le Spectacle du Monde* (April, 1969), pp. 91–92.

———, "Une Oeuvre retrouvée de Céline." *Rivarol* (February 6, 1964).

"A Propos de Céline" (unsigned). *Le Monde* (March 8, 1969).

Pulicani, André, "Chez Gen Paul, à Montmartre." *LH*, III, pp. 36–40.

Rabi, "Antisémite?" *Magazine Littéraire*, No. 26 (February 1969), pp. 10–11.

Dr. R. B. . . . , "Le Médecin de Meudon." *LH*, III, pp. 81–84.

Rebatet, Lucien, "D'un Céline l'autre." *LH*, III, pp. 42–55.

———, *Les Décombres*. Paris: Denoël, 1942.

"Révélations sur Céline" (unsigned). *Candide* (January 10–17, 1963).

Robbe-Grillet, Alain, "Céline." *Le Nouvel Observateur* (March 1965), p. 28.

Rolin, Dominique, "Ni avant, ni après, ni ailleurs." *LH*, V, pp. 289–291.

Rousseaux, André, "Justice pour Céline écrivain." *Le Figaro Littéraire* (July 8, 1961), pp. 1, 2.

Roux, Dominique de, "Céline: toujours dans les beaux draps." *L'Esprit Public* (March 1963), pp. 58–59.

———, *La Mort de L.-F. Céline*. Paris: Christian Bourgois, 1966.

Rudel, Y.-M., "Des Souvenirs rennais sur Louis-Ferdinand Céline." *Ouest-France* (February 29, 1963).

Salès Gomès, P. E., *Jean Vigo*. Paris: Editions du Seuil, 1957. Especially, pp. 156, 179.

Santayana, George, Extract from a letter about Céline, in Daniel Cory's *Santayana: The Later Years* (New York: George Braziller, 1964).

Sarraute, Claude, "Ecrire, c'est un truc qui vous tue le bonhomme." *Le Monde* (July 5, 1961).

Sartre, Jean-Paul, "Portrait de l'antisémite." *Les Temps Modernes,* I, No. 3 (December 1945), pp. 442–470.

Schuwer, Philippe, "La Passion de la médecine." *Magazine Littéraire,* No. 26 (February 1969), pp. 12–14.

Schwerin, Christophe, "Céline en Allemagne." *Le Monde* (February 15, 1969), p. v.

Schwob, René, "Lettre ouverte à L.-F. Céline." *Esprit,* No. 6 (1933).

Sénart, Philippe, "Céline: *Le Pont de Londres.*" *La Table Ronde,* June 1964.

———, "Gide et Céline." *Combat* (February 14, 1963).

Sérant, Paul, *Le Romantisme fasciste*. Paris: Fasquelle, 1959. Especially, pp. 64–80, 158–160, 247–249.

Shorter, Kingsley, "Expressionist Mosaic." *The New Leader* (March 31, 1969).

Sicard, Maurice Ivan, "Le Goncourt: Un scandale." *Le Monde* (December 9, 1932).

Spitzer, Léon, "Une Habitude de style, le rappel chez Céline." *LH,* V, pp. 153–164.

Stromberg, Robert, "La Source qui ne refraîchit pas." *LH,* III, pp. 268–271.

———, "A Talk with Louis-Ferdinand Céline." *Evergreen Review,* V, No. 19, pp. 102–107.

Suarez, André, "A Propos de Céline." *La Nouvelle Revue Française,* No. 104 (August 1, 1961), pp. 326–329.

Swaef, Paul de, "Toujours entre le trône et la potence." *Le Peuple* (June 11, 1964).

Thérive, André, *Essai sur les trahisons*. Paris: Calmann-Levy, 1950.

Tremblay, Laurent, "Céline malgré les trafics." *France-Observateur* (August 1964).

Trotsky, Leon, "Céline et Poincaré," in *Littérature et Révolution*

(Paris: Juillard, 1935). Extracts reprinted in *LH,* V, pp. 146–147.

Trotsky, Leon, "Novelist and Politician." *Atlantic Monthly,* Vol. 156, No. 4 (October 1935), pp. 413–420.

"Un Voile trop transparent" (unsigned). Report on *Nord* lawsuit. *Paris-Normandie* (March 8, 1963).

Vandromme, Pol, "L'Esprit des pamphlets." *LH,* III, pp. 272–278.

———, *"Rigodon* de Louis-Ferdinand Céline." *Le Rappel* (February 3, 1969).

Vanino, Maurice, "L'Affaire Céline." *La Résistance ouvre ses dossiers. Documents présentés par le Comité d'Action de la Résistance.* Paris: 1953.

———, *L'Ecole du cadavre, L'Affaire Céline.* Paris: Editions Créator, 1952.

Vignaux, Jean, "Le 'Cas' Céline," *Tribune de Genève* (March 6, 1969).

Villefosse, René Héron de, "Prophéties et litanies de Céline." *LH,* III, pp. 33–35.

Vinding, Ole, "Den maerkeligste Gaest Danmark har haft," *Copenhagen* (February 25, 1963).

———, "Vu par son ami danois." *LH,* III, pp. 69–71.

Voyage au bout de la nuit. Major critical articles at the time of publication. In *Oeuvres de Louis-Ferdinand Céline* (Paris: A. Balland, 1966–1969), Vol. I, pp. 777–815.

VII. Archives Relating to the Life and Work of Céline

Gallimard archives and press dossier, kindly put at the disposal of the author by the Editions Gallimard.

Newspaper archives of the Bibliothèque Nationale, Paris. For the study of the collaborationist press, 1940–1944.

CHRONOLOGY

May 27, 1894   Birth of Louis-Ferdinand Auguste Destouches, in Courbevoie (Seine). Father: Ferdinand Destouches; mother: Marie Marguerite Céline Destouches (nee Guillou).

Childhood spent in Paris.   The family lived in the rue Marsollot. Louis-Ferdinand's mother had a lace shop in the Passage Choiseul, near the Opéra; his father was employed in the Phoenix Insurance Company. The young boy attended public schools in Paris. After the completion of his Certificat d'Etudes, he was apprenticed to various commercial firms. His family hoped that he would enter upon a business career.

In 1908, the young Louis-Ferdinand was sent to Diepholz, Germany.

In 1909, his family sent him to England. Both trips had as their aim to teach him foreign languages which might be useful to him in a future commercial career.

He prepared for the baccalaureate degree on his own, passing the first portion of it in 1912.

In September 1912, the young Destouches enlisted in the 12th Cuirassiers (stationed at Rambouillet) for a period of three years.

1914   The first writings of the author date from this period. They are contained in a black notebook which Destouches had entrusted to a comrade in the army. Unknown to the public until 1965, they were identified by their owner at the time of the publication of *D'un Château l'autre* (1957), returned to Céline and finally appeared in *L'Herne V,* under the title "Carnet du cuirassier Destouches."

Ypres, October 25, 1914—Sergeant Destouches volunteered for a dangerous mission and was severely wounded in carrying it out. Shrapnel tore his right shoulder, resulting in damage to the arm and hand. There were, however, no head wounds and no trepanation was performed (although a legend, only recently proven false by J. Ducournaud, was created and sustained by Céline and many of his commentators which affirmed the existence of a head wound and trepanation). Destouches was decorated and cited by Joffre himself, receiving the Military Medal and War Cross for his heroism; the front page of the *Illustré National* carried a drawing of Sergeant Destouches advancing into battle, with a description of his exploit.

Treated for his wounds in various hospitals (the emergency ward at Hazebrouck, the Val-de-Grâce in Paris, Paul-Brousse at Villejuif, Michelet Hospital in Vanves), Destouches was finally released from active duty.

1915   Destouches appeared in London. He shared the lodging of a friend Georges Geoffroy and was employed at the Service des Passeports which is attached to the British Intelligence Service. Meetings with Mata Hari. Literary interests at the time: the German philosophers (Nietzsche, Hegel, Fichte, Schopenhauer); other interests: ballet, music halls, dancers, the milieu of pimps and prostitutes. A possible first marriage, annulled through the intervention of Destouches Sr.

ca. 1916   Trip to the Cameroons, in the occupation service. Destouches contracted chronic amoebic dysentery and malaria. Considered too ill, he was sent back to France. There, he passed the second part of the baccalaureate.

1918–1919   Destouches began his medical studies in Rouen. He also became part of the Rockefeller Mission and toured Brittany, lecturing on the prevention of tuberculosis.

Quintin, August 11, 1919.   Marriage of Destouches to Edith Follet, the daughter of the director of the medical school at Rouen.

June 16, 1920   Birth of the author's only child, Colette.

1920–1924   Destouches completed his medical studies and also became one of the researchers at the Institut Pasteur. He published several articles based on his research.

June 1923   Destouches passed his medical examinations.

May 1, 1924   Destouches was awarded his medical title and a bronze medal for his doctoral thesis *La Vie et l'Oeuvre de Philippe-Ignace Semmelweiss. 1818–1865.*

Until 1925   Dr. Destouches set up practice at the Place des Lices. The reputation of Dr. Follet, his father-in-law, ensured him success.

1925   He abandoned his comfortable life, as well as his wife and child, and became a doctor for the League of Nations.

1925–1927   Travel to the Cameroons; the U.S. (1926), Cuba, Canada.

In the U.S., he spent some time at the Ford factories in Detroit studying problems of social medicine. The experience would furnish him with material to be used in a pamphlet "La Médecine chez Ford," and would also appear (in transposed form) in his first novel, *Voyage au bout de la nuit.* According to all information, he also wrote his one and only play, *L'Eglise,* which was not to be published until 1933.

1928   Dr. Destouches had returned to Paris and resided at 36, rue d'Alsace, in Clichy. During the day, he worked in a clinic, le Dispensaire de Clichy. At night, he began work on his first novel.

1931   Destouches moved to 98, rue Lepic in Montmartre. It was here that his first work reached completion.

1932   *Voyage au bout de la nuit* was published by Denoël & Steele. The author assumed the pseudonym Céline. The work was dedicated to Elisabeth Craig, an American dancer.

1933   Publication of *L'Eglise* by Denoël & Steele. The play was performed only once by a group of amateurs in Lyon.

1934   Céline undertook another trip to the U.S. The reasons seem twofold: to search for Elisabeth Craig, who had returned to her country; to arrange for a film version of *Voyage au bout de la nuit.*

1936   Céline met Lucette Almanzor, a ballet dancer, who was to become his second wife.

Publication of *Mort à crédit* by Denoël & Steele. Publication of "Hommage à Zola."

Céline undertook a trip to Russia; upon return, he wrote a scathing attack upon communism, *Mea Culpa,* which can be considered the first of his violent "pamphlets."

1937   Publication of *Mea Culpa suivi de Semmelweiss* by Denoël & Steele. Céline dismissed from the clinic at Clichy. He visited the Isle of Jersey and was accused of attempted regicide. In December, *Bagatelles pour un massacre* appeared, the first of three racist, pacifist pamphlets which would be at the basis of the title of "collaborator" which the author received.

1938   Publication of *L'Ecole des cadavres* by Denoël: the second of these pamphlets.

1939   *L'Ecole des cadavres* condemned and withdrawn from circulation.

In August of the same year, war having broken out, Céline attempted to enlist in the French army, but was refused because of ill health. He found a post as ship's doctor on the *Shella.*

1940   In October, Céline moved to 4, rue Girardon in Montmartre. In the winter of the same year, the *Shella* was sunk in a naval encounter. Dr. Destouches began work in a clinic in Sartrouville.

1941   Publication of the third pamphlet *Les Beaux Draps* by Denoël; publication of *La Médecine chez Ford.*

1942   Trip to Berlin undertaken by Dr. Destouches.

1943   Marriage of Louis-Ferdinand Céline and Lucette Almanzor. *L'Ecole des cadavres* re-published by Denoël.

1944   Publication of *Guignol's Band, I,* by Denoël.

In July, Céline and his wife left Paris for Germany. They arrived in Sigmaringen in November of that year.

1945   At the beginning of March, the couple began their journey toward Denmark. They reached Copenhagen by March 27. "Foudres et flèches," one of Céline's ballets, was published at the beginning of December. On December 18, Céline's arrest and extradition was demanded. On December 20, the author was arrested and imprisoned at the Vesterfangsel in Copenhagen.

1947   Céline was freed on February 26. He remained under surveillance. Stayed in hospitals.

1948   In May, Céline and his wife moved to Korsør. Publication of *A l'agité du bocal,* a defamatory pamphlet in answer to the accusations of Jean-Paul Sartre in his "Portrait de l'antisémite."

1949   Publication of *Casse-pipe* by P. Chambriand, Paris.

1950   Condemnation of Céline (by the French courts) to national disgrace and the confiscation of one-half of his property. Publication of another ballet, "Scandale aux abysses," by P. Chambriand.

1951   April 26, Céline received amnesty and was exonerated. In August, the couple returned from exile. Céline signed a contract with the NRF (Gallimard) for the publication of his works. The writer and his wife moved to 25 ter, Route des Gardes (Bellevue), where Céline would reside until his death a decade later.

1952   Publication of *Féerie pour une autre fois,* by the NRF.

1954   Publication of *Féerie pour une autre fois, II. Normance.*

1955   Publication of *Entretiens avec le Professeur Y.*

1957   Publication of *D'un Château l'autre.*

1959   Publication of *Ballets sans musique, sans personne, sans rien,* with illustrations by Eliane Bonabel.

1960   Publication of *Nord.*

1961   Death of Louis-Ferdinand Céline on July 1, at his home in Bellevue. Burial in the cemetery of Bas-Meudon.

1963 Due to a libel suit, *Nord* was withdrawn from circulation. A revised edition (with libelous names altered) replaced it.

1964 Posthumous publication of a manuscript discovered by Céline's secretary: *Le Pont de Londres. Guignol's Band, II.*

1969 Posthumous publication of Céline's last novel, completed on the day of his death: *Rigodon.*

About the Author

ERIKA OSTROVSKY was born in Vienna but educated mostly in this country and in France. She is Associate Professor of French at New York University, and is the author of *Céline and His Vision*, the first major critical study of the novelist to appear in English.